Fascinating ... Gray helps  about and what's not.

Times

[Gray] is able to explore deeply relatable way.

Spectator

In a global food network, there are no black and white answers ... In the meantime, here are some food stories to munch over.

Sunday Telegraph

Fascinating and informative.

Delicious

Packed with insight, impeccably researched and skilfully narrated, this book is attuned to the contradictions and possibilities of the contemporary diet and ripe with appreciation for the visceral importance of plants.

Rob Percival, author of *The Meat Paradox*

Rigorous, incisive, warm and brave ... Gray combines moving, beautifully told insights with astute, no-bullshit journalism about the stories that really matter, now and for the future.

Lucy Jones, author of *Losing Eden* and *Matrescence*

Engaging stories and lively sanity for veg-forward eating in our complicated times.

Hattie Ellis, author of *What to Eat?*

Essential reading for anyone that eats, *Avocado Anxiety* takes you on a journey through food and its impact on our planet. Brilliant, just brilliant!

Jake Fiennes, author of *Land Healer*

In a quietly confident manner, *Avocado Anxiety* makes you think for yourself on matters that can only be described as universally urgent. Everyone should read it.

Caroline Eden, author of *Black Sea*, *Red Sands* and *Samarkand*

A fascinating book full of surprising facts that will force you to reconsider everything you thought you knew about fruit and vegetables. Truly, this is food for thought.

Cal Flyn, author of *Islands of Abandonment*

By turns fascinating, moving and funny, Gray gives readers the knowledge they need to make more informed choices about what to eat.

Emily Beament, author of *12 Small Acts to Save Our World*

Gray makes an overwhelming topic digestible ... *Avocado Anxiety* encourages understanding the science behind one's food and demonstrates the global impact of every meal.

Foreword Reviews

Each of the stories is an engaging essay written with punch and flair ... an intriguing read.

Read, Listen, Watch

Gray, a journalist who specializes in food and environmental issues, is not afraid to get her hands dirty ... With comprehensive research and intelligent, fair-minded writing, this is an informative, optimistic read.

Kirkus Reviews

A Note on the Author

Louise Gray is a writer based in Scotland. She trained with the Press Association and was a staff writer for *The Scotsman*. She covered UN climate change talks, GM foods and the badger cull during five years as the Environment Correspondent for *The Daily Telegraph*. Louise specialises in writing about food, farming and climate change. She has written for *The Sunday Times*, *Scottish Field*, *The Guardian* and *The Spectator*, among others, and has appeared on BBC television and radio.

Louise is passionate about environmental issues, increasingly focusing on how individuals can make a difference through the choices they make, such as the food we eat. Her first book, *The Ethical Carnivore*, won Best Food Book and Best Investigative Work at the Guild of Food Writers Awards and was shortlisted for the Fortnum and Mason Food Book of the Year.

AVOCADO ANXIETY

and Other Stories About
Where Your Food Comes From

Louise Gray

BLOOMSBURY WILDLIFE
LONDON • OXFORD • NEW YORK • NEW DELHI • SYDNEY

BLOOMSBURY WILDLIFE
Bloomsbury Publishing Plc
50 Bedford Square, London, WC1B 3DP, UK
29 Earlsfort Terrace, Dublin 2, Ireland

First published in the United Kingdom 2023
Paperback edition 2024

A catalogue record for this book is available from the British Library.
Library of Congress Cataloguing-in-Publication data has been applied for.

ISBN: Paperback: 978-1-4729-6962-0; Hardback: 978-1-4729-6963-7; Audio download:
978-1-3994-0628-4; ePub: 978-1-4729-6961-3; ePDF: 978-1-4729-6965-1

2 4 6 8 10 9 7 5 3 1

Typeset in Bembo Std by Deanta Global Publishing Services, Chennai, India
Printed and bound in Great Britain by CPI Group (UK) Ltd., Croydon, CR0 4YY

MIX
Paper | Supporting
responsible forestry
FSC® C171272

To find out more about our authors and books visit www.bloomsbury.com
and sign up for our newsletters.

For my grandmother, Beatrice Flockhart (née Rankin),
the daughter of a greengrocer

Contents

Roots

'Food is not an end in itself but a way of opening up the world.'
Angela Carter

The toddler screaming in the supermarket aisle is a familiar trope. But what if it is the mother, not the child, who is crying? She cannot throw herself on the floor and wail, much as she would like to. She must keep on walking, swallowing her tears. When I was weaning my daughter, I found myself, cheeks burning, having to speedwalk down the baby-food aisle before anyone noticed my eyes welling up. During those confusing first few months of motherhood, I had developed a nervous tick of twisting my hands around the rubber buggy handle until I could feel my palms burn. It was not that I was unhappy, but I was anxious. Here I was, with this perfect baby – the love of my life – and yet nothing I did ever seemed good enough.

The baby-food aisle with its colourful display seemed like a massive accusation. A voice in my head was shouting: 'What are you doing here? Proper mothers cook for their children. They put purees in special little ice-cube trays. It's

simple – why aren't you doing that? Look at all this plastic.
Do you really want to add more of this to the oceans? Oh,
hang on, it's all organic. Was that banana you fed her this
morning organic? I bet it wasn't.

As so often in early motherhood, I felt overwhelmed and
vulnerable and a little bit angry with myself for being either
of those things. I had done nothing wrong. I had simply
gone to the shops, tired and hungry, to buy some dinner for
my child. Yet it is not just new mothers who want to lie
down and bang their fists on the floor; shopping in a modern
supermarket can feel stressful for anyone, even someone
who has written books and articles about food: 'Is that meat
really high welfare? Shouldn't you be checking an app to see
if that fish is from a sustainable source? Did you know
almond milk uses up loads of water?

In the end, I bought my daughter a pouch of some apple
and parsnip puree, which she promptly vomited up. But it
had not been an entirely wasted journey. Somewhere in my
new sleep-deprived, hormonally charged mind, a seed of an
idea was beginning to grow … Why shouldn't I know
where the food my daughter is eating comes from? My
partner and I had already decided to try to limit the amount
of meat we would feed her as that felt like one of the easiest
ways to reduce our carbon footprint. But what about the
rest? In particular, what about all the fruits and vegetables in
the fresh produce section? The pears and parsnips, apples
and avocados that end up in infant food? My Instagram feed
was full of these 'clean foods' and the beautiful people who
claim eating plenty of avocados makes you 'glow'. But what
about the water used to grow these crops, the carbon
footprint of flying them halfway across the world and all the
packaging to make them ripen perfectly in your fruit bowl?

As I emerged from the supermarket, pushing my buggy
into the fresh winter sunshine, I felt a prickle of the 'old me'
return – the nosy, persistent journalist. Who says a carrot is
'clean'? What a preposterous notion! And actually, if I

stopped being jealous of their glowing complexions for a moment and asked them, I'm pretty sure the beautiful people on Instagram would like to know whether their 'superfood' smoothies actually are that 'super'? I decided I wanted to know exactly where the fruits and vegetables I would be feeding my baby over the next few months came from. And I knew just who to ask: Grandma.

My grandmother is the scion of a famous Edinburgh greengrocer, Rankins'. She grew up hearing the rustle of brown-paper bags, smelling the fresh strawberries every June and eating bananas before anyone else in the street. Speaking to her, I get a sense of the colour and smells that made buying fruits and vegetables a more sensory experience than today's sterile supermarket aisles.

Born in 1926, Beatrice Flockhart, née Rankin, grew up during what many people would see as the salad days of the UK's fresh fruit and vegetable trade. Rankins', set up by her father Willie Locke Rankin and his siblings in 1912, started as a barrow on St Patrick's Square. Willie, the son of a potter, had no background in the trade, but he was canny, and he liked to take risks. The family legend I am always told is that he raised the funds to set up the business by gambling on the boat back from serving in Greece during the First World War. I have since been given a more feminist interpretation, which is that Rankins' only survived because his spinster sister, Mary – or Aunty May, as she was always known – insisted it become a limited company in the 1920s to stop the boys from gambling away the profits. Whatever the truth, the business thrived. Digging around in the National Library of Scotland, I find a reference to Rankins' Fruit Market in the *Scotsman* as early as 1924, looking for a 'smart girl' to work in the first shop. There is a further reference to Rankins' alongside a map of the Established Trade Routes of the Port of Leith in the 1930s. Without the threat of German U-boats to worry about, and with refrigeration newly installed on ships, imports were coming in from across the Atlantic to the UK and snaking

through the islands of Denmark from the great ports of the
Baltic Sea like the roots of a tree. Rankins' could sell bananas
from the Caribbean, plums from Poland and oranges from
Spain. By 1935 the business had royal approval: 'Purveyors of
fruit and vegetables to His Majesty the King', an honour that
meant sending the finest white peaches down to Holyrood
Palace rather than the more common yellow varieties.
(Apparently, royal tastes have not changed too much; Prince
Philip always insisted on white peaches.) Later that year, there
was an advert for 'Macintosh Red' apples from Canada at the
Edinburgh Picture House, given out for free as you went into
the 'talkie', another sign of modernity. By the end of the
decade, Willie was so successful he had not only bought a
racehorse but won the Gold Cup at Musselburgh. Aunty May
might have disapproved, but now she had a chauffeur and was
getting her hair done on Princes Street.

Fruit and vegetables were more glamorous back then.
Grandma remembers the interwar years not as grey and
depressing but as a time that saw the arrival of red 'Mac'
apples from Canada, the lemons from Sicily, the tomatoes
from Lanarkshire, the potatoes from Jersey, the 'pimiento'
peppers ordered by the new wave of immigrants from Italy,
the pomegranates in paper, mandarins in silver foil and
Fyffes' brand 'bananas galore'. Even the paper bags – printed
with 'Rankins' of Edinburgh ... Branches Throughout the
City' in a distinctive 1930s script – look classy.

Rankins' survived the Second World War, thanks again to
Aunty May and the other women who must have stepped
into the men's jobs. Fruit and vegetables were not rationed,
but supply became restricted, and consumers were
encouraged to 'Dig for Victory' and grow their own.

Post-war, when the ships started coming back into port
and refrigeration improved further, the business thrived.
Rankins' became an Edinburgh institution, with warehouses
in the fruit market at Waverley Station, offices at the docks
and more than 20 greengrocers 'Throughout the City'. The

archives from this period start to show photographs of the interiors of the shops. To the modern viewer, it looks more like a department store than a greengrocer. A photograph of the flagship Rankins' in the West End of Edinburgh shows a linoleum 'terrazzo-style' floor, colourful tins stacked on the shelves and well-heeled ladies waiting to be served bunches of grapes for two shillings and sixpence. Self-service and selling fruit and veg pre-packaged rather than loose did not come in until the 1970s. Customers would queue at the counter before ordering a 'fourpit o' tatties', a hand of bananas or a couple of polished apples from one of the serving girls, then take their till tape to the cash kiosk to pay.

When I put some of the photographs up on my blog, I am surprised to find how many people still remember Rankins'. Those who worked in the fruit market at Waverley Station remember opening the doors of railway wagons full of strawberries from Hampshire and almost being knocked over by the scent. The smell in the humid 'banana rooms', where huge stems of green bananas hung on chains above naked gas flames to ripen, was even more overpowering. Every Thursday, there was a 'green market' where produce from the local area would be sold. My family on my father's side, the Dales, would bring up leeks, rhubarb and Brussels sprouts in a horse and cart from East Lothian. Market gardens within Edinburgh also provided local veg. More exotic goods came up on the train. Crates of peaches from France packed in ice, barrels of grapes from Spain packed in cork, and pomegranates from Italy packed in sawdust came in from Covent Garden in London, as well as the 'queer gear' – the alligator pears and custard apples that no one had any idea what to do with. When you got off the train at Waverley, you could smell the fruit market as you made your way up to the sooty streets of Auld Reekie.

Rankins' was a real treat for children, and many still remember tiny baskets of exotic fruit with legends such as 'just flown in from Jamaica' or 'newly arrived from Palestine'.

But my favourite story is told by Grandma about the day one of the workers brought her a hummingbird's nest from those hot, humid banana rooms, a tiny glimpse of another world, hardly bigger than a thruppence coin.

There is a sense of seasonality to these memories: strawberry jam-making in the last two weeks of June, marmalade oranges in January, and gorging on English cherries in July. Overall, you get a sense of fruits and vegetables as something special that changed through the seasons and that were grown with care by farmers all around the world. It is this sense of connection I would like to give to my daughter. But how do I reconnect to something that is gone? Like most high-street shops, greengrocers started to die out in the 1980s.

David Gillon, 80, my distant cousin, who worked in Rankins' throughout the post-war period, gets in touch to invite me for home-made gingerbread and an insight into the last days of the old-fashioned greengrocer. He says the decline was obvious as soon as people got motorcars and started to shop in bulk out of town instead of shopping for fresh fruit and veg every few days. More women were working and had to load up on fruits and vegetables for the week rather than popping into Rankins' or indeed sending a maid. Freezers in most homes and more tinned and processed goods made it easier to store fruit and veg for the week. Urban geography backs up his descriptions. In 1950 supermarkets were uncommon, taking up 20 per cent of the market and found only on the outskirts of big towns.

By 1990 the situation had more or less reversed, with supermarkets eating up 80 per cent of the grocery market.

The statistics on what we were eating also reflect the change in shopping habits. The world's longest-running record of what we eat, the British government's Family Food Survey, shows a rapid rise in the consumption of fresh produce during the heyday of the greengrocer all the way into the 1990s but ever since then, growth has stagnated as we rely more upon canned and frozen or processed food except in the case of 'exotic' fruit, like avocado and bananas, which are still rising in popularity.

As one of the company's younger members, David was sent to America in 1968 to see what the future might look like and to witness this new-fangled idea of 'self-service'. Much to Aunty May's dismay, he concluded that customers should be able to touch the fruit, even bag it up for themselves and take it to the counter.

Eventually, like most family businesses on the high street, Rankins' bowed to the inevitable, selling the remaining shops in 1985. They were just in time: another government report estimates that by 1997 there were 20,900 independent grocery shops in the UK, compared to 116,000 in 1961. The high street was dead.

The reality is that most of us buy our fruits and vegetables in supermarkets today. Even if you occasionally shop at the remaining independent grocer or order a veg box, you are likely to stock up on supermarket fare sometimes, which means being part of a vast and complex distribution system. Remember that old map showing the trade routes into Leith? Today it would look more like the complex fungal network, or mycorrhiza, that branches out from a tree's roots. Trade routes established in the last 80 years have become so fast and easy that they change daily, snapping and multiplying like a living system. Instead of coming into one central point – a wholesale market in the centre of towns, such as Waverley Station in Edinburgh or Covent Garden in London – fruits and vegetables are sourced directly by the supermarkets, several times a day from a network of warehouses across the country and indeed the world. It means that instead of a go-between like Willie Rankin choosing the best quality fruits and vegetables for the season from a wholesale market – the consumer is presented with what the supermarket can source for the lowest price direct from the producer. This model means prices have plummeted, and the same fare of the same size, shape and colour is available every day, but arguably diversity has diminished. Yes, you have strawberries all year round, but you do not experience a changing palate with the changing seasons.

In future, the supply chain will become even more frenetic, with customers able to order online from the retailers or cut out the intermediary entirely and order direct from the supplier. The new technology could see drones deliver groceries door to door. Every customer will be able to see precisely where each fruit or vegetable was sourced by tapping their phone. They may even be able to get a read-out on water, chemicals and labour. How many of us will tell our children and grandchildren about the fruits and vegetables we used to buy with any sense of wonder?

There is another reason I want this connection to fruit and vegetables – it connects me back to my mother. The first people to know about the birth of Marianne Rankin Gray, née Flockhart, in 1951 were the workers at the fruit market. As she was born so early in the morning, the only person up to hear the good news was her grandfather Willie Rankin. Like most people in my family, Mummy was a 'fruitaholic' who ate more than one apple a day, tasted avocados when everyone else thought avocado was just a bathroom colour and fed her four small children grapes 'like baby birds'. It is one of the few things I know about her.

Marianne died when I was very young, so young that I remember very little about her other than what I have cobbled together from photographs and dreams. I have always been desperate to know more. To write about her in a book about fruits and vegetables seems like a stretch. For me, though, food is always mixed in with emotion. As a heroine of mine, the great American food writer M.F.K.

Fisher wrote: 'When I write of hunger, I am really writing about love and the hunger for it, and warmth and the love of it and the hunger for it...'

When I write about fruit and vegetables, I am really writing about an effort to be a better person, to leave a lighter footprint on the world and connect more to the natural world around me. An effort, perhaps, to emulate my mother.

Part of my reason for meeting David Gillon and other people who remember Rankins' was to ask them, furtively, at the end of the interview, 'do you remember my mother?' (David did; he remembered a vivacious young woman walking along India Street.) All my life, I have greedily scavenged information and objects associated with her.

One of my most treasured possessions is her recipe book. It is a battered hardback with a bright orange cover illustrated with brown leaves and purple brambles, the kind of psychedelic design that could only be sold in the 1970s. It contains just a few recipes, written in my mother's attractive sloped handwriting, for basics like rough puff pastry, sponge and scones, the kind of recipes a young mother might like to learn as she starts to cater for her family. But after that, it peters out. I recognise my Scottish granny's handwriting in a few additional recipes for shortcake and drop scones. Then it is empty. Despite carrying it to every kitchen I have ever cooked in, I have never written a recipe in it. Nothing seemed good enough.

Now seems like the right time to bring it out. I have a year to get my head around fruit and veg, and I need something – or someone – to act as my ballast, my inspiration. The recipe book is a place to write down what I learn month by month and the recipes I pick up. Trying to untangle the complex truth around our fruit and vegetables is going to be tough. But everyone has to start somewhere, and I could start with my roots. I am the great-granddaughter of a greengrocer, after all. Maybe if I do manage to grow something decent in the allotment or make a delicious meal, I can write up a recipe and finally start to fill that battered old orange and brown recipe book. I could learn something about my mother, about myself, as well as fruits and vegetables. Everyone has to have roots, to feel grounded, to know where they are in the world, to grow.

CHAPTER ONE

Old Beans

British-grown broad beans: 0.89kg CO_2e per kg[1]

'Hallo, Old Bean …'
P. G. Wodehouse, *Indiscretions of Archie*

Mike Stringer didn't particularly like feeding broad beans to farmed salmon. He used to look at his field beans brightening up the Yorkshire Wolds with pretty black-and-white flowers every summer and think: 'Surely there must be another use for this crop other than feeding cattle and farmed fish?'

I remember thinking the same thing walking a crop of beans in Scotland with my dad one day and finding out they all go to Egypt or North Africa, where fava beans are part of the staple diet. The cream of the crop is sold during Ramadan when there is demand for the best beans. 'If they are good enough for a religious feast,' I thought, 'why aren't we eating them in this country?'

Still, farmers don't have much time to think about the endpoint of their crops, especially hardy Yorkshire farmers

---

[1] CarbonCloud.

like Mike, farming at 250 metres above sea level. So he pulled on his woolly hat, climbed back on his combine harvester and got on with his job, providing the commodity that the market demands.

Until one afternoon, two enthusiastic young men came bounding into his life, asking quite an obvious but unexpected question: 'Why can't we feed your beans to British people, Mr Stringer?' For Mike, the thought that he could feed the crop he put so much effort into to his friends and neighbours was a lovely idea. But it was not a new idea.

Broad beans, fava beans, horse beans, field beans – whatever you like to call them – have been grown in the British Isles for thousands of years. The crop was one of the first to be domesticated when humankind began farming in the Fertile Crescent,[2] and it soon arrived in Britain. The earliest archaeobotanical evidence we have is some 'Celtic beans' from the Bronze Age found at Glastonbury. More recently, archaeological digs along the new HS2 rail route have found further evidence of Britons including it in their diets. The Roman chronicler Pliny claimed that peasant farmers 'live on beans'. When the word bean appears in European texts before 1492, it is almost always the fava. By medieval times, there was written evidence in recipes and even songs. The earliest collection of recipes in the English language, 'The Forme of Cury', from the fourteenth century, includes a recipe for spiced fried beans – 'benes yfryed' – although spices such as clove and nutmeg are not what we would use in baked beans today. Pottage, a stew made with peas or beans, is mentioned in several texts, and I sing the nursery rhyme 'Pease pottage hot, pease pottage cold' to my daughter.

---

[2] In 2015, the oldest-known domesticated fava beans (about 10,000 years old) were discovered on an archaeological dig in Israel.

Beans were thrown into everything from beer, to bread, to plain old gruel.

But around the eighteenth century, peas and beans went out of fashion. With the gradual industrialisation of agriculture, grains were being produced on a massive scale, as well as being imported from America, making bread cheaper. At the same time, potatoes were becoming more popular. Later, with the development of refrigeration and canning, meat and dairy – sometimes from across the world – became more accessible. Our diets changed to the 'meat and two veg' we know today. Only poor people ate pulses, so it became stigmatised as a 'poor man's food'. One only has to read Dickens to understand what Victorians thought of 'gruel'.

Beans and peas were forgotten in Britain except for animal feed grown by farmers like Mike, field beans grown for export and the 60,000 tonnes of baked beans[3] we import from Canada, the US, China and Ethiopia every year. Until those enthusiastic young men came along.

Josiah Meldrum and Nick Saltmarsh still exude the puppyish excitement of people who have discovered the answer to the world's problems and just need 'EVERYONE ELSE TO KNOW ABOUT IT!' In this case, their answer is to solve climate change by eating more beans. Although they are now an established and award-winning food business, they retain the excitement of a green start-up – but maybe that is just the wild hair and the woolly jumpers. The pair met while working on East Anglia Food Link, a non-governmental organisation set up to find a way to feed the local community

---

[3] The average UK household consumes 10 tins of baked beans per week. The Food Foundation claim that 17 per cent of the 'vegetables' children eat in this country is made up of pizza and baked beans.

without driving climate change. Their job was to find new sources of low-carbon food for the local city, Norwich. At first, they came up with all the usual ideas, like setting up Community Supported Farms on the outskirts of the city to supply seasonal vegetables. But while they were driving around looking at all those carrots, they noticed acres and acres of beans growing around the city. Could they use them? 'No,' they were told by perplexed grain merchants. 'Absolutely not.' 'Animal feed.' Then one day, a farmer said something that got them thinking: 'That? Oh, that's foreigners' food.' Hang on, so people eat these dried beans in other countries, but for some reason, we don't eat them in the UK? They did a bit of digging and found out that the UK is growing around 250,000 tonnes of beans every year, which are all exported, mainly to North Africa and the Middle East, where they are a crucial part of traditional diets.

Digging a little deeper, they discovered that historically fava beans would have been a staple crop for local peasants from as far back as Roman times. Fava beans grow well in East Anglia, a rich arable area in eastern England, and are a good source of protein and fibre. The crop is also good for the environment. Unlike other combinable crops, such as wheat or oilseed rape, beans do not need nitrogen fertiliser. This is because legumes like peas or beans produce the nitrogen themselves. The plants suck nitrogen from the air, and then, through bacteria living in nodules on their roots, they 'fix' the nitrogen into nitrates the plant can absorb. When the plant dies, the nitrogen fixed in the roots is left behind, further enriching the soil for the next crop. As early as 37 BC Marcus Terentius Varro recommended in his *Rerum Rusticarum* that legumes be planted in poor soils. Today modern farmers do it because it will save them money. By growing beans in a rotation every five years, farmers can reduce the nitrogen fertiliser they use by a fifth, saving energy and cutting pollution from nitrogen run-off. For environmentalists like Nick and Josiah, growing this crop once again for food seemed like the obvious answer to the question of how to feed the local population well without destroying the planet. It also fits into the broader argument that eating less meat reduces an individual's carbon footprint[4] and helps fight climate change by providing a delicious alternative protein.

Josiah persuaded a local grain merchant to give him some sacks of the 'foreigners' food', dumped them in his living room and sat on them for weeks. Eventually, he cut the 'bean bags' open and transferred the dried fava beans to the kitchen for some culinary experimentation. Being partial to a kebab, Josiah tried his favourite, falafel, on his flatmates, and it was a great success. He took the beans into the office and persuaded his colleagues to try this new ingredient, culminating in a 'bean feast'.

'There was this moment when we all brought in the food we had made from fava beans,' he says. 'The table was groaning under all these dishes – falafel, hummus, ful medames, baked beans, stews, dips, salads – and we thought: "We have something here. They are all delicious!" We just could not understand why more people were not eating them.'

Nick and Josiah realised it was nothing more than an image problem – not just the Victorians but also the 'hippies' and environmentalists eating beans and pulses during the 1970s, 1980s and 1990s. It was what Neil ate, the hilariously depressed hippy in *The Young Ones*. And then there is that scene in the 1970s film *Blazing Saddles* ... (more on that later). Food made with pulses was associated with righteousness, not flavour. Yet things were changing. Yotam Ottolenghi, the Israeli chef who makes pulses zing and pop with his Middle Eastern recipes, was just emerging as a celebrity chef, most kids were familiar with hummus and falafel, and vegetarian cooking was joining the mainstream. Could it be time to rebrand the bean?

---

[4] For more on the argument for eating less meat, read my first book, *The Ethical Carnivore* (Bloomsbury, 2016).

With the support of Transition Town Norwich, another NGO that helps communities transition to a fossil-free way of living, the pair decided to ask the public what they thought. They bought a tonne of fava beans from a surprised grain merchant and sat around Josiah's kitchen table, putting them into little paper bags. It was vital at this point that these packets of rather uninspiring dry brown beans looked more appealing, so they got an illustrator on board, Carol Kearns, to paint pictures of broad beans' black-and-white flowers, reminiscent of orchids, that people would see in agricultural fields all around them. They popped a postage-paid illustrated postcard with a few questions on it into each packet: would you eat them again? What did you think? What recipe did you use? At first, there was nothing. Then there was a trickle, then a stream, and then hundreds of enthusiastic replies started arriving. 'My family loved them!' 'I made falafel for the first time.' 'It's so easy.' 'Are these really from the beans growing outside my house? They are delicious!' The most common response was: 'Why has no one done this before?'

Josiah, Nick and a local farmer called William Hudson realised they had an idea for a business. Gambling that the 'stigma' has passed, they set up Hodmedod's in 2012 to distribute British-grown peas and beans. More beans were ordered from a (still very cynical) grain merchant and sold through shops and restaurants.

'It was just a matter of imagination. Of imagining it was possible,' says Nick. 'Of making beans associated with worthiness and blandness [seem] exotic, delicious and colourful.'

In the decade since then, Josiah and Nick have certainly turned around the image of the bean. Hodmedod's has seen sales of some of their products grow by 50 times, and their goods are now available in independent shops across the country. During the Covid-19 crisis, when the public was discouraged from going to shops, the website repeatedly sold out because of the demand for foods that could store well and make a filling supper. And it looks like the trend will continue now that people have learned to enjoy cooking with store-cupboard staples. Hodmedod's has expanded its range to include British-grown quinoa and lentils and championed saving seeds and rediscovering 'lost' varieties such as Borlotto Lingua di Fuoco and the Canadian Wonder.

On shelves in his office, Josiah has chosen to display the beans he is selling: jars of pink Flamingo peas, Ayocote Negro beans, green marrowfat peas, white Soldier Beans, blue peas, Swedish Brown beans, Black Badger Carlin peas, Eye of Goat beans, Red Fox Carlin peas, Good Mother Stallard beans, split yellow peas and Gogmagog beans. Even British-grown quinoa and lentils. He has undoubtedly made the dusty old bean more colourful.

Food writers who turned up their noses at 'repulsive pulses' now include beans and peas in their recipes. Celebrity chefs like Jamie Oliver promote British fava bean falafel, and Ottolenghi has ensured we all know the joys of a decent broad bean salad. It's not just hippies any more; people across Britain are eating local beans again, just like their ancestors in Bronze Age Glastonbury.

As idealistic environmentalists, Nick and Josiah have achieved their dream by allowing people to source protein near where they live to cut carbon, reduce food miles and reconnect with what they eat. But the most satisfying thing is the influence they have had on farmers. And not just Mike Stringer. Other farmers across the country are introducing pulses to their crop rotation to reduce their use of nitrogen. Field beans are also a good source of protein for livestock, instead of soy imported from South America, which may be grown on deforested land. Next time you drive around the countryside, look out for strips of pulses as 'companion' crops or even mixed randomly into other crops, creating 'messier' and more diverse fields than the ones we are used to in our neat countryside. Just like in the culinary world, pulses have become fashionable, and they are helping the environment.

For Nick, engaging farmers with consumers is key to protecting the countryside: 'When farmers reconnect with the food they are selling and ultimately the consumer, they are more invested in looking after the land and the environment.'

Perhaps Nick's enthusiasm is infectious. It has undoubtedly inspired Mike Stringer to look at his land again, where he credits growing beans for humans with making his farm much more diverse.

'Most of our combinable crops are going into a nameless, faceless commodity market,' he says. 'I am just really enthusiastic about growing them for human consumption. It's nice to be able to eat and enjoy what you grow.'

As a biochemical engineer, Madalina Neacsu seems to have a more scientific approach to beans than Josiah and Nick. The Romanian scientist, who specialises in the 'functionality of food', spends most of her time in a lab coat examining the molecular properties of our food. Her job is to find food that 'works' not just for our health and the environment but also for the commercial food industry. Her remit might make food sound more like a necessary chemical input than a daily joy. But by the end of our conversation, she is excitedly sharing recipes with me, as enthusiastic as everyone else about the humble bean.

The first question I ask her is one that vegetarians and vegans are plagued with every day, particularly by the sort of enthusiastic carnivores who seem personally offended by others' choice not to eat meat: 'Is there as much protein in plants as meat?'

'Yes,' she answers unequivocally. 'It is a different sort of protein, but you can get all the protein you need from a plant-based diet.'

Put simply, the human body needs certain amino acids found in different proteins to function well. The protein in animal products is more likely to have a wider range of these amino acids than the protein in plants. For instance, a steak has a more 'complete' range of amino acids than a patty made out of one sort of bean. However, combining different plant proteins allows us to find the full range of amino acids we need. Often the best combinations have come about over centuries of cooking and experimentation. For example, an essential amino acid, methionine, is missing in chickpeas but is present in sesame. Reader, I give you hummus. Dhal made with lentils is complemented by the flavour of naan bread – and the amino acids found in wheat protein. For Madi, who eats meat, it is about diversity and balance – and joy – in the diet.

'Yes, it is easier to put a steak on the griddle, but a more colourful plate with different plant proteins can also give you a range of amino acids – and flavour,' she says.

There is also the question of other nutrients easily available in animal products, such as Omega-3 fatty acids and vitamin B12. Again, these can be found in plants, though it is often necessary to cook the food in a particular way to make it available to the human body.

'You have to think about what you eat a bit more perhaps,' says Madi, 'but you can get everything you need from plants.'

Especially beans. In terms of protein, they provide a lot. Fava beans are 20 per cent protein, 11 per cent dietary fibre and just 4 per cent fat. There are also plenty of micronutrients such as potassium and iron.

In her role as a research fellow at the Rowett Institute at the University of Aberdeen, Madi could see distinct advantages to including more plant protein in our diet, particularly in relation to heart disease, diabetes and cancer. Pulses contain more fibre, less fat and no cholesterol. Plants tend to have less salt and fewer cancer-causing substances than processed meat. For weight loss, pulses are a low-glycaemic index food, meaning they stabilise blood sugar and insulin levels, making them suitable for people with diabetes and ideal for weight management. Fibre slows the digestion of food, which slows the release of energy into our blood and keeps our digestive system strong and healthy.

'In the Western world, we over-consume protein but tend to under-consume fibre,' says Madi. '[I wanted to find out], could replacing meat protein with plant protein help people lose weight and stay healthy?'

In her 2014 study, published in the *American Journal of Nutrition*, Madi and her colleagues looked at the efficacy of a high-plant-protein diet in helping obese men lose weight compared to a high-protein diet including meat. Dieticians had long known that a high-protein diet helped people feel fuller for longer. Many people will be familiar with the most popular version, the Atkins diet, which recommends eating eggs and bacon for breakfast but cutting out the toast. The low-carb, high-protein diet was popular in the 1990s but later accused of increasing the risk of heart disease because it relies on high-fat and high-salt foods, such as cheese, butter and bacon.[5] In Madi's study, she replaced the meat in a high-protein diet with plant proteins that tend to be much lower in fat and higher in fibre. Compared to the participants on a meat-protein diet, the plant-based protein participants still felt fuller for longer, helping them eat less and lose as much weight. Madi also found the participants on the plant-based protein had more evidence of a healthy gut.

The next question Madi asked was: what kind of plant protein? Her earlier studies had used soy as the vegetarian protein, but soy comes with environmental problems. It is usually imported, which adds food miles; a lot of it is

---

[5] Dr Atkins died in 2003 following a fall outside his home. A medical report leaked shortly afterwards suggested he had a history of heart attack and hypertension, though doctors in the Atkins Physicians Council say this is not correct.

genetically modified, and it is often grown on land cleared of rainforest and important biodiverse areas.

The Rowett Institute began a study investigating the nutritional and health impacts of plant-based foods that can be grown in Scotland by supplementing volunteers' diets with green pea, fava bean, hemp and buckwheat. The plant proteins were not only chosen because they are high in fibre and low in fat but because the crops could be grown locally and reduce nitrogen use. Over three months, the study replaced half of the animal meat protein typically eaten in each diet with fava bean and other plant proteins. Not only did participants lose weight and see their cholesterol go down, but a month afterwards, they were still eating the plant protein in their diet because it was delicious. Madi admitted that initially, participants found it hard to give up bacon and sausages for hemp bread and Moroccan fava bean stew, but they switched much more willingly than the scientists expected.

'It does not take long,' says Madi. 'If you show people how to cook with ingredients like fava beans once, they soon start to enjoy it. We need cultural change and innovative solutions. Food can be medicine.'

As part of the study, the Rowett Institute did something they had never done before: they published a recipe book. I download and cook from *A Taste of Plants* during Veganuary. Fava bean flour makes it much easier to get protein from the bean without eating anything too 'beany'. I particularly enjoy fava and apricot muffins and fava bean frittata.

'It was very important they were simple and could be replicated, so you have pancakes and flapjacks and soups and stews,' explains Madi. 'Nothing too fancy.'

The recipes show how we could introduce more plant protein into our diets, and they helped the volunteers that took part in the Rowett Institute studies. But Madi is a food technologist at heart, and she wants to make a difference on a bigger scale. How can she get plant protein into the diets of people who struggle to find the time to cook these recipes from scratch? At the moment, Madi and her colleagues are working on ways to get the protein and micronutrients from fava beans and other plants into processed food. So, buckwheat flour pizza or chicken nuggets coated with fava bean flour. Sure, she would prefer people to eat whole foods; studies show that is the best way. But while so many people need convenience and affordability, why not?

'If people have things they can buy and eat, they will do it. It is about familiarity and convenience. Personally, the health impacts are so great that I think it is worth doing.'

Madi has proven how healthy beans can be and even ways to 'sneak' them into our diets occasionally via processed foods, but to really get the benefits, we have to make them part of our diets regularly. We have to *want* to eat them. This is where Jenny Chandler comes in.

When Jenny Chandler got a call asking her to be the United Nations Ambassador for Pulses, she thought it was a joke.

'The caller had a heavy Italian accent, and I just assumed it was my husband playing a practical joke,' she says. 'So I replied in a silly accent. There was silence at the end of the line …'

Jenny realised she had made a mistake. The Food and Agriculture Organization (FAO) really did want her to tell the world about the many benefits of eating pulses. For Jenny, it was a dream job. As a cook, she had been extolling the virtues of pulses since her student days, when she swapped baked beans in Surrey for *lentejas con chorizo* in Spain. Now it seemed the whole world had officially got on board.

The FAO is a very respectable organisation based in Rome where scientists from every UN nation meet to decide on the best way to tackle hunger and malnutrition worldwide. Having promoted pulses for years without anyone really noticing, the men in grey suits made 10 February World Pulses Day. UN committees were convened to collate the latest information on the benefits of pulses to human and planetary health. UN reports concluded pulses should be promoted in developing countries as they are cheap, can grow in dry conditions and provide protein and essential nutrients such as iron, folate and vitamin C for children. Pulses are already one of the first foods flown into disaster zones because they can store well without losing nutrients. With climate change on the horizon, the FAO wanted to promote a crop that uses less fertiliser and water and could allow more biodiversity. There was only one obstacle: trying to convince the world that pulses are nice to eat.

A modern home cook and food writer from southern England, Jenny initially seems like someone who could not get further from the ancient Mediterranean and Middle Eastern tradition of pulses. But she has all the zeal of a convert. Brought up eating 'not very hot chilli' in 1970s England, she was blown away when she first travelled to Europe and ate *pasta e fagioli* in Italy, *lentejas con chorizo* in Spain and *cassoulet de canard* in France. Travelling the world as a chef on yachts, she discovered Indian dhal, properly hot Mexican chilli and Japanese edamame.

'You look at world cuisine, and people have been finding wonderful ways to cook with pulses for centuries,' she says. 'Not only do they often make up a complete protein in a meal such as hummus or dhal and breads, corn and squash and beans, but the flavours work so well together.'

Jenny talks about a vibrant food that can make meat go further and create a healthy, tasty meal that lasts all week with batch cooking.

'It's just really difficult to convince people that something that has been such a mainstay is not boring but modern, exciting and delicious,' she says.

In 2019 she wrote a recipe book about pulses, *Super Pulses*, and admitted that her food-writing friends were initially cynical. 'Pulses are associated with tie-dyed tepees and nut loaf,' she cheerfully admits. It took Greek baked butter beans with feta, Californian bean burgers and adzuki bean ice cream to win them over. 'Gradually, they realised this is not something you eat because you are a hairy hippy in the 1970s; it is because they are simply delicious.'

It also took a bit of work persuading people that beans are easy, especially dried beans. As Jenny says, 'Why should soaking beans overnight be such a hassle? We manage to charge our phones at night.' The food writer Rachel Roddy recommends leaving beans by the corkscrew, so you always remember to 'skittle some beans' into cold water when you open a bottle of wine at night.[6]

Jenny had another ace to offer the FAO: she was brave enough to take on the uncomfortable digestive issue epitomised in *that* scene in *Blazing Saddles*. Yes, beans are good for your heart, and yes, there is also the possibility that the more you eat, the more you fart. Like most nursery rhymes, there is a grain of truth to the saying. In fact, it is not the beans themselves that produce gas in the digestive tract; it is bacteria as it struggles to break down a group of sugars called oligosaccharides that are present in beans. The harder the bacteria works, the more gas is produced. Two studies have tried to determine if there is anything the individual can do about this.

The first was a recent study in America commissioned to support the American Dietary Guidelines' advice to eat more plant-based protein. There was concern people would not follow the guidance unless their minds were put at rest over the possible side effects. Participants were asked to eat more beans and peas over a two-month period. But only half reported more flatulence, leading the study to conclude

---

[6] And there is nothing wrong with tinned beans.

the concern about stomach issues may be exaggerated. Moreover, 'it is important to recognize there is individual variation in response to beans'. In other words, it depends on who you are.

The second study, from the 1960s, was carried out by NASA because of concern about astronauts releasing gas in space and causing an unexpected explosion. Again, the study found that beans do make you produce a bit more methane, but it varies a lot depending on the person. That may be because some people have a more diverse microflora in the gut, making it easier to digest beans or simply because they have gotten used to it. Whatever the reason, I am haunted by the idea of the wannabe astronaut being refused their dream job because of a propensity to fart a lot.

In summary, beans may be easier to digest the more you eat, but it may also just be your own stomach and something perhaps the people you live with have to put up with. Unless you are an astronaut, in which case, get another job. Jenny points out that, once again, traditional cooking comes to the rescue: in Europe, they add cumin, bay leaves or summer or winter savory; in Japan, they include seaweed kombu in bean recipes, while in India, they add asafoetida, and in Mexico, they add epazote. All these herbs and spices are known for aiding digestion, though I am unaware of any peer-reviewed studies to prove it or explain why.

It is the last stigma attached to beans, and Jenny reckons we can get over it: 'The stigma has disappeared because people have realised they can be delicious rather than something you eat because you are obsessed with sustainability.'

She is hugely passionate about beans, and her year with the UN made her more so. 'I did not realise the "miraculous" stuff it can do in helping in war zones and climate change,' she says. 'It can be convenient, sustainable and delicious and all of these things.'

Jenny reins herself in for fear of sounding 'worthy' again – something she hates. As a sensible home cook, it is not about being worthy but about a rational argument. It looks like it might be working.

That is what the Honest Bean company are hoping for. Adam Palmer grew up eating hummus in lunchbox sandwiches or barbecue dips. 'We are a massive hummus family,' he says enthusiastically. The Yorkshire farmer had already made a name for himself by being one of the first people in the UK to start cold-pressing rapeseed oil, establishing the Yorkshire Rapeseed Oil company in 2008. When thinking of a product to make with the rapeseed oil he was pressing on his farm, he immediately thought of hummus. He tracked down some chickpeas and started to experiment. It was only when he saw the Cyrillic script and 'produce of Russia' on the sack that he started to wonder why they had to come from so far away? He looked around for a plant protein closer to home before realising the answer was just over the gate in his neighbour Mike Stringer's fields: fava beans.

Adam got his sister Zoe Oates on board, and the pair started experimenting with fava beans. Over three or four years, they developed recipes using fava beans and rapeseed oil, all grown within a few miles of the farm. The Honest Bean company was born in 2016 and started to sell hummus in independent shops and online. They have recently expanded into roasted fava bean snacks for a 'post-workout protein hit' or with something cold to drink. With its trendy packaging and lively social media presence, it is already taking off among young people looking for vegan, protein-packed, climate-friendly foods.

Zoe is passionate about food and explains how the rapeseed oil is cold pressed rather than using chemicals or heat to extract the oil. This process means the oil retains more flavour and nutrients, including Omega-3s. It also has a lower carbon footprint because less energy is used to make the oil, and because the company does not use tahini, the finished product is 90 per cent British-made.

'I can tell you where each ingredient came from, from start to finish,' says Zoe. 'It's a story, and people want a story with their food.'

In terms of a story, Hodmedod's certainly has a good one to tell, with a product history spanning back 10,000 years and a sense of purpose in helping farmers connect to their crops and consumers connect to their food. At the end of our lengthy conversation, I ask Josiah what Hodmedod means. It is a forgotten word, he explains, just like the fava bean was a forgotten bean. It means snail in old Suffolk dialect, or ammonite, or a curl in a girl's hair, or anything in a spiral, curled up, ready to grow …

Further reading
The Ethical Carnivore by Louise Gray (Bloomsbury, 2016)
Beans: A History by Ken Albala (Bloomsbury Academic, 2017)
Super Pulses by Jenny Chandler (Pavilion, 2019)

Hummus in homage to 115 Egerton Road

In my first student digs, we used an old door on bricks as our
dining room table. When it was damp, which it was often,
slugs would crawl out from under the MDF and ooze across
the table strewn with king-size rizla and tobacco. We didn't
eat many meals around that table except scrambled eggs with
magic mushrooms and Donk's roast chicken dinners that
were put together by midnight, by which time everyone was
stoned and absolutely ravenous. Kate and Olivia, who were
from London, occasionally made French onion soup with
cheese on toast floating in it – the height of sophistication. I
once cracked an egg into a tin of soup to make a 'meal' after
my sister told me that's what French girls do, but it was just
soup with bits of scrambled egg floating in it. It is a constant
source of amazement (and not a little amusement) to the
people who lived in that flat that I am now an award-winning
food writer.

Mostly we ate hummus, usually on burned toast (there
was a sock over the fire alarm), sitting on the countertop,
chatting about Bronisław Malinowski or aestheticism. No
one ever actually made hummus; we bought it in some
corner shop on the Curry Mile. I'm not sure we had much
idea of what was in it or had ever heard of tahini. We just
thought it was delicious on burned toast.

Today the average student has possibly got more idea of
the ingredients in hummus – and they may even have tables
on which to eat it – but they still probably don't own a
blender. So this is a really simple recipe adapted from one by
Nick Saltmarsh at Hodmedod's that requires no equipment,
as the beans just dissolve themselves.

In the UK, fava beans cost around £1.99 for a 500g pack,
which is much cheaper than buying five pots of hummus
and uses much less plastic. Climate-aware students may also
enjoy knowing they are eating a relatively low-carbon dish
that can even benefit the environment by reducing the use
of nitrogen fertiliser.

To make this hummus even more delicious, sprinkle some British dulse seaweed on top. That should also aid digestion if you are one of those people who got rejected from NASA because you fart a lot.

- 100g of split dried fava beans
- 2 tbsp of tahini
- 2 tbsp of olive oil
- 2 tbsp of lemon juice
- 1 clove of garlic (chopped or crushed)
- ½ tsp of chilli powder (or paprika, if you prefer)
- A sprinkling of lemon zest
- A pinch of dulse seaweed to garnish

1. Skittle the split beans into a large pan, add plenty of cold water and bring to a boil. Simmer them for 30 to 40 minutes. You want the beans to get soft enough to mash into a paste.
2. Drain the beans in a sieve and once the steam has evaporated, mash them in a bowl using a fork or wooden spoon.
3. Add the tahini, olive oil and lemon juice to the bowl, stirring them into the mashed beans with a fork or spoon until you have a creamy consistency. Stir in the chilli, lemon zest and garlic. You can adjust the amounts of these last three ingredients according to taste.
4. Transfer to a serving dish that makes it easier to share the dip and perhaps looks a bit more sophisticated, if you have one. Drizzle with a little more olive oil and garnish with dulse.
5. It will taste much creamier than shop-bought hummus and is delicious served with toast (burned or not).

CHAPTER TWO

Bananageddon

Bananas shipped from Latin America: 0.7kg CO_2e per kg[7]

'Bananas are the product of the industrial machine.'
Alistair Smith, Banana Link

A killer disease turns up out of the blue. It moves by 'stealth transmission', spreading before symptoms even show. Once it takes hold, it is already too late to stop it. There is no cure. Life will never be the same again. Sound familiar?

I am not talking about Covid-19; I am talking about Fusarium Tropical Race 4 (TR4). I first came across the disease when interviewing Fernando García-Bastidas, a Colombian banana expert based in Holland, on Zoom. Fernando is an engaging and rather eccentric scientist prone to emotional outbursts about the future of the world's favourite fruit.[8] At any other time, I would have switched off when he launched into a long and detailed description of a

---

[7] Mike Berners-Lee, Lancaster University.

[8] Technically, the banana is a berry, and the banana plant is a herb. One banana is 0.1kg CO_2e per kg.

pathogenic fungus. But our conversation was in March 2020, and something in his description stopped me in my tracks.

'So, we think this disease started in South East Asia, in an area of deforestation?' I asked.

'Yes.'

'And it moved through the soil, largely undetected?'

'Yes.'

'And it blocks the plant's vascular system, preventing movement of life-giving nutrients?'

'Yes.'

'And it has now spread all over the world, thanks to globalisation and world travel?'

'Yes.'

'So, it's a …'

'Yes, it's a pandemic.'

I'm not sure I had thought much about that word before, or even used it. Before March 2020, global viral outbreaks had seemed a distant phenomenon, like something out of science fiction. Now it was on the news every morning, it was stopping me from seeing loved ones, it was preventing me from leaving the house. Suddenly it seemed very important to understand how a pandemic had taken hold – even in the context of plant disease – and, more importantly, how to stop it. But first, I had to understand the history of bananas.

Bananas are originally from the jungles of South East Asia. Some of the earliest evidence of farming is banana groves dating from 5000 BC in Papua New Guinea. The fruit soon spread with Arab[9] traders from Asia to Africa, where bananas became a staple, and eventually via the first explorers to the

---

[9] The word banana derives from 'banan', meaning 'finger' in Arabic.

New World. At first, bananas were grown in the Caribbean as food for enslaved people, but as land became scarce, cultivation spread to Central America, where at the end of the nineteenth century, a new breed of North American prospector realised bananas were the new gold.

In his book *Banana*, Dan Koeppel describes some of the characters at the start of the banana trade. They are vicious gangsters more at home in the popular mob movies of the day than in agribusiness. They arrived in South America with guns, money and the express purpose of 'making bananas more popular than apples'. Quite a challenge when you think that apples grew on every farm in North America and bananas had to be shipped in from the tropics. But the new 'Banana Men' realised sooner than most that fruit traded in bulk could be sold cheaper than local small-scale fruit. They cleared the rainforests, bribed the government – or had them removed[10] – picked bananas green using cheap labour and set up a network of refrigerated warehouses to link into new refrigerated ships. The train network built to link banana plantations to the ports was so comprehensive – and oppressive – it became known as 'El Pulpo' (The Octopus). All they had to do now was convince nice Victorian ladies that it was OK to eat the phallic-shaped[11] bananas by placing photographs of very elegant ladies doing just that in the press. It worked. By the turn of the twentieth century, cheap bananas had outsold apples – and oranges.

The fruit was not only cheaply grown (if you did not include the cost to the environment of cutting down the rainforest to create the plantations in the first place), bananas

---

[10] The replacement of Guatemala's second democratically elected president, Jacobo Árbenz, by a military coup in 1954 is largely thought to have been influenced by the United Fruit Company, who were unhappy about proposed land reforms.

[11] Despite the phallic symbolism of the banana, the part we eat is feminine.

were also relatively easy to transport and store. Unlike pears or plums, bananas all ripen at the same rate; they are picked green, kept in stasis using a cold and controlled atmosphere for shipping and then, once in the shops, they will cycle from yellow to flecked with brown in almost exactly seven days.

Banana fleets were the first vessels to have built-in refrigeration, and banana companies were the first to use controlled atmospheres and piped-in chemicals to delay ripening. They were also the first to employ the methods of other big commodities for fruit: work on a large scale, control transportation and distribution, and aggressively dominate land and labour. None of these now widely used innovations existed in the fruit industry before bananas. In fact, there was no such thing as a fruit industry before the widespread distribution of bananas. Apples, oranges, cherries and grapes were picked locally and distributed regionally. Bananas showed what could be done with fruit on a global scale, and it made the Banana Men very rich indeed, specifically the four leading companies that still dominate the market today: Fyffes, Chiquita (previously the United Fruit Company), Dole and Del Monte.

There was only one problem: all the bananas were the same. Initial growth of the banana trade, up until the 1950s, was thanks to a particular variety of bananas, the Gros Michel or 'Big Mike'. It was a bigger banana than the banana we know today, and apparently, it tasted like those banana foam sweets you get in pick and mix. The Gros Michel was popular with traders from the beginning because it grew in big bunches, did not bruise easily and ripened slowly. It could also be easily propagated and grown at scale.

Unlike most other fruits, bananas are not grown from seed but cloned. That is because the seeds in most popular varieties have been bred out or become so small they are non-viable. In contrast, it is easy to clone a banana plant. Rhizomes, stems that grow underground, can be cut off and replanted. These 'banana pups' – or suckers, as they are known – are identical twins of the parent. They are even more identical than human twins. Every banana we eat is a genetic twin of every other, whether that banana is grown in Costa Rica or Iceland.[12] That means every banana is equally tasty, equally easy to transport, store and ripen – and equally susceptible to disease.

So when disease struck the banana industry in the early twentieth century, it spread quickly from Asia to Panama, gaining the name Panama Disease. Central America was covered in vast swathes of Gros Michel at the time, each banana as susceptible to disease as its identical twin next door. If the banana plants went down, they would go down like dominoes.

The Banana Men smelled trouble, and the search began for an alternative variety that could satisfy the demand for this new fruit while also being robust enough to be traded in bulk. Botanists around the world started searching for the 'million-dollar banana'. In the end, the answer was a variety quietly cultivated in an English greenhouse by a farmer's son. The Cavendish was grown by Joseph Paxton,[13] the head gardener at Chatsworth House in Derbyshire. Possibly inspired by a picture of a banana plant on some wallpaper in the house, he bought a banana plant for £10 and planted it in the greenhouse. When it successfully bore fruit, he named it after his employers, the Duke and Duchess of Devonshire, who go by the family name Cavendish. There is still a banana plant at Chatsworth House today, and still members of the Cavendish family to enjoy it, although I believe they

---

[12] The Icelandic grow bananas in greenhouses powered by geothermal energy. This provides home-grown bananas and allows for research. Contrary to popular belief, however, Iceland is not a major banana exporter.

[13] Joseph Paxton went on to use the expertise he developed constructing experimental greenhouses at Chatsworth in designing the famed Crystal Palace in London.

seldom eat home-grown Cavendish bananas. The banana
was not quite as tasty as the Gros Michel, but it travelled
well, and soon it was cultivated in the Canary Islands and
Jamaica. When it became clear it could resist Panama Disease,
it became the dominant variety on the plantations of South
and Central America. Today most of the bananas we eat in
Europe, China and America are Cavendish.[14]

The banana had survived its first crisis, but the problem
was not solved completely. Panama Disease was not the only
pathogen out there. Cavendish bananas may grow in uniform
bunches, taste OK and travel well, but they are delicate
creatures. To keep the banana business booming, it was
necessary to farm in a whole new way.

The new Cavendish needed chemicals – a lot of chemicals
– to thrive. To keep the monoculture alive, the Banana Men
had to douse bananas in fungicides, herbicides and
insecticides. Banana plantations were one of the first places
where aerial spraying was used, and plantation owners took
full advantage of the post-war development of highly toxic
substances to control plant disease. It kept their bananas
cheap but resulted in an industry that damaged the local
environment and, arguably, local people, too. For Alistair
Smith, the chairman of the charity Banana Link, it is not so
very different today.

'Bananas are the product of the industrial machine,' he
states at the beginning of our conversation. We are sitting in
a cafe above a student bar in Norwich and, I must say, I am
a little shocked. There is something about bananas –
something most of us would recognise in cartoon characters
like Banana Man or the tutti-frutti hat worn by 1940s
Hollywood star Carmen Miranda – that feels silly and fun.
I mean, just thinking of someone slipping on a banana skin

---

[14] In India, where Cavendish are known as 'hotel bananas', they only
make up a quarter of the market since the 670 varieties of local bananas
taste so much better.

makes us laugh. As I sat there, I wondered whether any of the students around us had any idea how the fruit they slice into their cereal is produced. Perhaps not. They may, however, understand the story of bananas as a lesson in cut-throat capitalism.

In the style of a firebrand union leader, Alistair describes the life cycle of the modern banana. Bananas are grown on vast monocultures, up to 300 acres in size, where plants and people are rigidly controlled. The banana plants are grown in regimented rows and harvested all year round. Since each is a clone, they can be relied on to fruit at neat nine-month intervals. During the lifetime of a banana plant, it will be sprayed with fungicides up to 70 times, usually by planes flying over the massive plantations (and their workers). Insecticides are also sprayed by hand, herbicides are used to clear the land between the rows, and nematicides are used on the soil. Plastic bags embedded with insecticides are put over the growing fruit throughout its gestation. Alistair says bananas are the number-one user of pesticides of all crops in the world.

On a typical plantation, workers are rotated around the fruiting banana crops throughout the year. Their work starts early in the morning, and shifts will last at least eight hours per day. The bananas are cut when green and sent down the lines on zip-lines or mules, depending on the size of the plantation. Wages are low, primarily because workers' unions are banned in many of the principal banana-growing countries. In some cases, even mentioning a union can get you sacked – or worse. Banana Link says that since 2007 at least 68 trade unionists have been murdered in Guatemala alone.

And who drives this system of low wages and high pesticide use? You. According to Alistair, it is because supermarkets in the UK insist on such a low price for the fruit. Bananas are a 'value product', a staple item that supermarkets think consumers will notice if the price changes. Supermarkets, therefore, compete to keep bananas priced very low. In June 2007, Asda and all the other big UK supermarkets cut the cost of their loose bananas to 59p per kg – 45 per cent lower than five years before. In 2009, Aldi sold theirs for 37p per kg. Today, the price has crept back up to 78p per kg, a little better perhaps but clearly still a loss leader when apples cost £2.70 per kg. At the time of writing, we now typically pay 11p for a loose imported banana compared with 18p a decade ago, whereas a loose apple grown in the UK now costs us 20p. Is it any wonder bananas are the biggest-volume item sold in supermarkets when they are so cheap?

For Alistair, it does not add up.

'The product may be cheap,' he says. 'But the cost to the environment and the workers is too high.'

I am so shocked by the description of growing bananas that I ask him if he ever eats the fruit. He doesn't answer.

'OK, what about pineapples?' I ask.

'Chemical timebomb,' he replies. 'I wouldn't touch them.'

In the fight for fair conditions for banana workers, Alistair took Harriet Lamb (at the time, Head of Campaigns at the World Development Movement) on a trip to Costa Rica, where she met a woman called Maria. Thirty years later, Harriet recalls her shock to me.

'I never really recovered from that,' she says. 'Maria has stayed with me all my life.'

The story of Maria is one of thousands of workers who claim to have suffered life-changing illnesses due to the chemicals used on banana plantations. During the 1980s, Maria's husband, Juan, had the job of injecting the pesticide dibromochloropropane (DBCP) into the ground around banana plants to stop a worm-like parasite from attacking the plants. Little did he know then, but the US Environmental Protection Agency had banned the chemical in 1977 after it was linked to the infertility of 35 male workers at a Californian factory. Yet the chemical continued to be exported to countries like Costa Rica for use on banana plantations. When Maria and Juan had a son with severe congenital disabilities, they blamed DBCP – and the banana industry.

In her book *Fighting the Banana Wars*, Harriet wrote: 'As we sat there and Maria showed me pictures of her baby, rage bubbled up inside me because the companies knew of the dangers of this chemical, but they ignored them. I have never, ever forgotten.'

A 1999 study of women in banana-packing facilities conducted by the National University of Costa Rica found that the rate of leukaemia and congenital disabilities was twice the national average.[15]

Harriet vowed to do what she could to help Maria by setting up a fairer way to sell bananas. Her opportunity came when she took over as Executive Director at the Fairtrade Foundation. She believes at the heart of the injustice suffered by people like Maria is a simple fact: we sell bananas too cheaply.

'It is appalling, shocking and unfair the way bananas are produced to make them a tiny bit cheaper as part of a battle between the supermarkets,' she says.

In the 1990s, Harriet began fighting for a system of certification that asked producers to pay workers a minimum price and offered a premium in return for a new 'Fairtrade' logo. The 'extra money' – or simply fair wage – meant that farmers could feed their families and improve their working conditions. Fairtrade bans the internationally recognised 'dirty dozen' most dangerous chemicals to humans and wildlife. The workers decide for themselves how to spend the premium, whether on a new school, healthcare or roads.

---

[15] *Banana*, Dan Koeppel (Plume, 2007).

Despite the fact Fairtrade bananas cost slightly more, Fairtrade certification took off. In Switzerland, up to 50 per cent of the market is Fairtrade, and in the UK, it is a third. For Harriet, it has proved that consumers will pay more to know the fruit they are eating has been produced in a fair way.

'If we eat on average 10kg of bananas a year, then eating Fairtrade instead of normal bananas would add only £3 per annum onto your grocery bill,' she points out.

It seems like a small price to pay. Fairtrade has given consumers a way of treating banana workers fairly, even if supermarkets will not make that call. You can buy a banana now with a Fairtrade logo and know that the person picking your fruit has received a fair wage.

However, it has not solved the environmental problem with bananas or the looming crisis with disease.

Panama Disease did not stay away for long. As early as the 1990s, there were stirrings of an extremely virulent new strain of the disease in Taiwan, known as Tropical Race 4 or TR4. This time the Banana Men were ready, and they introduced measures at the first sign of the disease. Infected banana plants were ripped out. Workers were asked to sanitise boots in a foot bath to stop the spread of the disease, and plantations were put into quarantine – the banana equivalent of washing our hands and lockdown. But, like with Covid-19, some have questioned whether any of these measures were helping. Even with 'banana social distancing' in place, it was impossible to stop the spread of the disease via a tiny sample of soil in the water course, on machinery or the bottom of boots. TR4 is a fungus that lives in the soil, so even if you can identify all the infected plants, you can't possibly track down where the invisible infection has spread. In the same way that

Covid-19 continues to spread via people who are asymptomatic, TR4 continues to spread via seemingly harmless soil. TR4 infects bananas via the roots and clogs up the vascular system that distributes water up the main stem, effectively choking the plant to death.

The banana community was becoming increasingly nervous: if this new disease destroyed Cavendish, the whole industry would go down. That was not only bad news for supermarkets but also for world development. Bananas are the fourth most important food crop in the least developed countries.[16] Around the world, 400 million people rely on bananas as a source of income and nutrition.

Scientists worldwide began working on a vaccine or a fungicide to fight TR4 but to little effect. Although bananas are such an essential crop for millions of people, most of those people are poor. There is little funding for investigations into disease compared to research around the staple crops for developed countries. TR4 has evolved alongside bananas for thousands of years and had ample opportunity to find multiple ways to adapt to any form of resistance. It can survive in the soil for decades and mutate into new strains. If someone was going to tackle TR4, they needed to be banana-*obsessed*, a kind of banana superhero. That man is Fernando García-Bastidas.

Fernando wears banana socks, lives in a flat surrounded by banana houseplants, and has been known to dress up as a banana. He is also a talented cartoonist and creator of #bananatoons who often depicts himself as 'Dr Banana' fighting the dreaded TR4. Growing up in Colombia, Fernando was aware of bananas as a source of both pride and significant problems. Bananas are the third most important official agricultural export from Colombia, after coffee and flowers, and are a substantial source of income for the developing nation. But the history of bananas in the

---

[16] CGIAR.

country is brutal. The 'banana massacre' of 1928, when the Colombian army shot down workers at the United Fruit Company for taking part in strikes, remains one of the most well-known acts of 'state terrorism' in South America and was fictionalised in the works of the Nobel Peace Prize-winning novelist Gabriel García Márquez. Chiquita (the new name for United Fruit Company) has been accused of paying money to terrorist groups in Colombia as recently as the 1990s.

As a boy, Fernando almost dropped out of school, preferring to play football and read comics. He only stayed because his mother had sacrificed so much for his education. Thankfully, he found science, first taking a job on a coffee plantation before finding his true calling in bananas. He completed his PhD on TR4 at the University of Wageningen in the Netherlands before moving to a Dutch plant-genetics company trying to tackle the disease. In the fight against TR4, he found a mystery to be solved and a fight against a foe as shape-shifting and wily as the best baddie in a graphic novel. It was Fernando who discovered TR4 outside Asia for the first time in Jordan in 2013. Ever since, he has been 'crossing his fingers' that it would not hit developing countries, where bananas are a staple food.

'Bananas are undeniably among the most important fruits in the world and are a major staple food for millions of consumers,' he says. 'We cannot underestimate the impact the current TR4 pandemic could have on food security.'

But in 2013, TR4 was spotted in Mozambique. Fernando was getting increasingly nervous it would make it to South America, and his beloved Colombia, endangering the whole industry. In 2019, his worst nightmare came true: a farm in Colombia called to say that banana leaves were wilting 'like a lady's skirt', and they wanted to send him samples.

'It was like a bad dream,' he says. 'One minute I am on the farm, the next in the lab, the next explaining to the Colombian government minister that the worst has happened. For a very long time, I could not sleep well. It was heartbreaking.'

Fernando did not give up. Like the Banana Men in the 1950s, he started searching for resistance to the disease. Unlike the Banana Men, however, he was not searching for just one banana. Very early in his research, Fernando realised that the big problem for bananas is the homogenous nature of the crop. As long as the industry continues to rely on one clone, disease will be a problem.

That is one of the reasons he steers clear of genetically modified bananas. Yes, it may provide a cheap, resistant banana in the short run, but what happens if/when the fungus mutates in the long run? You are back to square one. In Australia, scientists have developed a genetically modified (GM) Cavendish banana resistant to TR4, as yet unavailable to the public. The Bill & Melinda Gates Foundation also supports ongoing research into GM bananas. But at the moment, the global public is unlikely to buy a GM banana. Fresh GM fruit and vegetables have never been sold in the EU, where strict laws restrict the sale of such products, and there is little sign of that changing. Even in the US, where GM papaya and other fruits are available, public opinion remains sceptical.[17] Instead, Fernando and his colleagues in the Netherlands are using the latest techniques in DNA sequencing to identify genes resistant to TR4 and breeding several non-GM bananas that may be able to withstand the disease and be commercially viable.

In the flat, damp expanse of Gelderland, Fernando has created his own oasis, a greenhouse of more than 600 banana plants. Here he is experimenting with crossing the ancestors of the Cavendish banana with more than a hundred wild varieties collected from all over the world to try to create

---

[17] Only a minority of Americans perceive scientists as having a strong understanding of the health risks and benefits of GM foods, according to Pew Research Center.

the 'future banana'. It is a long, slow process. Although he has already created hybrids with resistance to TR4, it will be another few years before the plants bear fruit – and then, of course, they will have to taste right and fit into the existing trade infrastructure.

'I feel like we are creating something completely new [in the greenhouse],' he says. 'You are combining two parents and making an offspring. We do not know how it will go yet, but it could be the future banana …'

Right now, 'every seed is a treasure' while Fernando and his team work tirelessly towards creating future bananas that taste good, look good, travel well and, crucially, resist both strains of Panama Disease.

We also need to eat more of the diverse bananas we already have. Fernando points out there are more than a thousand edible bananas in the wild with different tastes, smells and sizes. Why not use them? Supermarkets could stock Dwarf Red bananas, which taste a little like raspberries, Lady Fingers, which are smaller and sweeter than Cavendish, or Blue Java, which taste like vanilla ice cream. As Fernando says, more than a hundred apple varieties and 25 watermelon varieties are commercialised and found in supermarkets. Why only one banana? Eating different types would not only support smaller farmers and businesses but also create a more resilient banana crop better able to weather disease as there would always be at least one variety able to fight back. Different varieties are already available in Asian or Afro Caribbean supermarkets. The makers of an inspiring new film, *Bananageddon*, exploring the dark history and possible future of the banana, have set up a 'banana list' (see page 55), where you can find suppliers of different varieties in your local area. In future, you could buy Praying Hands, Raja Puri, East African Highland, Senorita or even that old favourite, Gros Michel.

It is not just TR4 that threatens the future of bananas; climate change does too. In 2016, the UK government sponsored Dan Bebber at the University of Exeter to investigate the impact of climate change and disease on bananas. The UK eats 5 billion bananas every year, and there was genuine concern that a staple fruit could disappear from our tables. The BananEx project (officially known as Securing the Future of the UK's Favourite Fruit) produced unexpected results.[18] It found that, since 1961, climate change has actually increased banana yields in 27 countries, accounting for 86 per cent of global production. However, these gains will reduce or disappear by 2050 if climate change continues unabated. Crucially, the world's largest producer and consumer of bananas, India, and the fourth largest producer, Brazil, are predicted to see crop yields significantly decline.

Climate change is already impacting bananas because of extreme weather events. Next time you are in the supermarket, look at your bananas. The optimum colour of bananas is yellow, but if there are shortages, you will see more green on the shelf. In other words, the greener the bananas, the more stress the supply chain is under. In 2017, following hurricanes Irma and Maria in the Caribbean, you may have noticed a lot of green bananas as the storms hit the main production area for organic bananas.

For banana plantations to survive, they must be resilient against climate change *and* TR4. For Dan Bebber and the team at BananEx, this means farming in a completely different way.

'In the early days, in Latin America, bananas were sprayed 40 to 80 times on one plantation,' he explains. 'Just imagine what that does to the soil microbiota.'

Dan says that many banana plantations cannot fight against TR4 if there is no army of good bacteria in the soil

---

[18] Published in *Nature* in 2019.

to protect against pathogens. Just as we have to retain 'good bacteria' in our guts to stay healthy, soil needs active microorganisms to fight infection. The good news is that by feeding these organisms with organic matter and protecting against erosion, we can bring soil microbiota back to life. Banana farmers have plenty of tools at their disposal. They can make compost from rotted banana leaves and stems. They can prevent erosion by planting seasonal crops between rows of bananas and planting trees along waterways. They can even use remote satellites to spot the spread of disease and prevent deforestation.

Rainforest Alliance claims they are ensuring many of these measures are carried out on banana farms. The non-profit organisation was set up in the late 80s to stop the destruction of rainforests by creating a certification scheme for tea, coffee, bananas and other tropical foods that ensured farms did not clear rainforests to grow the crops. To display the label, farms must also meet specific environmental and social standards, such as planting native trees and providing safety equipment for workers. Many shoppers will recognise the label showing a key rainforest species, the tree frog. But a 2016 report by Banana Link[19] questioned whether the certification scheme can be rigorous enough when the cost of bananas in supermarkets remains the same. For Dan, changes cannot be made without significant investment, which will mean we pay more for bananas. We cannot just stick a pretty label on bananas.

'I would say eat bananas, but be prepared to spend as much as you can on them, like coffee and chocolate,' he says.

It doesn't matter how much you pay; bananas are still under the threat of a pandemic. And, as we all know, a pandemic can last a long time. When I first started writing about bananas, I thought I might be in lockdown for a few

---

[19] 'Rainforest Alliance and the Discount Supermarkets: Low prices and easy standards?', September 2016.

weeks. A few years later, we have all learned a lot about pandemics. We have learned just how much damage a microscopic virus can do to the world economy, our daily lives and our mental health. We have also learned how to take the plight of the environment more seriously. In lockdown, while we were isolated from family and friends, many of us found nature a solace. At the same time, it became clear that destroying nature is what got us into this mess in the first place. In 2020, a report by WWF International and the UN linked the destruction of nature to an increase in the risk of pandemics. The study found that deforestation and trade in wildlife make the leap from animal disease to humans more likely.

As we emerge from the Covid-19 pandemic, questions are being asked about how we can protect against future pandemics by looking after our environment. In the same way, the banana pandemic is making people think about how we farm our favourite fruit. Extensive monoculture farming and the destruction of rainforests have allowed TR4 to spread. Globalisation has speeded up its spread even more. The only way to stop it – or at least to survive it – is to take better care of the soil, pay workers fairly and introduce more diversity to the market. We need a 'new normal' for bananas.

Further reading

Banana by Dan Koeppel (Plume, 2007)

'Panama Disease in Bananas: Spread, Screens and Genes, Thesis' by Fernando García-Bastidas (Wageningen University, 2019)

Where to buy Fairtrade bananas: fairtrade.org.uk/buying -fairtrade/bananas/

Where to buy different varieties of bananas: bananageddon2018.wixsite.com/home/banana-list

Bananageddon the film: bananageddonfilm.com

Pandemic banana bread

Like everyone else during lockdown, I had too many bananas and too much time, so like everyone else, I started baking banana bread. Usually, I bake to please people. Baking is such a fail-safe way of expressing love, without any of the messy expectations of saying 'I love you'. Just a sweet treat that offers uncomplicated joy. During the first lockdown, stuck in a remote part of the Highlands with just my partner and a young baby, I was baking because I missed people.

My only friends at that time were the red deer outside the window. Like me, they were tired of the scorched vegetation and hungry for spring. One day I noticed them nibbling at the gorse flowers coming into bloom. 'If they can eat them,' I thought, 'why can't I?' It turned out that gorse flowers were perfectly edible, and plucking the delicate flowers from their spiky stalks was the perfect task for the toddler at my feet.

Another reason baking makes you happy is the meditative process of weighing, measuring and mixing. A study in the *Journal of Positive Psychology* found that such small creative tasks can help people feel more relaxed. A walk outside to gather some gorse petals adds time in nature to the mental health benefits of baking.

Gorse flowers smell of coconut on a sunny day, and although the petals don't taste of much, they do retain their colour in a bake. I have added desiccated coconut and pineapple to reintroduce this 'tropical' feel. I love the idea that by adding foraged ingredients, you are thinking of the nature outside your door, as well as the diversity in nature that allowed us to grow the bananas. I could not share my banana bread with those I loved during the pandemic, which makes it extra special to share this recipe with you now.

- 225g of self-raising flour
- 2 tsp of baking powder
- 50g of desiccated coconut
- 50g of granulated white sugar or caster sugar
- a couple of handfuls of gorse flower petals
- 3–4 Fairtrade bananas, as black as possible (how my dad likes to eat them)
- 75ml of cooking oil
- 50g of chopped, tinned pineapple
- 1 tbsp of tinned pineapple juice

1. Go for a nice walk and pick some gorse flower petals. This recipe is vegan, but you can add gorse flowers to any favourite banana bread recipe.
2. Smear a teaspoonful of oil in a tin and preheat the oven to 180°C.
3. Mix the dry ingredients (the flour, baking powder, coconut, sugar and gorse flowers).
4. In a separate bowl, mash the bananas (frozen bananas defrost as very soft, black and sweet bananas, making mashing them even easier and cutting food waste). Mix the bananas in with the remaining oil, pineapple chunks and juice. Then add these wet ingredients to the mixed, dry ingredients. If you need more moisture, add more pineapple juice.
5. Bake for 40 minutes or until a knife or skewer pushed into the bread comes out clean.
6. Sprinkle with flower petals and share with loved ones.

CHAPTER THREE

The Valuable Esculent

British-grown potatoes: 0.3kg CO_2e per kg[20]

*'Upon this handful of soil our survival depends. Husband it
and it will grow our food, our fuel, and our shelter and surround
us with beauty. Abuse it and the soil will collapse and die,
taking humanity with it.'*

Sanskrit scripture *c.*1500 BC

When potatoes first arrived in Europe in the sixteenth
century, they were considered just plain rude. Members of
the clergy banned their parishioners from planting the tubers,
saying they were unworthy of human consumption because
they came from the dark underground and were not
mentioned in the Bible. An early edition of the *Encyclopaedia
Britannica* described the potato as a 'demoralising esculent'.
Remember that the first potatoes to arrive in Europe were
not the uniform, round, dirt-free tubers we see in the
supermarket today. They were red, pink or purple and came
in all sorts of weird, bulbous shapes. At the time, herbalists

---

[20] Mike Berners-Lee, Lancaster University.

linked the form of a plant or vegetable to its medicinal properties. For example, walnuts were seen as beneficial for the mind because of their brain-like shape. Potatoes, with all their embarrassing protuberances, must surely have something to do with sex? Shakespeare even referred to potatoes as an aphrodisiac. In *The Merry Wives of Windsor*, he has Falstaff, dressed as a stag, greeting Mistress Ford as 'My doe with the black scut! Let the sky rain potatoes!'

The first potatoes brought to the Old World from the Americas arrived at the end of the 1500s. The myth commonly told in the British Isles is that Sir Walter Raleigh served Queen Elizabeth I a plate of boiled potatoes on his return to England in 1581. Most modern historians dispute the claim, pointing out that potatoes did not grow in most of the places Raleigh visited. It is far more likely the Spaniards – who Raleigh and other British pirates were busy looting – brought the potato to Europe.

At first, the potatoes stowed on the ships of the early conquistadors were botanical curiosities, hardly noticed alongside the piles of gold and silver. Only when all the gold was looted, and most of the indigenous people were dead, did the conquistadors turn their attention to the strange 'truffle' the remaining locals grew underground. As they began to settle in the New World, European colonists discovered they could grow potatoes more easily than their imported strains of wheat and barley, and potatoes seemed to be far better at keeping the new population alive. Even in its ancient forms, the tuber is a superfood. Although it is mostly water (79 per cent), the remainder is an exceptional all-round package of food with a carbohydrate:protein ratio that ensures anyone eating enough potatoes to satisfy their energy requirement will automatically ingest protein too. An average-sized potato contains almost as much vitamin C as an orange, as well as good amounts of calcium, iron, phosphorous and potassium. The potato also grows under challenging conditions, mainly because the indigenous people of the Americas spent 8,000 years selecting and nurturing different varieties of potato for different environments to ensure a successful harvest every year. If disease struck – or they had a particularly cold year or even drought – then at least one variety should survive. Potatoes could also grow at different altitudes and in different soils. In the Andes today, people will still grow up to a hundred varieties on each plot. They have more than a thousand names for the different potatoes they grow regularly. My favourite is *papa Ilunchuy wagachi* – the potato that makes the new bride weep because it is so difficult to peel.

Towards the end of the eighteenth century, the emerging industrialists realised just how useful the potato could be to Europe and encouraged peasants to plant it. Frederick the Great of Germany had potatoes grown in a field and arranged for a guard to watch over the plants. Sure enough, the peasants assumed potatoes must be valuable and stole them. And when Marie Antoinette of France wore potato flowers in her hair, it sealed the elevation of the potato as a fashionable product.

The potato swiftly became a staple crop as Europeans realised the tuber would withstand heavy winters and provided a much more nutritious return per acre of land than grains. As farming shifted to producing raw materials like wool, potatoes enabled people to grow their own food with much less land. Even an acre of land can grow enough potatoes to feed a family. As the Industrial Revolution took off, the potato was vital in supporting the population growth and, in turn, the stream of workers needed in factories.

In Ireland, the population boom was most extreme. In the early 1600s, before the potato arrived, no more than 1.5 million people were living in Ireland. By 1800, the population had risen to 5 million, and by 1845 to 8.5 million. On the fertile lands of Ireland, a patch of potatoes and a cow should have been enough to keep a family alive. There was only one problem: unlike their Andean counterparts, Irish farmers were only growing one variety of potato, the lumper, and when disease hit Irish crops, the effects were devastating. Between 1845 and 1852, the Irish potato famine killed a million people and forced another million to emigrate to the US and Canada.

Accounts of the time describe shocking scenes of skeletal men and women, starving children and cannibalism. Already the potato had fuelled the Industrial Revolution, and now it was forcing a shift in the population across the world.

You might think the famines would have slowed the spread of the potato, but this was the Victorian era when many believed invention could solve most problems. The botanists of the day got to work developing blight-resistant potatoes, allowing agriculture to continue growing the crop. At first, it was a somewhat random process. Gentleman botanists searched the world for new varieties, pollinated in the wild, and simply cloned the best specimens by planting seed potatoes. A popular potato at the time was known as the Fluke. As science developed, botanists deliberately cross-pollinated potato seed, inventing more sophisticated varieties better suited to European palates, including the Victoria, the Prince Albert and of course, the King Edward.

With the approval of the Royal family, the potato shifted from peasant food to a staple within all classes of society. In 1861, in her *Book of Household Management*, Mrs Beeton described the potato not as a 'demoralising esculent' but as a 'valuable esculent'. The potato had arrived.

It may have taken us 300 years to learn to love the potato, but now we really, really do. In the UK, we eat 7 million tonnes of potatoes annually, most of which are grown domestically. The humble potato has become not just a staple in our diets but the stodgy heart of British culture. Our national dish is fish and chips, and we eat more crisps than any other European country.[21] Yet few of us know how

---

[21] We eat around 6 billion packets of crisps annually. That's more than everyone else in Europe put together – around 150 packets per person each year.

the modern potato is farmed or the impact growing it has on our most precious resource, the soil beneath our feet.

To find out for myself, I visit James Thorp, a leading potato farmer in the Fens in eastern England. In my experience, young farmers are often keen to show off the latest technology they are using to try to farm more sustainably, such as the snazzy GPS on a shiny new tractor or the drone footage of their fields. But we start with something much more important: the soil.

To illustrate the importance of the soil, James takes an apple out of his pocket. It is usually a demonstration he gives to school children, and at first, I am not sure it is really necessary. He cuts a quarter out of the apple as he tells me: 'This is how much of the Earth's surface is land, rather than water.'

'Yes, I am familiar with basic geography.' Now I really feel like a school child.

He splits the quarter in two. 'Half of that land is inhospitable places like the polar ice caps, deserts or mountain tops.' Then he cuts that eighth of the apple into four pieces, and as he puts three of them to one side, he says, 'Those are the land we use to build cities or motorways, or where it is simply too hot, too cold, too wet, too dry for growing crops.' He holds the small slice he has left – the remaining 1/32nd of an apple – between his finger and thumb. 'This is all the land left to grow the crops needed to feed more than 7 billion people.' I am beginning to think it is a rather good way to demonstrate the vulnerability of our planet. James carefully peels off the skin of the remaining apple. 'In fact, all we can use is the topsoil.' He dangles a tiny sliver of apple under my nose. 'Not much, is it? And every day, it is slowly being eroded by water, by wind, by humans, by you and me. Every single day …'

Popping his penknife back into his pocket and tossing the apple pieces into the hedge, James gestures to the farmland around us. We are standing in the lowest land in England; from here, it is pretty much uphill in every direction. Above the ground around us, the big skies of the Cambridgeshire

Fens stretch out uninterrupted by hills or even a slight bump.
Below us is the 'black lands', some of the most fertile soil in
the British Isles, built up over thousands of years by sediment
washing in from the surrounding chalk and limestone
uplands. More than half of the grade-one agricultural land in
England, which will grow the best crops in the country, is in
this corner of East Anglia. Around 30 per cent of the fresh
vegetables grown in the UK come from here.

We jump into James's truck to drive across the Fenland
farm. At the first stop, James bends down to pick up a
handful of soil. It looks like the compost you can buy in a
garden centre: dark, rich and crumbly.

'Black gold,' he says proudly. 'You can grow anything in
this stuff.'

Since the seventeenth century, people have worked hard
to farm the prized soil of the Fens intensively. First, they
used windmills to pump water away from the lakes and
wetlands and out to sea, leaving the sediment-rich soil
below. Later, the pumps were powered by steam, then by
diesel and nowadays electricity. Towards the sea, dykes
create a wall so the fertile land can extend even further. At
400,000 acres, the Fens is Britain's largest human-made
landscape.

It has a strange kind of beauty. From the air, a gridwork of
drains and ditches; from the ground, just two simple lines:
land and sky, like a Rothko painting. As a woman who
escaped the flat lands of East Anglia to live in the mountains
of Scotland, it is difficult to understand the appeal, but it's
clear James loves it. He points out that the best potatoes in
the world all come from within sight of Ely Cathedral. That
sounds ridiculous until you come to the Fens and realise
that it is so flat, you can see the spire of the cathedral
interrupting those big skies for miles around.

The trouble is that the black lands are turning brown. At
our next stop, James jumps out of the truck again to dig up
a very different kind of soil. This time it is a shade lighter,

heavier, more like clay. The beautiful black gold is gone, and the geography lesson is turning into a history lesson.

The draining of the Fens may be seen as a triumph of agriculture, but like most human intervention, it has come at a cost. Firstly, the loss of wetland habitat and species such as eels, freshwater fish, frogs, rare butterflies, insects and birds, which are only just returning as some farmland is reclaimed as nature reserves.[22] Secondly, it has led to the loss of the soil.

Good soil is full of organic carbon. Remember that lovely black crumbly soil? Generally, the blacker it is, the more carbon it contains. But carbon exposed to the air will turn into carbon dioxide and escape into the atmosphere. Through ploughing the land, we have speeded up this oxidation process further. At the same time, nutrients built up in the soil are lost every harvest, which is why the soil in James's hand looks less like John Innes No. 1 compost and more like the clay lands of Essex where I grew up. I roll some around in the palm of my hand, and it forms a neat ball.

Farmers understand better than anyone the need to keep the carbon in the soil; for generations, they have done this through traditional methods. The rotation of livestock and crops meant that land was not ploughed every year, and nutrients were returned to the soil via animal dung. Organic matter was returned as grass or straw ploughed into the earth. But in recent decades, these traditions have been forgotten. Chemical fertiliser has perhaps made it too easy to plant the same crop year after year without waiting for nutrients to build back up in the soil. Tractors meant the earth could be turned over faster, and compaction was more likely from the heavy machinery. Changing labour patterns and farm ownership also influenced the management of the soil. As small farms became more marginal and land prices rose, good land like the Fens was bought by pension funds

---

[22] The Great Fen Project is one of the largest habitat restoration projects of its type in Europe.

and financial institutions. Fields grew larger and were farmed on a more industrial scale. Less labour was needed because of larger and larger machines.

Consumers primarily benefited from these changes. After the Second World War, agricultural production in the UK boomed, and food became much cheaper. Potatoes were eaten not only as part of a family meal but in processed foods and the new fast foods. But as we ate and ate – and ate – the soil naturally diminished. It is only now that both farmers and the school children they meet are looking at the skin of an apple and the ground beneath our feet and wondering how we keep eating potatoes if there is no soil left? It is estimated that the peat of the Fens is eroding at an average rate of 2cm per year.[23] In some areas of the Fens, the peat has disappeared completely, exposing the grey clay soils that were once underneath it.

The soil is not only losing nutrients and structure; it is diseased. Some 60 years of intensive potato production have taken its toll. A parasite called potato cyst nematode, or eelworm, has infected the soil in many areas where potatoes are grown across the British Isles. Farmers have little choice except to dose the soil with highly toxic chemicals or leave the land free of potatoes for at least six years.

James is refreshing in his frank admission of what has happened, but he is also optimistic about the future. Like many modern farmers, he does not push against intensification but sees it as part of the solution. As we tour the farm, he returns to those snazzy GPS systems and drone footage, the modern-day methods for preserving the soil, as well as the tried and tested methods being brought back from the past. In the autumn, following the potato harvest, green waste collected from the local towns is added to replace lost organic matter. Over the winter, cover crops such as the pretty purple phacelia and clovers are grown to try to stop bare soil from being eroded by the wind and rain. The tractors today have

---

[23] The Great Fen Project.

tyres to minimise the compaction of the earth, while computers on tractors ensure pesticide use is much more targeted. Rotations for potatoes are more like every 10 years, rather than every six, to rid the soil of diseases without using toxic chemicals. New varieties of potatoes with better disease resistance[24] are replacing the old favourites like King Edwards. For James, his job is not only producing potatoes but preserving the soil for future generations.

'I see myself more as a soil manager than a farmer,' he says.

The world only has around 5–20cm of topsoil, the precious layer of 'living soil' – James's 'apple skin' – containing all the nutrients to grow food. But we remove those nutrients every time we plough the soil and harvest a crop. If the nutrients are not replaced, the topsoil – our life source – will deplete. Even before the industrialisation of farming, humans were destroying the soil and, in turn, themselves. The Sumerian society in Mesopotamia (the world's first literate culture) flourished from 3000 BC but ended because of over-cropping and over-irrigation of their soils. The Easter Islanders allegedly died out after chopping down all the trees and causing erosion of the soils. Both Plato and Aristotle warned of the consequences to civilisation of allowing the soil to degrade. More recently, a newspaper article[25] in 2014 warned that in the UK, we have less than a hundred harvests in the soil before we run out.

It is a terrifying figure, so I decide to track it back to its source. But when I read the paper[26] by the University of

---

[24] In 2021, a number of UK retailers signed up to the Robust Potato Pledge, promising to stock organic, disease-resistant potatoes grown using fewer chemicals.

[25] 'The UK only has 100 harvests left', *Independent*, 2014.

[26] 'Urban cultivation in allotments maintains soil qualities adversely affected by conventional agriculture', *Journal of Applied Ecology*, 2014.

Sheffield from which this shocking prediction allegedly came, I find no reference to a hundred harvests. Confused, I contacted the lead author, and she told me it was never in the report – a press officer added the sentence. Is it fake news, then?

It takes a little digging to track the figure back to its source. In 2012, John Crawford, then a Professor of Agriculture at the University of Sydney in Australia, told *Time* magazine that there were only 60 years of topsoil left before the world ran out. The UN later used his figure to highlight the threat to the world from unsustainable intensive agriculture. Previously scary statistics on the rate of soil erosion had been available to the public, including a report that warned all of the topsoil could be gone from Europe, except the valley floors, in the next hundred years.[27] But what did that mean to ordinary people? This new figure captured the public's imagination. It suddenly made soil sexy because we could understand the danger we were in and still are.

John is now in a new post at Rothamsted Research in England, from where I interviewed him about his famous prediction. He tells me the figure was an 'order of magnitude' calculation put together after a coffee with other scientists. He was surprised and pleased that it had ended up being quoted by politicians and 'stimulated thinking'.

'The point is not that we have 60 harvests left,' he says. 'The point is that soil is a finite resource, and all the evidence we have currently [suggests that] we are using it in an unsustainable way. The rate of degradation is scary.'

Since 2014, several peer-reviewed papers have confirmed the figure was along the right lines, including a report that the world was losing 10 million hectares of cropland a year due to soil erosion and that the rate of loss is between 10 and 40 times the rate of formation.[28] In 2020 a report

---

[27] *Earth-Science Reviews*, 2009.

[28] College of Agriculture and Life Sciences, Cornell University. Published in *Agriculture*, 2013.

looked at soils around the world, and while it found that rates of erosion vary widely, some 16 per cent have less than 100 years left,[29] and areas of intensive agriculture are much more in danger.

A report by the Committee on Climate Change (CCC) found the UK has lost 84 per cent of its fertile topsoil since 1850, with the erosion continuing at a rate of 1–3cm a year, which doesn't sound like a lot until you realise it could take a thousand years for another 3cm to form.[30]

'The most fertile topsoils in the east of England – where 25 per cent of our potatoes and 30 per cent of our vegetables are grown – could be lost within a generation,' warned Lord John Krebs, Chair of the CCC, referring to the Fens where James Thorp grows his potatoes.

So not fake news then, at all, news that we really ought to be listening to.

One crop in particular works the soil harder than any other: potatoes. For James Thorp, this is part of the challenge – how to ensure a good growing medium without losing nutrients. Even years before the potato is planted, crop rotation must be planned so that the soil has time to recover from any pests. Certain crops in the rotation, such as peas or broad beans, can add nitrogen to the soil. Others, such as mustard, can help 'biofumigate' pests in the soil. Then, months before the potatoes are planted, the soil must be cultivated. In most parts of the country, the stubble land will be ploughed and left to weather over Christmas. But in the Fens and other parts of the country where farmers are

---

[29] 'Soil lifespans and how they can be extended by land use and management change', *Environmental Letters*, 2020.

[30] 'Reducing emissions and preparing for climate change: 2015 CCC Progress Report to Parliament'.

taking a more modern outlook, cover crops are planted to retain that precious organic carbon in the soil. In spring, a nitrogen-based fertiliser will be applied and possibly some lime, the latter to make the soil more alkaline if the pH is too acid. The field will then be broken up further with a grubber, a great paw of a machine with metal claws that are raked across the field to break up the earth into smaller pieces and let in the air. A few weeks later, deep ridges, known as tatty rigs or beds, will be created with a 'hiller' or a cultivator, another machine dragged across the field to mound the earth into straight rows.

From my interview with Professor John Crawford, I know that disturbing the soil is not very good for storing carbon, but I can't help loving the plough. Perhaps it is because I am a farmer's daughter, but there is something so beautiful about how the low winter light catches the underside of freshly turned soil, turning it purple.

Farming families tend to be sentimental about ploughing. Every autumn across the country, there are ploughing matches, ostensibly to judge who can plough the straightest furrow with a tractor or horse, but in reality to tinker with vintage Fergie tractors, admire Suffolk Punch horses and catch up after the harvest.[31] My own family still talks with pride of the land at East Lothian in Scotland, where we have ploughed for generations. My great-great-great-grandfather took on Auldhame in 1837 as a 21-year-old tenant. Like most farmers of his time, he invested in the soil, adding manure every year, seaweed from the beach and even night soil[32] from the nearby towns. His hard work paid off: in 1920, my great-grandfather bought the farm, and some of the land is still in the family today. I was brought up to be proud of this heritage. I even have a copy of an old black-and-white

---

[31] The Irish National Ploughing Championships has grown into one of the largest outdoor events in the world.

[32] Human sewage.

photograph from around 1950 of the last Clydesdales that helped make a success of the farm. Somehow the name of the ploughman has been forgotten, but we know the name of the horses, Bob and Dick. They are magnificent beasts, jangling in brass and blinkers, their manes combed out and their white fetlocks bright against the freshly turned soil.

My great-grandfather Jack loved ploughing. There is a famous story in my family that when his wife Mary went into labour, instead of stopping farming, Jack asked for a towel to be dangled from the window of Auldhame's farmhouse when the time came. It was two towels: my great-aunts Stella and Flora.

Today, of course, a much bigger plough is pulled by a tractor,[33] and the farmer can sit in an air-conditioned cab and listen to a podcast. I can't be sure where Bob and Dick pulled the plough, but I found a field nearby in April when the bed tiller was working away, sieving the soil so that only the fine grains are on the top of the mounds while the larger chunks sit in the dips. I bend down and run my fingers through the soil. It feels like icing sugar. I love the words associated with soil: friable, tilth, protozoa. A skylark is singing, and wagtails and seagulls follow the tractor. It is a perfect countryside backdrop and, at the same time, an industrial scene. The potatoes have not been planted yet, and already at least four tractors, each using at least 100 horsepower, have had to go over the field to create this perfect growing medium.

After the soil has been prepared, the chemical applications are introduced. Despite its rugged Andean ancestry, the modern potato – *Solanum tuberosum* – is a delicate, tender

---

[33] My great-grandfather wouldn't like it, but there is even the possibility of growing potatoes without ploughing. A recent experiment in Cambridgeshire has grown 'no-till' potatoes under a straw mulch.

and highly bred creature. We have bred out all its tough genetics for fighting blight in favour of flavour, looks and size. As a result, commercially grown potatoes are one of the most chemical-heavy crops we grow in this country.

Potatoes are constantly under attack from aphids, eelworms, blight and scab. The supermarkets want them perfect, so they have to be protected from all these diseases. I have already described how the soil is made perfect in places like the Fens, but how is the potato protected from any possible attack?

Before the modern seed potato is even planted in the ground, it will have been treated with fungicide to try to keep away any blight. Where there are potato cyst nematodes in the soil, a nematicide will also be put in when the potato is planted to stop an attack by eelworm. Just before the baby potato plants emerge, a herbicide is put onto the soil to kill any weeds trying to come up at the same time to give the potato a head start.

Yet, no matter how good a start the potato plant is given, the blight is always a threat. The spores of late blight, or *Phytophthora infestans*, are virtually everywhere. There could be some near you right now. All it needs is the right conditions to strike. For potatoes to be infected, the temperature needs to be above 10°C, and it must be humid. These weather conditions are not unusual in the UK, so throughout the season, the farmers have a 'blight alert' to tell them to spray when the conditions are right. Many will spray just to be safe.

Usually, when the potato plants reach the 'rosette stage' (around the size of a hand), they will be given their first spray of fungicide, which is repeated pretty much every week through the growing season. In a bad season, fungicides can be sprayed up to 20 times on the plants, which means taking tractors into the field 20 times, not to mention the chemical use. Farmers will also often spray insecticide once or twice to get rid of aphids that can cause the spread of blight.

As well as the energy used to apply chemicals, potatoes need to be irrigated, especially in dry areas with less blight. As soon as the tubers start growing, most potatoes grown in the British Isles are given water regularly.

When the potato plants are ready, the 'shaws' are sprayed off with herbicide and allowed to die. The potatoes are left four weeks to 'set', so the skins harden off before they are ready to harvest. The crop will have been treated with chemicals more than a dozen times since it was planted. Most of the energy to manufacture the chemicals and drive the tractors will come from petroleum oil. As the American ecologist Howard Odum said: 'Industrial man no longer eats potatoes made from solar energy; now he eats potatoes partly made of oil.'

Potatoes grow in six to 14 weeks, making them one of the most efficient ways to get maximum nutrition out of the soil in the shortest possible time. As breeding has improved, potatoes have become even more popular, despite the heavy chemical and energy input. Since the 1960s, the potato has become the fastest-spreading major food crop in the world. Today potatoes are grown in 148 of the 192 countries represented in the UN. They are grown from latitudes 65°N to 50°S, from sea level to altitudes of 4,000 metres, and potatoes have become the third most important crop after rice and wheat in terms of consumption.[34]

The British may claim to grow the best seed potatoes in the world, but the biggest producers today are China and India. While potato consumption is falling slightly in Britain and the rest of Europe due to competition from other carbohydrates such as rice and noodles, and perhaps the trend for low-carb diets and avocados, in developing countries, potato consumption is growing. The Chinese, in

---

[34] International Potato Centre.

particular, are promoting potatoes. The People's Republic sees potatoes as a way of feeding more of the population using less land. The crop takes less water than rice and produces less greenhouse gases while providing more nutrients. For now, it is an uphill battle trying to persuade the Chinese to eat a 'peasant food' they consider inferior to rice – rather like the early Europeans' perspective with potatoes and bread. But propaganda, including a singing 'potato lady' and cartoon characters, promises to transform it into a staple food. The Chinese are already beginning to eat French fries as the potato fuels a different way of eating and a new approach to agriculture that works the soil harder than ever.

The problem is that soil is not an inexhaustible resource, and it is running out. So how do we farm without destroying our soils? Many would argue that organic farming is the answer. The organic movement certainly cottoned on sooner than the rest of the world that the headlong industrialisation of farming was depleting the soil. In 1946, when the British government was driving intensive agriculture in places like the Fens, a bunch of eccentric farmers were going in the opposite direction. The Soil Association was set up on a farm in Suffolk by Lady Eve Balfour to try to prove that traditional methods such as adding compost to the soil and rotating crops – were superior to using synthetic fertilisers. She argued that the soil needed careful management to remain healthy and that adding fertiliser that leaches into the water courses will fail to build up structure and nutrients. The Haughley Experiment she set up was the first to compare organic and conventional methods and prompted many of the questions we are still asking today. Perhaps it was her background (her uncle was the prime minister), her relationships with women or her spiritualist beliefs, but Lady Balfour was never taken seriously. It was only in the late 1960s, when consumers became concerned about the pesticides used in conventional agriculture ending up in their food, that the Soil Association became more mainstream. In 1967, the organisation set up the world's first organic certification scheme. The famous trademark that we look out for on food is now what the Soil Association is most famous for, as well as campaigning work on improving school meals for children and perhaps a bit of an 'elitist' reputation because of its continued links with the aristocracy and more recently rich celebrities.

The lifestyle associated with organic food may have gone beyond the original purpose in some areas, but the belief in the soil and the experimental spirit of Lady Balfour has continued. Although it barely makes up 4 per cent of the land farmed in the UK, the organic movement is still forward-thinking. Despite the image of 'muck and mystery', many of their methods have been proven correct. Green waste, ploughed back in the stubble and compost, is increasingly used by farmers like James Thorp to maintain structure and carbon in the soil. Globally, many studies have shown that small farmers, who cannot afford to buy a massive amount of energy-heavy artificial chemicals, are better off improving yields using organic methods. A University of Essex study covering 286 projects in 57 countries and including 12.6 million farmers found a yield increase of 79 per cent when farmers shifted to primarily organic practices like nutrient cycling and increased crop diversity. A 2016 report in *Nature Plants* found that organic farming could fare even better as the climate changes in many areas of the world. It is also accepted by scientists that organic methods boost biodiversity on farms and help the soil retain water. An Oxford University study found that, on average organic farms support 34 per cent more plant, animal and insect species.

So why aren't we all going organic? It is an ongoing debate in the farming world. The most common answer is that yields are lower[35] in organic farming, meaning that

---

[35] Various studies have estimated the yield of organic potatoes to be lower by 5–40 per cent. However, it is worth noting that in many crops, the gap between organic and conventional yields is closing.

more land is needed to produce the same amount of food. Then there is the cost. Organic potatoes are generally more expensive. Perhaps it is because I am the daughter of a 'conventional farmer',[36] or maybe because I don't always buy organic potatoes for my family I remain, like many people, 'on the fence' looking at two fields of potatoes grown in very different ways.

Perhaps the answer is to combine organic methods and conventional farming to grow enough food while maintaining the soil? Rothamsted Research, where Professor Crawford is now based, has more rigorous experiments than the early efforts of Lady Eve Balfour. For 175 years, fields have been monitored for the best growing mediums to produce the highest quality crops. And the answer? Like most things, it is a little bit of both: in this case, organic and conventional farming.

We don't have a name for that yet. Some people call it 'regenerative' farming, farming that not only maintains the soil but repairs it if necessary. Some have even tried to certify it. LEAF (Linking Environment and Farming) has been successfully combining organic and conventional farming for 30 years to produce food certified in a similar way to the Soil Association. Some people call it 'agroecological' farming, which works with nature to keep the soil alive. Some people just call it 'good' farming. Whatever we call it, organic methods will be part of the future. Despite all the horsepower and chemicals introduced since my great-great-great-grandfather grew potatoes, organic methods he used, such as manure and crop rotations, are now coming back into the system as we realise that no technology can replace knowledge and care of the soil.

'We need to move towards a more organic system,' says Professor Crawford. 'We need more organic matter cycling

---

[36] I have yet to meet anyone who would describe my father as 'conventional'.

through, creating a nutritional circular economy that allows food waste or waste, in general, to feed into the soil.'

James Thorp takes this approach, adding organic matter to the soil, increasing rotation times and essentially using organic methods to try to reverse the soil degradation on the land he manages.

Returning to the Fens in October, I watch a harvester move across the field in a cloud of dust, digging up the soft ridges, dead potato plants and perfect potatoes. As the potatoes pass on a riddle, workers on the back of the machine pick out the dead plants and any rotten potatoes or stones. The potatoes ending up in the crates are indeed perfect, not only because of chemicals but because of a long rotation and care of the soil.

'We are intensively farming; there is no doubt about it,' says James. 'But a lot of thought goes into what we do. We are preserving soils for the next generation.'

What will the soil look like for the next generation? According to Hollywood, it could be red. Anyone who has seen *The Martian* starring Matt Damon will know the storyline of the stranded astronaut planting potatoes to stay alive or having to 'science the shit out of this', as he memorably puts it. It is not as far-fetched as it sounds. Since the 1980s, NASA has been working on a 'Biogenerative Life Support System' to use in space – in other words, 'grow your own veg'. A stand of potatoes large enough to provide as much as each person needs per day will also supply all the oxygen they must have and remove all the carbon dioxide they exhale. Trillions of dollars, billions of hours and the success of humanity's most ambitious and complex enterprise to date will ultimately depend upon the astronauts' ability to grow potatoes.

In Peru, where the story of the potato started, NASA is growing potatoes in 'Martian-like' soil to try to find the best varieties for growing on the red planet. The plans involve cultivating 65 selected varieties in extreme Mars-like conditions in the Atacama Desert that could eventually pave the way to building a dome on the planet for farming the tuber. After all, what could be a better way to survive than growing your own locally?

The slightly scary fact is that we are not just planting potatoes in a tent in the searing heat of the desert because we will be living on the red planet any time soon; frankly, it could just be a clever way to get media attention. The more pertinent reason we are trying to grow potatoes in degraded soils is that that is how we may need to farm potatoes on *this* planet very soon. Already we are struggling to feed the world with the soil we have. If droughts and floods become worse with climate change, or if we destroy the microbial life in the soil with damaging farming methods, it will be even more difficult. The answer could be to grow potatoes in degraded soils.

It will be some time before humans can farm on Mars, and in that time, we will need to grow all our food here – for a population set to reach 9 billion by 2050. To do that, we need to look after our soil. The potato has influenced our history, fuelling the Industrial Revolution and mass migration to the Americas. It has driven globalisation, spreading industrial farming and the ability to feed millions of people in developing areas. In the future, it could fuel our colonisation of Mars. But its most important contribution could be what it tells us about the soil. If we do not learn to look after the soil, if we do not learn to farm more sustainably, we will have no potatoes or any other food to eat. A valuable esculent indeed.

Further reading

The Living Soil by Lady Eve Balfour (Faber & Faber, 1943)
The Untold History of the Potato by John Reader (Vintage, 2009)
The Martian by Andy Weir (originally self-published, 2011)
'Healthy Soil, Healthy World', Professor John Crawford, TED@Sydney 2012

Crispy potato 'worms'

Charles Darwin discovered the fossils of lost species. He encountered birds with bright blue feet, sharks with T-shaped heads and giant tortoises. He defied the Church by publishing the theory of evolution and became the most famous biologist of all time. He also spent a lot of time with worms.

When he wasn't circumnavigating the globe or picking fights with Creationists, Darwin liked nothing better than crouching down to look at worms. Every morning, when the ground was still wet with dew, he would set out with one of his 10 children to look at the earthworms at the bottom of his garden. Over 40 years, he noted how the earthworms aerated the soil with their burrows and created humus by ingesting organic matter. Like the slow process of evolution, he saw that the slow process of soil passing through the gut of worms creates the world we know and rely on.

While his more controversial work on natural selection enraged the Church and changed the world, he quietly worked away on the less controversial but no less important theory that worms are crucial to our civilisation because they create the soil that is vital to growing our food. Six months before he died, Darwin published *The Formation of Vegetable Mould through the Action of Worms, with Observations of their Habits*. Surprisingly, it sold 6,000 copies in its first year, selling faster than *On the Origin of Species* had when it was first published. The Victorians were fascinated by worms and the benefits they could bring to their gardens.

Today, observing worms is still a fun thing to do with young scientists, and it tells you a lot about the soil. Just take an ordinary garden trowel and dig around until you find some worms. If you have unhealthy soil, you won't have many worms. Sadly, a recent survey of fields by farmers found 42 per cent were seriously deficient in earthworms, and in some fields, they were missing altogether.[37] That

[37] 'Soil health pilot study, 2019' *Plos One*.

could be because of specific farming methods, such as ploughing, chemical use and use of heavy machinery. If you have healthy soil full of organic matter and microbial activity, you should have two to four worms per spadeful.

With their inherent wisdom, children love worms, but it can be a bit messy spending all morning digging in the dirt. This recipe makes potato peelings, which would otherwise go to waste, into worms. Children love to use their hands to mix the 'worms' in oil, and making these is an excellent way to celebrate potatoes and the worms that make them possible.

- potato peelings (the longer and wormier, the better). You can use any peelings you have from making potatoes for a bigger meal (like mukimo on page 100).
- vegetable oil to lightly coat the peels. Start with one tablespoon for four medium potatoes worth of peelings, and add more if needed.
- salt, to taste
- flavourings, such as paprika, rosemary or lemon

1. Preheat the oven to 180°C.
2. Toss your potato peelings in a bowl with the vegetable oil, so they are thinly coated.
3. Once they are all covered in oil, transfer the peelings to an oven tray, ideally arranging them skin side up and not touching one another.
4. Bake for 10 minutes and then keep an eye on them, turning the skin or rotating the tray if necessary. You can use a fish slice to loosen the skins before giving the tray a shake. They should take around 15 minutes. Keep an eye on them and take them out when they are browning at the edges and look like well-done crisps.
5. Once cooked, toss the 'worms' in a good sprinkling of salt and add flavourings such as a dusting of paprika or some black pepper. I like to add a squeeze of lemon and a sprinkle of chopped fresh rosemary.

CHAPTER FOUR

Miciri

Kenyan green beans: 15kg CO_2e per kg
UK-grown green beans: 0.15kg CO_2e per kg[38]

*'[Eating local] may seem difficult and dull, but it is in
fact liberating.'*
Mike Small, *Scotland's Local Food Revolution*

The rolling hills of the northern Rift Valley are known as
the 'bread basket' – or rather the 'maize basket' – of Kenya.
This is good fertile land, and most farmers here grow maize
for the traditional dish, *ugali*. But look closely and you will

---

[38] A 2006 DFID report stated that airfreighting produce such as green
beans from Sub-Saharan Africa to the UK produces 15kg CO_2e per kg.
The same report noted that shipping produce would create 0.1kg CO_2e
per kg, while transport in an articulated lorry from Spain would produce
0.15kg CO_2e per kg. Since we transport UK-grown green beans around
the country by lorry, it is safe to assume UK-grown green beans create
around 0.15kg CO_2e per kg. Another DFID report stated that cultivation
before the transport of green beans in Kenya or the UK produces
around the same amount of CO_2e per kg because while UK farms use
more fossil fuels due to mechanisation, they produce much higher
yields, and therefore it balances out.

see splashes of a brighter green amid the farm terraces; French beans, mange tout, snow peas and cabbage nestle among the corn. These tender crops are Joshua Etyang's pride and joy and his family's route out of poverty. Two years ago, when he specialised solely in maize farming, Joshua could barely meet the basic necessities of his family with the four 90kg sacks of maize he'd harvest after six months. This would force him to take up casual jobs on neighbours' farms to supplement the family's meagre income. He could not afford the basic costs of uniforms and equipment to send his children to school.

Like most young people in Kenya, Joshua had little choice. The country has a high unemployment rate in the under-35 age group, with one in five struggling to find work. Agriculture, which employs 70 per cent of rural people, is the best hope for many, yet traditional maize farming is failing to provide them with enough money – or nutrition. Changing weather patterns and depleted soils mean harvests have been poor. Meanwhile, the withdrawal of national government purchases of maize has led to a massive drop in income.

Enter Farm Africa. In 2016, the charity started the Growing Futures project specifically aimed at helping young farmers in western Kenya to improve their livelihoods by moving into the production of horticultural crops. Vegetables not only grow well in the fertile land of Trans-Nzoia County, but they can fetch a good market price and provide more than one harvest a year. The crops also supplement the family's diet with highly nutritious food.

As part of the project, Joshua was trained in producing horticultural crops such as French beans (also known as *miciri* in Kenya), sugar snaps, snow peas, garden peas and cabbages. He was given support in the form of seeds and materials for implementing drip irrigation. He was taught the best way to rotate crops and apply both organic and inorganic fertilisers. He was also trained in record-keeping and farm management. Farmers linked to the project in the local community have formed a network to sell into markets, swap seeds and share information.

Joshua and his wife, Maximilia, worked hard, spreading cow manure on the crops, digging trenches to prevent flooding and picking off pests by hand. Finally, they could reap a good harvest, and Joshua could ask his neighbours to help him this time. Within a few years, Joshua was making good money from selling his crops and was able to start feeding his family better food. He could even buy a cow and send his children to school.

'My household is now happy since we can comfortably afford the basic needs we couldn't buy before,' he told Farm Africa.

It is a rare good-news story of knowledge transfer helping a family to become healthier, happier and more resilient to climate change. But there is one uncomfortable question: where are those green beans going?

Some of them go to a supermarket near you after flying to the UK in the belly of an aeroplane pumping out lots of carbon dioxide. Green beans from Kenya may be a good-news story for international development, but for some people, they have become a symbol of Food Miles, which are seen as one of the worst excesses of our profligate food system and a driver of climate change.

The term 'Food Miles' was first coined more than 20 years ago by Tim Lang and colleagues at the Sustainable Agriculture, Food and Environment (SAFE) Alliance (later to become Sustain, the Alliance for Better Food and Farming) to describe the hidden distance that food travels before it 'miraculously' appears on the supermarket shelf. The campaign group could see the impact supermarkets stocking food from all over the world throughout the year had on the environment, our town centres, our food security and even our health. In a report[39] published in 1994, SAFE

---

[39] 'The Food Miles Report', *Sustain* (2011 reprint).

described the ecological impact of burning fossil fuels to transport food and the plastic pollution from over-packaged foods. It blamed supermarkets providing food from all over the world during every season at lower and lower prices for putting small retailers and farmers out of business. And one of the very worst culprits? Green beans being transported some 4,000 miles from Kenya.

Even before the internet, the report went viral. *Farmers Weekly* began a Food Miles campaign informing readers that 'Local Food is Miles Better'. The Soil Association flirted with banning any food that was airfreighted, and several food companies began including 'low food miles' as a boast on labels. Tesco and Marks & Spencer started to put an image of a little black aeroplane on airfreighted food so that consumers could spot Food Miles. In Scotland, the Fife Diet, which invited people only to eat local food, became Europe's biggest such food initiative, with copycat 'local food revolutions' popping up all over the British Isles. Again and again, Food Miles was shown as the key to all that was wrong with our food system – and the 'poster vegetable' was Kenyan green beans. As concern about our carbon footprint went up the agenda, the number of Food Miles your lunch had travelled became even more important. Food Miles became a 'water cooler' topic, taught as a concept in the geography syllabus and was a storyline on *The Archers*. It even made it into the *Oxford English Dictionary*, something Tim Lang admitted 'even impressed my mother'.

Then came the backlash.

Following so much public concern, in 2005, the government ordered a study into Food Miles.[40] It found that food transport produces 1.8 per cent of the total reported UK CO_2 emissions from all sectors. So, yes, the environmental impact of transporting our food is significant enough to need solving, but not necessarily how you think. The largest

---

[40] 'The Validity of Food Miles as an Indicator of Sustainable Development', Defra, 2005.

proportion of our carbon footprint taken up by food transport was not green beans flying from Kenya but all the other food we move around the UK in big smelly trucks or cars. Since 1978, the annual amount of food transported in the UK by HGVs has increased by 23 per cent, and the average distance for each trip has increased by more than half. This means more carbon and an increase in congestion, air pollution, accidents and noise. At the same time, the number of car journeys to pick up food from the shop has increased. Each year, the average UK adult travels about 135 miles (217km) by car to shop for food, which adds up to an estimated total of 3 million shopping miles (or 4.8 million shopping km) per day. Road transport accounted for more than three-quarters of the carbon emissions arising from food transport. In comparison, airfreight only accounted for 11 per cent.

A 2007 report by the International Institute for Environment Development (IIED) focusing on African horticulture broke it down further. Their report estimated that the airfreight of fruit and vegetables is approximately 0.2 per cent of total UK greenhouse gas (GHG) emissions. Additionally, within the airfreight sector, produce coming from Africa is no more than half of the total, so the total airfreight component of African fruit and vegetables, like Kenyan green beans, is a maximum of 0.1 per cent of the UK's total GHG emissions. The IIED report made the point that food-related car travel is 0.38 per cent of UK emissions; hence air transport of all African fruit and vegetables (0.1 per cent) is equivalent to one-quarter of the emissions of total UK consumer supermarket trips. In other words, cycling to the shops may do more to help than cutting down on green beans from Kenya. The report calculated that one packet of Kenyan green beans is equivalent to 12 school runs in the car. A return flight from London to Barcelona is 420 packs.

Both these reports emphasised the need to look at more than just Food Miles to estimate the carbon footprint of food. Instead, the reports suggested that consumers should look at the entire life cycle of a product, 'from seed to plate', including what chemicals were used to grow the plant, how much energy was used to harvest and process the product, how it was transported to your house, and how it was cooked. Looking at the total life cycle of a food item, rather than just the Food Miles, gives a more accurate indication of carbon footprint and where the hotspots are. The Defra report cited a case study that showed that at certain times of the year when tomatoes have to be grown in heated greenhouses in the UK, importing tomatoes from Spain, where they are grown under polytunnels with no heating, can be the lower carbon option. It also said that organic food could be lower carbon than conventionally grown UK crops because organic farmers use less energy-intensive chemicals. Another study suggested apples shipped from New Zealand had a lower carbon footprint than British apples at certain times of year because the scale of orchards in the Southern Hemisphere meant that it takes less energy to produce each apple.

The Defra and IIED reports were jumped on. Some might say this was because they were making an important point about the complexity of the carbon footprint of our food. Some might say it was because those reports could be used as a way to protect against those pesky environmentalists ruining our right to eat what we want when we want.

In a speech in 2007, Gareth Thomas, then Minister for Trade and Development, made the government's position on Food Miles clear: 'Food Miles alone, or the distance food has travelled, is not a good way to judge whether the food we eat is sustainable,' he stated. 'Driving 6.5 miles to buy your shopping emits more carbon than flying a pack of Kenyan green beans to the UK.'

After other studies suggested that eating less meat could be the best way to cut the carbon footprint of your food[41]

---

[41] Diets containing meat have carbon footprints around twice that of plant-based diets – *Climatic Change*, 2014.

rather than cutting Food Miles, the argument shifted to the carbon footprint of meat. A US study found that switching less than one day per week's worth of calories from red meat and dairy products to chicken, fish, eggs or a vegetable-based diet achieves more GHG reduction than buying all locally sourced food.[42] Another study[43] found that cooking food in a microwave, pressure cooker or slow cooker are lower carbon options than using an oven. In summary, cycling to the supermarket, eating less red meat and cooking food in the microwave rather than in the oven could reduce your carbon footprint more than cutting out green beans. Though arguably, you could do both.

Suddenly the concept of Food Miles was not so trendy. Both the *Observer* and the *Daily Mail* published columns questioning the idea. Jay Rayner, the well-known food critic, was on the BBC explaining why the concept of Food Miles was over-simplistic: 'What matters is how your food is produced, not where,' he said.

The Soil Association dropped its plans to ban airfreight,[44] and some supermarkets refused to put the little black aeroplanes on labels, as they felt it was not a reflection of the environmental impact of a product. Most recently, the first database to break down food emissions from each stage of the food chain, published in *Nature Food*, concluded that transport is a small part of a food's carbon footprint compared to the emissions from food waste and food packaging.

The question is, is worrying about the distance your food travels really all about carbon? Or is it about something else?

---

[42] *Environmental Science & Technology*, 2008.

[43] *Nature Food*, 2020.

[44] On 25 October 2007, the Soil Association announced that all airfreighted organic food will have to meet the Soil Association's ethical trade standards.

When Mike Small started the Fife Diet, it was all about reducing carbon emissions. His second son had just been born into a world where every summer seemed to break a new record for heat.[45] As a father, he felt a growing need to do something about climate change. He looked around for a way to change his lifestyle and settled on the statistic that the food chain was responsible for a third of the UK's GHG emissions and even a little bit more if you also added out-of-season fruit and vegetables – such as green beans from Kenya.[46] Mike, who had just moved from Glasgow to Fife, looked out the window and saw plenty of food growing in the fields in his local area but very little of that food in his fridge. Why couldn't he cut his family's Food Miles by eating those potatoes, cabbages, buffaloes[47] and rabbits? Inspired by the growing 'locavore' movement in the US, where a book on the '100 Mile Diet'[48] had sparked enormous interest, he decided only to eat food from his home county of Fife (barely 50 miles, or 80km, at its widest point). Mike later extended the radius to be more like 100 miles (160km), including East Lothian for most of the fruit and veg.

From day one, the Fife Diet garnered enormous media interest. The community feast in Falkland Village Hall, where Mike expected a few members of the Green Party and the town busybody to join the locals, was attended by *ITN News* and journalists from the national newspapers. Over its first seven years, interest never really let up. The public was fascinated by this 'bonkers idea' (Mike's wife Karen's description of the Fife Diet, not mine). Within a few years, 'followers' of the Fife Diet had swelled from 14 to

---

[45] 2007 was one of the UK's top-10 hottest years.

[46] *Scotland's Local Food Revolution*, by Mike Small (Argyll Publishing, 2013).

[47] Scotland's biggest buffalo farm is in Fife.

[48] *The 100 Mile Diet: A Year of Eating Locally* by Ailsa Smith and J. B. Mackinnon (Vintage Canada, 2007).

more than a thousand. Maybe it was concern about all those green beans being flown in from Africa, but people wanted to know about a young family eating locally. What on earth did they eat? How did they survive? Good grief, how were the children coping without sweets? (This was genuinely the line of questioning during a BBC Radio 5 Live interview.)

The answers were predictable enough. Yes, they ate a lot of tatties and oats, brassicas and turnips, the staples of a traditional Scottish diet. But they also enjoyed soft fruit (including jams and frozen berries preserved from the summer), meat and fish (probably a little more than they otherwise had done because it was a nutritious source of food found locally), dairy (including local cheeses), organic wheat grown and milled in the Howe of Fife, and local beer and cider and even fruit wine.

It was not actually that hard, Mike admitted. Fife and its surrounds offered enough food for the family to 'survive'. What was hard was the additional effort it took to fit sourcing all their food locally into modern life. As working parents, Mike and Karen had to spend more time sourcing, preparing and cooking food. They could not just bung on pasta and pesto. They had to plan around a veg box and a piece of meat. They became proficient in batch cooking and making soups and ate a lot of omelettes. They cut out snacks (yes, including sweeties for the kids). A typical day might include porridge for breakfast, a bacon roll for lunch and for dinner, fish pie with purple sprouting broccoli followed by raspberries and cream.

Within a few years, the Fife Diet morphed into something more doable. Mike conceded he could not live without coffee, so he allowed the inclusion of spices, tea, rice and pulses. He decided on an 80:20 ratio of local to further afield to allow people the 'luxuries' of bananas and chocolate and things they personally felt they couldn't live without. This combination was popular with people.

The Fife Diet swelled further to 5,000 and became Europe's biggest local food project. The message was no longer only about eating local produce but about limiting meat and dairy consumption, eating more organic produce, reducing food waste and composting more. At the end of the experiment in 2015, Mike calculated that the Fife Diet had saved 1410.47 tonnes of CO_2e – the equivalent of driving from Scotland to India – by encouraging people to eat only locally sourced food.

However, the diet's most significant impact was about something else entirely. In a survey of people who took part in the Fife Diet, the thing they spoke about most was not how much carbon they saved but how it made them feel. Yes, they felt good about cutting their carbon footprint – however slightly. More than that, they said the diet helped them feel less stressed in an age of anxiety.

Mike wondered if that was because participants enjoyed having limits imposed by the seasons and geography. Supermarkets give you 55,000 options, including green beans from Kenya; the Fife Diet had 500 products over the year. On the face of it, this could seem like a limitation, but many participants found taking a holiday from supermarket choice freeing. Angus from Lochgelly wrote: 'Understanding for the first time what it would mean to live here, to actually live here in this place in this time, I felt re-rooted.' Others enjoyed eating 'what my granny cooked'. Mike cited a 2004 book by American psychologist Barry Schwartz: *Paradox of Choice: Why More is Less*. Schwartz argued that too much choice leads to decision-making paralysis, anxiety and perpetual stress. When it came to food shopping, the Fife Diet took some of this away.

There were other reasons the Fife Diet made people feel happier. It may take more work to source food locally, but it forces more social interaction at the farmers' market, with a veg-box producer, with a local farmer or even cooking with your partner. It connected people to the seasons by forcing them to understand what food was in season and to their local landscape by pushing them to see what was grown, where and when. It opened their eyes to the fertility of the soil and richness of the seas around Fife, the buffalo mozzarella, the foraged nettles and the polytunnels full of strawberries. And it encouraged them to try new recipes like beetroot chocolate cupcakes, broad bean and caramelised onion pesto or grilled tomatoes with sage butter. It was not about restriction but rediscovering the abundance on their doorstep.

Other locavore initiatives started to pop up around the British Isles. One of the most successful, Growing Communities in London, came up with a handy diagram to explain the principle of a 'bioregional' approach or 'local and seasonal first'. The Food Zone looks like a target. The inner ring is hyperlocal foods such as salads, leafy greens and fruits grown on city farms or rooftops. The next ring is market gardens in the peri-urban setting. Cereals and livestock can come from the next ring out, the 'rural hinterland' within 100 miles of where you live. Next is the rest of the UK. The not-for-profit company think it is realistic to aim for 80 per cent of food from within the UK, with 60 per cent within 100 miles of where you live. Growing Communities supplies fruit and veg to Londoners from small-scale organic farms via veg boxes and collection points. It also supports market gardens within the city to train the next generation of growers and provide affordable organic fruit and veg to low-income families. One of the farms, called Grown in Dagenham, grows green beans that are transported just 12 miles to a collection point for consumption. In its annual report, Growing Communities does not speak much about carbon; instead, it talks about supporting small farmers and bringing the community together. Every year it has expanded, taking on more farms and more customers and providing food for more vulnerable families.

Many people want to be able to be locavores or at least eat from their local 'foodshed' (the area where you could naturally source your food, like a watershed). During the pandemic, demand for veg boxes soared. A Food Foundation survey of 101 veg-box schemes across the UK found they doubled the number of veg boxes ordered weekly during the first lockdown. Riverford, which never airfreights their produce, saw a 70 per cent increase during the peak of lockdown. I'm sure some of that was thanks to being stuck at home and concern about Food Miles, but it was also about getting back in touch with the community (10 per cent of box schemes offer cheaper boxes for those suffering financial hardship and give members the option of paying a bit more to help others who are struggling) and nature (most box schemes are organic and try to minimise the use of chemicals).

In my own life, I try to get an organic veg box whenever I am home in Edinburgh for long periods. I am lucky enough to have access to a veg box from East Lothian transported into the city in electric vans.[49] It is always wonderful to discover the delicious leafy greens and root vegetables that can be grown on my doorstep throughout the year. Even better is picking vegetables at my local community garden.[50] As Schwartz suggests, I do like choice being taken away within this limited context and having to be creative with what is available (though I still struggle to get my head around celeriac). I also enjoy 'eating the seasons' and find I eat more vegetables when I get a veg box. Every so often, there is a bottleneck, and I have to cancel the veg box while I work through old potatoes and shrivelled beetroot. I can't pretend that I eat totally seasonally and locally or even manage the '60 per cent within a 100-mile radius' and '80 per cent within the UK' model that Growing Communities suggests, though I would like to do better. My local veg box company doesn't offer green beans because they are so labour intensive to pick. From mid-summer to

[49] Thank you, East Coast Organics.
[50] Thank you, everyone at the Blue Door garden.

autumn, I buy green beans from the UK, where they are harvested using machines in and around the Fens; I always keep a pack in the freezer,[51] and I have bought them from Kenya. I have completely failed to grow them at the allotment. As Mike and his family suggested, for all its benefits, it is tough to fit 'locavorism' into a busy modern life. As a nation, we are 54 per cent self-sufficient in vegetables and 15 per cent in fruit.

Mike readily admits there is a long way to go. Indeed, the Fife Diet partly ended so he could concentrate on campaigning on the big systemic issues at the heart of the food industry. He wants to see the government make it easier – and cheaper – for us all to eat seasonally and locally by supporting British farmers and local shops. But he does not dismiss the power of the narrative created by the Fife Diet, which proved local does not have to be boring. His favourite moment from the Fife Diet experience wasn't being interviewed on the *Ten O'Clock News*, doing a TED Talk,[52] or even proving how much it reduced carbon. It was one of the many community feasts where he sat down with his family and others taking part to enjoy Kingdom of Fife Pie,[53] borscht, spicy vegan stew, fish cakes, pork sausages and cranachan – all sourced locally, of course.

On Twitter, Jay Rayner, the food writer and a leading voice in the backlash against Food Miles, admitted that perhaps the power in the locavore movement is the story of our food: 'The best reason for local is narrative.'

Yet the trouble with narrative is that it depends on who is telling the story. From the perspective of Farm Africa, green beans mean more stories like Joshua's. Kenya was one of the

---

[51] To my knowledge, no study has been done on the carbon footprint of freezing green beans.

[52] TEDxGlasgow 2012.

[53] Rabbit pie.

first countries in the world to develop an airfreight trade in
fresh fruit and vegetables, mainly with the UK. As a former
colony, it had links to businesses and consumers, and it had
the advantage of regular flights to and from Heathrow
because of tourism. Why not bring green beans back in the
belly of the planes after delivering tourists heading to Kenya
on safari? There was a fourfold increase in UK imports of
green beans between 1990 and 2004, from 8,300 to 33,000
tonnes. An estimated £200 million is injected into rural
economies in Africa through the fruit and veg trade with
the UK alone.

Mary Nyale, head of all programmes in Kenya for Farm
Africa, said that – unlike other exports – fruit and vegetables
tend to help the rural poor because much of the produce is
still from small farms. In sub-Saharan Africa, 50,000–60,000
small-scale producers are growing vegetables for people in
the UK to eat. There are also jobs in larger farms and in
processing green beans, though the industry does not come
without problems.

In 2013, Oxfam published a report voicing concern
about labour rights, sexual harassment and zero-hour
contracts on large farms. While admitting that horticulture
could empower women in Kenya, it concluded that
improvements must be made in working conditions and
human rights. Ultimately, the charity is not against
exporting horticulture from Africa, but it calls for 'Fair
Miles' rather than 'Food Miles', where workers are paid a
minimum wage in a similar way to Fairtrade bananas. Food
waste is also a problem, although this is now better thanks
to the campaigning work of Feedback that pushed Tesco to
stop topping and tailing green beans in 2016, saving 135
million tonnes of food waste.

For Mary, horticulture for export is the lesser of two
evils. The airfreight in fruit and veg may make up 0.1
per cent of the UK's GHG emissions, but it supports a

million farmers in Africa. She points out that most of the vegetables grown in Kenya are consumed locally. But the value of the 5 per cent that is exported is almost equivalent to all the rest, so the foreign earnings that Kenya gets from the export of vegetables like green beans go very far to get the economy going.

For many, supporting green beans grown in Kenya is about 'climate justice'. The average carbon emissions per person per year globally is 3.6 tonnes; the African average is 1 tonne; the UK average is 9.2 tonnes. Don't Kenyans have a right to emit carbon in the name of development that will benefit many people? ActionAid and other charities have said that taking jobs away from African farmers for a slight reduction in our carbon footprint does not seem fair.

Farm Africa has helped more than 4,000 young farmers in Kenya to enter the export growers' market and farm green beans for sale in the UK. Mary said most of the suppliers are small producers like Joshua and his family, whose lives have been transformed by the opportunity to diversify their crops.

Mary and I are chatting on Zoom, and I can see the bright African sunshine through the window behind her. 'Yes, the rains are late this year,' she admits.

'Is that due to global warming?' I ask. 'And if so, isn't the carbon footprint of airfreight a cause of that?'

Mary cannot say for sure. What she can say is that Farm Africa is helping to cut energy use on farms by installing solar power and training farmers in more energy-efficient methods such as drip irrigation. The charity is also assisting the farmers in dealing with weather extremes by farming methods like digging drains to stop soil from washing away in floods and adding organic matter to the soil to prevent it from drying out in a drought.

'We are very well aware of the devastating effects climate change is having across eastern Africa. We are helping communities to build resilience. Export horticulture does bring benefits in terms of improving livelihoods,' she says. 'These farmers have hope, and that is a good-news story.'

The story is very different from the perspective of a hardened climate campaigner and locavore like Mike Small. Looking at both the Defra and IIED reports more closely, it is clear they are not quite saying that the carbon footprint of airfreight is negligible. Yes, it may be comparatively small right now, but when the target for cutting carbon emissions in the UK is net zero by 2050, every little helps (to quote a well-known supermarket). Just 0.1 per cent of the UK's carbon footprint may not seem very much at the moment, but by 2050, when every sector has to cut its footprint by 90 per cent, this figure will look a lot higher, especially since airfreight is predicted to increase.

The Defra report points out that transport by plane generates 177 times more GHG emissions than shipping, and it's the fastest-growing way of moving food around. The IIED report also acknowledges airfreight is growing and has a heavy carbon footprint for the amount of food produced. The 1.5 per cent of fruit and veg transported by air makes up half of all the emissions from fruit and vegetable transportation from farm gate to the retailer. In other words, while green beans may not account for a big part of your overall carbon footprint, it is significant if you want to cut your shopping trolley's carbon footprint. Both reports agree that if the UK is to meet its 2050 target, cutting airfreight (or finding a way to offset those emissions) will be part of the equation. Already retailers are considering bringing in green beans by sea, using modified-atmosphere packaging to ensure freshness.

On the point of climate justice, it may seem fair to allow Kenyans the 'right' to emit carbon in the name of development. But what about their right to live in a world that is not suffering climatic extremes like drought and flooding? Unless every sector cuts its carbon emissions, there is little chance of avoiding that scenario. In 2020, a paper in *Science* stated that the world cannot meet its target to keep global temperature rise below 2°C by 2050 unless we tackle emissions from food production. That will include the emissions from airfreight.

Tim Lang, the 'father of Food Miles', stands by his original thesis that the distance food travels matters. He would still encourage people to take a 'bioregional approach', choosing local and seasonal first. Not just for the relatively small amount of carbon saved but for the food system it encourages by supporting nature-friendly farms using less chemicals. But he acknowledges that distance travelled does not tell the whole story. Ideally, every product needs a complete Life Cycle Analysis that tells the story of a food item from seed to plate. The trouble is that this can be an extremely complicated analysis of up to 51 criteria. What do you include, and what do you leave out? The fertiliser spread by the tractor? The petrol put in the tractor? The energy to build the tractor?

To clarify things and counter some of the criticism of Food Miles, Professor Lang and his colleagues have come up with a new concept: 'omni-standards'. Unfortunately, 'omni' – meaning 'everything' in Latin – has not been embraced with the same enthusiasm as Food Miles by the world press.[54] This is not an opportunity to bash Greens but a chance to get our heads around the profoundly complex issues surrounding our food system, including carbon emissions, biodiversity loss and labour rights. Sadly, that is simply not as sexy (though, believe me, I am doing my best). Omni-standards is a labelling system that would tell consumers how food impacts the environment and society.

---

[54] The *Guardian* did a piece.

The label looks like a 'food flower' with each 'petal' representing an area of concern. One 'petal' might represent the carbon footprint of a food item, another might be nutrition, another labour rights, and so on. Each 'petal' would be colour-coded, so a green petal would indicate the food product did well in this area, whereas a red petal would show it is failing on a critical issue. Green beans from Kenya are a perfect example. They are healthy and would have a green nutrition petal, and if they are grown in partnership with Farm Africa, they will show a green petal for Fairtrade. However, they would have a red carbon footprint petal because of airfreight.

Professor Lang admits this labelling system would be a lot for a parent to process while standing in a supermarket aisle with a screaming toddler, but that is not the point. The most urgent need is to set standards everyone can recognise and that hold retailers and producers accountable. Lang and his colleagues have set up a not-for-profit group, Omni Action, to begin the work of collating these standards. They are bringing together an independent body of experts to gather the vast amount of data that is now available and set the new standards. Professor Lang says the world can address these 'omni-problems' in the food system by coming up with 'omni-standards'.

'What a food system needs, if it is to be good, is to tick lots of boxes. We must not trade off the environment for health or social justice and labour rights for cheapness,' he says. 'We've got to have all of the criteria the world needs to be addressed in its food system addressed at the same time. It's got to be multiple actions at multiple levels across multiple sectors, from production to consumption.'

Omni Action hopes this 'multicriteria' approach would produce a food label everyone understands. More than that, it would be a narrative everyone understands. The question is: which story do you choose?

Further reading

'A life cycle analysis of UK supermarket imported green
beans from Kenya', Department for International
Development, 2006

'The Food Miles Report', Sustain (2011 reprint)

A Greedy Man in a Hungry World by Jay Rayner
(HarperCollins, 2014)

Feeding Britain: Our Food Problems and How to Fix Them by
Tim Lang (Penguin, 2020)

Mukimo

It was pilau rice that did it. Dennis Mwakulua had never tasted better than his mother's until, exhausted after a shift working as a kitchen porter, he tasted the chef's pilau rice.

'Immediately, I wanted to know what was in it,' he says. 'And I wanted to go home and make it.'

Dennis had come to London to study business in the hope (or rather his parent's hopes) of becoming a banker. (A semi-professional gig as a rapper in Mombasa had not quite worked out.) But first, he needed money, so he took a kitchen porter role at Merrill Lynch. It was there that he discovered his passion for cooking. He made a deal with the chef to stay in the role of kitchen porter if he taught Dennis how to cook, and then he worked his way up. He is now an award-winning chef who has worked in a seven-star hotel in Dubai, and he is passionate about encouraging other young men from Africa to join the catering profession.

Dennis also takes part in charitable work, including supporting a primary school outside of Mombasa. He supports Farm Africa because he has been impressed by how it encourages young people into farming. Like cooking, many people in Kenya still see farming as a low-status job suited to women and older people. Dennis sees it differently. He has proven what is possible with chefing and has seen for himself how farming can provide employment and opportunities by visiting Growing Futures projects with Farm Africa. Dennis acknowledges the carbon footprint of airfreight, but he balances it against economic development in his own country. Ultimately, he would like to see more of a domestic market emerge in Kenya so that green beans can become a 'locavore crop'. He has worked with Farm Africa to develop recipes that appeal to Kenyan families and top-end restaurants.

'Green beans are delicious and a great source of protein,' he says. 'I would like to see them eaten more in Kenya; there is no reason they cannot be a local dish.'

Below is a recipe for *mukimo*, a traditional Kenyan dish served on its own or as a side dish for meat or fish. Generally, you make it by mashing potatoes with the best vegetables of the area mixed in, from ground peanuts to cabbage or collard greens. It looks a bit like bright green mush, and it is wonderful comfort food. Depending on the season and the 'story' you choose, you can make it with green beans from Kenya or the UK.

- 3 onions (300g), finely diced
- 3 cloves of garlic (12g), crushed or finely chopped
- 100g of unsalted butter
- 4 medium-sized potatoes (600g), peeled and cut into quarters – whatever kind you get in your local veg box is fine; Maris Pipers are good for mash, but try not to get too hung up on varieties as the ones more resistant to potato blight might be just as good and use less fungicide. Use your potato peels to make crispy potato 'worms' (see recipe on page 79)
- 300g of green beans, finely chopped – UK green beans are in season from mid-summer to autumn and have a lower carbon footprint; use Kenyan or frozen green beans if you want to cook this out of season.
- 150g of sweetcorn kernels (canned is fine)
- 2 large handfuls (100g) of spinach, washed and finely chopped
- A small bunch of fresh coriander (12g), finely chopped
- 1 spring onion (9g), finely chopped
- A small bunch of parsley (9g), finely chopped
- salt

1. Blanch the green beans in a pan of salted boiling water for approximately one minute, then take them out, keeping the boiling water in the pan, and rinse the beans in cold water to refresh them.

2. Put the peeled, quartered potatoes into the pan of boiling water, bring them back to a boil and gently simmer for 20 minutes. Take off once they are soft enough to mash, then drain and set to one side.

3. While the potatoes are cooking, in a large frying pan or wok, sauté the onions in the butter on medium heat for three minutes until they are translucent. Add garlic and cook for another minute, then add the sweetcorn and cook for another five minutes.

4. Add the spinach, and once it has wilted, add the drained boiled potatoes, the green beans, coriander, parsley and spring onions. Mash the mixture until the potatoes are smooth and not lumpy.

5. Season the mash to taste, and serve immediately. It is delicious as a side with sausages or stews. Adding leftover veg to the mix is a good way to cut food waste, a bit like an African bubble and squeak.

CHAPTER FIVE

Humblebees

UK tomatoes grown in season: 1.3kg CO_2e per kg
Tomatoes driven from Spain: 2.5kg CO_2e per kg
Tomatoes grown in UK hothouse: 4.6kg CO_2e per kg[55]

*'If the bee disappeared off the surface of the globe, then man would
have only four years of life left. No more bees, no more pollination,
no more plants, no more animals, no more man.'*
Attributed to Albert Einstein, but there is no evidence he said it.
The original source for the sentiment behind the quote is probably the Belgian writer Maurice Maeterlinck or Charles Darwin.
Variations have since been repeated in beekeepers' journals and
attributed to Einstein, who we know was an admirer of bees.[56]

Besides the British, the Belgians are one of the few countries
with a passion for pigeon racing. But there is another sport

---

[55] Mike Berners-Lee, Lancaster University.

[56] The 'Einstein quote' suggests only honey bees pollinate crops when
other bees, including bumblebees, are important, as well as other insects.
Also, not all plants require insect pollination. I included it because
humans need a diversity of crops, for which we need insects, and it
illustrates well the importance of bees in that symbiotic relationship.

in Belgium that, to my knowledge, has never taken off in the UK, and that is bumblebee racing.

Every spring and summer, small boys – and girls, one presumes – cycle around the Belgian countryside, catching bumblebees from their nests. The bottom of the bumblebee is painted to identify its 'owner', like the silks worn by a racehorse jockey or the leg ring on a racing pigeon. At the starting pistol, satchels buzzing with a very angry insect, the children cycle a mile or so and release 'their' bumblebee. Like pigeons, bumblebees have a homing instinct and will always return home. By racing back and waiting by the nest, the bumblebee owners can hopefully see which bumblebee returns first and thence identify a winner (and even win a bet).

Unlike honey bees, which live in a hive, bumblebees breed in a nest. Every spring, a queen bumblebee creates her own little colony by collecting pollen mixed with some nectar to store and then lays her eggs. Once her offspring emerge, they become her worker bees, collecting pollen and nectar to bring back to the nest for at least one more brood from their queen.

Perhaps it is not so common now, but in the past, it was a known countryside pursuit in Belgium to take advantage of this amazing natural history happening at the bottom of gardens by catching some of those worker bees to watch them 'race' home to their queen again.

As a boy, Roland de Jonghe was a passionate bumblebee racer, going so far as to breed prize bumblebees in his garage to race them. And he never really grew out of it. Well into adulthood, he was improving his system of cardboard 'nests' that queen bumblebees would be happy to use and breed a colony inside. As a young veterinarian, he transferred these nests of bees to his greenhouse so they could help pollinate his tomatoes – every year, he got a bumper crop. Aware of the burgeoning tomato industry in 1980s Belgium, he suggested to some farmers that they use his bumblebees in their glasshouses too. Within a few years, Roland's bumblebee nests were being used on commercial farms. In 1987, he set up Biobest Group, the first company in the world to sell bumblebee nests to tomato farmers. Little did he know then, but the hobby he had as a schoolboy in shorts was about to transform how we eat our most cultivated fruit[57] or vegetable.[58]

Like potatoes, tomatoes were brought to Europe from South America by the conquistadors, and like potatoes, Europeans initially distrusted them. The small, lumpy, misshapen tomatoes that arrived in Europe were from the same deadly nightshade family, Solanaceae. Rather than red, they were more often orange or yellow – hence their Italian name *pomodoro*, meaning 'golden apple'. If tomatoes were going to be eaten at all, they were first boiled for hours, though the time taken to do this may have had as much to do with the purity of the water supply. Fortunately, in southern Europe, the warnings against deadly nightshade were largely unheeded, and consequently, we have pizza, pomodoro pasta and gazpacho. The Italians, God bless them, discovered that tomatoes are a significant source of umami flavour and gave them a central role in peasant cooking. Whereas in chilly northern Europe, tomatoes only became a staple when we worked out the technology to grow them indoors.

The tomato plant was first grown in England as a horticultural curiosity in the 1590s, and the fruit was enjoyed by the few who could afford an orangery or a building with large glass windows. Large-scale cultivation of crops under glass

---

[57] Whether tomatoes are a fruit or vegetable is still a matter of some debate. Botanically, it is accepted as a fruit, but many think the savoury flavour makes it a vegetable.

[58] In 1893, the US Supreme Court ruled the tomato was a vegetable after a trader tried to claim it was fruit to get out of paying taxes (*Nix v Hedden*).

only got underway during the second half of the nineteenth century, when the Victorians discovered greenhouses. The Crystal Palace Exhibition in 1851 showed the world 100,000 objects made possible by the Industrial Revolution. It also showed that greenhouses could be built quickly and at scale. Within a few decades, plate glass was cheap enough for huge commercial greenhouses to start popping up around the British countryside. The most famous place for hothouses was Worthing in Sussex, where grapes, cucumbers and tomatoes were grown to sell to the burgeoning middle classes of the London suburbs during the first half of the twentieth century. Swanley in Kent and along the Lea Valley in London were also areas famous for their tomato houses. Sepia-tinted photos remain of Edwardian ladies standing amid the vines and young men in flat caps and braces pushing barrows of tomatoes to Covent Garden Market.

The mining of coal made it easy to heat the greenhouses, and tomatoes became a luxury many more could afford after the First World War. Even in Scotland, tomatoes became a 'local' food. The Clyde Valley became famous for the Lanarkshire tomatoes my grandmother remembers from Rankins'. At one point, the crop supplied all of Scotland and had sufficient left over for export. Breeds like Ailsa Craig were developed, and fresh local tomatoes were a treat everyone could enjoy throughout the warmer months. Perhaps it is no coincidence that at the same time, 1950s home cooks discovered Mediterranean cooking through the work of writers like Elizabeth David, as northern Europe was beginning to enjoy the flavours of the Mediterranean thanks to glasshouse technology.

The trouble is that we then started to go on holiday to the Mediterranean. As travel routes opened up, so did trade routes from Mediterranean countries like Spain, making imported tomatoes cheaper than home-grown tomatoes. At the same time, coal became more expensive as the British mines started closing down. The British tomato industry struggled to compete with cheaper imports, and the famous hothouses began dying out in the 1960s and 1970s. The glasshouses of Worthing and the Clyde Valley were knocked down in favour of housing developments around the major conurbations of London and Glasgow, respectively. Increasingly, the UK relied on tomatoes from Spain, often picked unripe to help them store and travel well, but as a result, sometimes colourless and flavourless tomatoes – or 'tennis balls', as I have heard them described. The Germans call such tomatoes *Wasserbomben* (water bombs). Again, this was reflected in our cooking habits as we moved to more processed food and reached a low point in the British diet. Those sepia-tinted British tomato houses were forgotten in favour of Spanish tomatoes and, later, a smaller, tastier tomato that would come from a most unexpected source.

Today most of the imported fresh tomatoes we eat are from the Netherlands, where glasshouse technology has allowed fresh tomatoes to be grown within 1,600km of the Arctic circle. This tiny little country next door to Belgium does not have a massive amount of land. It is half the size of Ireland, and much of it is built on a flood plain. But somehow, it has managed to become one of the world's leading producers of fruits and vegetables. Perhaps the drive to produce more food comes from the memory of famine during the Second World War.[59] (As a prisoner of war travelling through the Netherlands during the German occupation,[60] my grandfather told a story of how the locals pressed sweets into the hands of Allied soldiers, even though they were near starving themselves.) Or perhaps it is because, if you have a large population and only a certain amount of land above sea level, you learn how to make the most of it.

[59] Up to 20,000 people died in the 'Dutch hunger winter', during the last months of the German occupation.

[60] My grandfather Alexander (Sandy) Flockhart was one of the Allied soldiers captured after parachuting into Arnhem.

While the British let their glasshouses fall to pieces, the Dutch took hothouse horticulture to a whole new level. When coal started to become more expensive, Dutch growers switched to renewable technology; when the wood in their glasshouse frames began to decay, they replaced it with aluminium; when the soil became diseased, they replaced it with rockwool; and when the workers began to drift away, Dutch growers started using robots. The Netherlands is now the second-biggest exporter of fruits and vegetables worldwide (after the United States). This windswept part of Europe produces more tomatoes per acre than any other country.

The vast glasshouse complexes of the Netherlands are now considered a significant human-made phenomenon, large enough to be visible from space. A photo montage published in *National Geographic* shows swathes of glasshouses, some 70 hectares in size, snaking across the Dutch countryside. At night, many glow with artificial light to create longer growing days and ensure tomatoes can be grown through winter.

The plate glass invented by the Victorians has been improved, so now, instead of letting in 70 per cent of light (as your kitchen window might), this new glass lets in more than 90 per cent of light. The floors of the greenhouses are covered in white sheeting to reflect yet more light up onto the plants. The ceilings are high enough to let tomato vines climb for 13 metres, producing 33 clusters of tomatoes for every plant in so-called 'vertical farms'. Soil has been done away with in favour of hydroponics or growing in a soil substitute such as rockwool, coconut fibre, clay pebbles or perlite. Nutrient-film technique uses no substrate at all. Precisely the right amount of water, nitrogen, potassium, phosphate and oxygen is fed into the inert material via tiny pipes. Computers control the climate to ensure precisely the right temperature, humidity and levels of CO_2 to boost growth. The boys in flat caps and braces have been replaced by robots that remove side shoots and monitor growth. Mini-railways run between the rows to transport pickers and move them up and down the vines on cherry pickers. In time, the robots will even do the picking.[61]

The Dutch have taken technology that started in the UK as part of the Great Exhibition 150 years ago to unimagined levels of expertise and ingenuity. For British growers, it was time we invested in our horticulture once again.

The British were not left behind for long. In the early 2000s, what was left of the UK tomato industry started to think about scaling up. In Kent, where much of the UK salad crop used to be grown, a consortium pitched an ambitious plan to build 'the biggest greenhouse in the British Isles'. At first, there was strong opposition. Locals complained they missed the cauliflowers and oilseed rape that would 'naturally' grow in the Kent soil and the hares that would lollop across the muddy fields. Newspaper articles warned of a 'super-sized plant factory' and cautioned against 'Franken foods' (forgetting we were once quite happy to eat tomatoes grown in coal-fired glasshouses). For a traditional farming area like Kent, the idea of a greenhouse city was scary. Still, it was now an area suffering from chronic unemployment, so ultimately, the development got the go-ahead.

A decade later, Thanet Earth has proved the British can grow tomatoes as well as the Dutch can, which is not surprising given it is a joint venture between the Fresca Group (a British conglomerate of fruit and veg producers) and a consortium of Dutch growers. The company claims to grow 400 million tomatoes every year, while APS, the UK's biggest producer of tomatoes, grows an additional 500

---

[61] Although tomatoes are not picked by robots in most greenhouses, the technology is being developed and expected to become more common.

million tomatoes a year in vast greenhouse complexes on the Isle of Wight, Cheshire, Teesside and Kent.

It is a good food story, except perhaps when you come to carbon. In the previous chapter, I mentioned the controversial 2005 Defra report[62] that pointed out tomatoes grown in UK greenhouses could have a heavier carbon footprint than equivalent tomatoes driven to the UK from Spain. That's because burning fossil fuel, in this case, natural gas, to heat British greenhouses outside of the summer months produces more carbon dioxide than transporting tomatoes from Spain in trucks. According to carbon experts, tomatoes driven to the UK from Spain produce 2.5kg CO_2e per kg, whereas tomatoes grown in a hothouse in the UK produce 4.6kg CO_2e. Tomatoes grown in the UK in season outdoors or under plastic sheets only produce 1.3kg CO_2e per kg.[63]

The Defra report did, however, point out that improvements in energy efficiency could mean that British tomatoes should use less energy in the long term. Like many modern glasshouses, Thanet Earth is heated by the excess heat from electricity generation in a system known as Combined Heat and Power. Each greenhouse has its own natural-gas power station pumping electricity into the grid, while the heat generated is pumped into the greenhouses. The carbon dioxide that is a waste product from burning the gas is also pumped into the greenhouse to boost the growth of the plants. Other greenhouses in the UK use 'waste' heat and CO_2 from industrial processes, such as APS Produce in Teesside, which uses waste CO_2 from fertiliser production. Waste heat and carbon from the British Sugar factory in Suffolk used to power tomato production but now is used to heat a greenhouse growing medicinal cannabis. An anaerobic

---

[62] Defra report 2005, p. 84.

[63] If you really want to eat low-carbon tomatoes, eat beefsteak instead of cherry tomatoes as studies have shown cherry tomatoes, with their lower yields, have a higher carbon footprint.

digester on the APS Cheshire plant produces gas from the tomato crop's leaf waste and then manufactures punnets and bio-plastic from the left-over leaf-fibre cellulose.

There is also the question of other environmental factors. Spanish tomatoes may use less fossil-fuel-based energy, but the yield per hectare is lower, so it takes a lot more land to grow the same amount of food, land that could have been habitat for wildlife. Water is scarce in many areas where Spanish tomatoes are grown, so desalination is necessary, requiring a separate, additional use of energy. In comparison, Thanet Earth is 85 per cent self-sufficient in water, thanks to rainwater harvesting. In Spain, tomatoes are generally grown beneath plastic tunnels, which must be replaced every four years.

In contrast, the input of fertilisers and any pesticides can be tightly controlled in a glasshouse environment using hydroponics, minimising chemical use.[64] In terms of socio-economic benefits, the UK now employs 3,500 people in the tomato industry. In Spain, the industry relies on a migrant workforce from Africa, many of whom claim they are often not treated well. In the latest reports, migrants claimed to be facing systematic labour exploitation before and throughout the pandemic, such as non-payment of wages and being kept on illegal contracts.[65]

Thanet Earth cannot replace the fruit and veg we source from Spain, and we should continue to push for improved working conditions.[66] But it can be part of a sustainable supply grown on our doorstep. After a 50-year hiatus, British

[64] The *New York Times* bestseller *Tomatoland* by Barry Estabrook (Andrews McMeel Publishing, 2012) claimed some tomato fields are sprayed with more than 100 different pesticides to ensure a good crop.

[65] 'We Pick Your Food', *Observer*, 2020.

[66] 'Ethical Consumer is calling on UK supermarkets to make sure their suppliers uphold workers' rights. Their website provides links to lobby supermarkets, sign petitions and crowdfunding opportunities that support their work.

tomatoes are back. The British Tomato Growers Association estimate that around a fifth of the tomatoes eaten in the UK are grown here in the UK, and in the summer, half of the tomatoes we eat are grown here. The British Tomato Growers Association wants to increase the proportion of fresh tomatoes grown in the British Isles from 20 to 50 per cent by 2030. Demand is growing too because, let's face it, tomatoes taste better than ever before.

I remember tomatoes bought in the UK in the 1990s, and they were horrible, pale *wasserbomben* that tasted of the back of the fridge. Nowadays, cherry tomatoes are available all year round and, at least from April to October, they are juicy and sweet. Lots of people take credit for this transformation. In the early 2000s, the Israelis claimed to have 'invented' the cherry tomato, sparking outrage in many quarters. The Greeks claimed the Santorini tomato was the first small tomato (though it is small because of the nutrient-poor volcanic soil where it is grown, not because of breeding). The Dutch claimed to have invented the cherry tomato in their enormous labs. Even Marks & Spencer, the bastion of the British high street, laid claim to the cherry tomato. In a fascinating exploration of food and nationalism, Anna Wexler[67] tracked the history of the cherry tomato back to its source in Central America, where the Aztecs and Incas first cultivated the fruit. She found references to cherry tomatoes as early as the Renaissance period and in popular media, as early as the 1970s when President Nixon was reported to have enjoyed the fruit. The modern cherry tomato has been a mainstay of our salads since the 1990s, thanks to supermarkets selling more robust, tastier breeds. Wexler argued that the Israelis claimed to have invented the cherry tomato to counter negative images of Israel in the international press. Such is the power of a bite-size fruit. In truth, the cherry tomato was probably 'invented' by several nations, including

---

[67] *Gastronomica*, May 2016.

Israel, the UK[68] and the Netherlands, all intensively breeding tomatoes for flavour for the last 60 years.

What next for tomato breeding? It was the first fruit or vegetable developed commercially as a genetically modified crop and licensed for human consumption. The Flavr Savr, created to improve shelf life, was launched in 1994. It was even briefly sold in the UK as a tinned sauce in clearly labelled cans. But coverage of GM foods in the press and public distrust of the new technology meant that sales crashed, and it was removed from commercial sale in 1998. A plant scientist I know keeps an old can from Sainsbury's in his garage to remind him of the days when the public was less afraid of GM.

Genetically modified tomatoes continue to be bred, but mainly to develop traits for health food or medicine. Professor Cathie Martin at the John Innes Centre in Norwich took the genes from a snapdragon to create a purple tomato unusually high in antioxidants.[69] When cancer-prone mice were given Cathie's purple tomatoes as part of their diet, they lived 30 per cent longer than mice fed the same quantity of ordinary tomatoes. The mice were also less susceptible to inflammatory bowel disease. Cathie had all this data more than a decade ago. The results of her tests were published in 2008 in *Nature Biotechnology*, but her efforts to get the purple tomato sold commercially have largely been in vain, though there is interest from the US in purple tomato juice. In Europe, the idea of selling a genetically modified fruit juice – even one with cancer-fighting properties – is a long way off. Instead, scientists are using gene-editing, which enhances desirable traits a lot more quickly than traditional breeding processes but does not introduce new DNA from another species. This 'Crispr'

---

[68] Bernard Sparkes first started supplying Marks & Spencer with cherry tomatoes in the 1990s.

[69] The same antioxidants you get from foraged blackberries. See chapter nine.

technique has been used recently by the John Innes lab to create a tomato with high levels of vitamin D.

Tomatoes have become a technological feat. We farm them in glasshouses that can be viewed from space, we grow them in melted rock, we feed them artificial nitrogen, we pick them with robots, and we have bred out their faults and altered their genes. But there is still one thing tomato farmers cannot do without, and it is buzzing about in a greenhouse not far from my home.

On a May morning, when the first orange-tip butterflies are feeding on the wildflowers left on the road verges, I drive down to the Borders to visit Scotland's biggest tomato farm. At first, I think I have missed it. As I park up at Standhill Farm, I can see Holstein cattle – another Dutch import – grazing the fields and bales of silage stacked against the old stone walls, but no sign of a greenhouse. It is only when I approach the farmhouse that I see the flashes of glass nestled in a field behind the steading. It is a bit like travelling forward through time. One minute I am in a dairy farmer's kitchen, leaning against the Aga and chatting about milk prices, mucky overalls hanging at the door and the smell of wet grass, sour milk and manure in the air. The next, we are sanitising our boots and walking into a 'food factory' growing Annamay cocktail tomatoes and Sweetelle baby plum tomatoes, where the warmth and scent of tomato vines remind me of holidays in Tuscany.

Jim Shanks is a typical modern farmer in many ways, with one foot in the old and one in the new. As a fifth-generation dairy farmer, he has worked hard to maintain a herd of cattle despite ongoing crises in the sector. He is rightly proud that his cows produce 70,000 pints of milk for Tesco every week. But as an innovative Nuffield scholar and Scotland's only major tomato farmer, he is also proud of embracing new technology. Jim decided to diversify after visiting similar farms in Europe and the US. Returning home, he saw that the cattle he so loved could be part of the solution if he just looked at them a little differently. In cow slurry, he had energy, and in his fields, he had space to use that energy to grow tomatoes.

Jim installed an anaerobic digester to capture methane from the cow slurry and burn it for electricity. After the methane has been extracted, the remaining slurry is rich in nitrogen and spread on the fields to help the grass grow. The excess heat from the engine on the anaerobic digester is used to dry woodchip that, in turn, powers a biomass boiler to heat the greenhouses. Again, the heat is renewable, coming from sustainably managed forests nearby. Finally, the tomatoes are fed by rainwater harvested from the roof of the giant greenhouse.

'Everything you see around you is powered by cow shit,' he says. 'Even the car, an electric Tesla.'

The greenhouse is just like the behemoths pictured in *National Geographic*, built with modern glass that allows in 97 per cent of the light and lined on the floor with white sheeting. The F1 hybrid tomato plants are grown in bags full of rockwool and irrigated by drip-feeding. Computers constantly monitor the atmosphere to ensure the perfect amount of light, heat and CO_2 to speed photosynthesis and 'turbocharge' the growing tomatoes.

As I float up on a cherry picker past clusters of Piccolo cherry tomatoes, I feel a little like David Attenborough heading up into a rainforest canopy. It is humid and warm, and the green leaves filter the light around me. Workers in shorts and T-shirts scoot up and down the rows on trolleys, shouting insults and instructions. It is a tough job, but Jim has found 10 full-time employees in the local area and employs 12 more locals during the picking season. Perks include being one of the few places in Scotland where you get to work in shorts. From my vantage point up high, I look across

1.5 hectares of plants at different stages of growth. If I squint slightly, I can see a cow in the distance through the glass.

When I come back down to earth, Jim offers me a freshly picked tomato. It is sweet and warm, which reminds me of picking tomatoes off the vine in the greenhouse at the community garden (I can never wait to get home to put them in a salad). He shrugs off criticism that tomatoes grown in industrial greenhouses are not the real thing. This is farming, he says. This is how his family have managed to stay on the farm for a fifth generation: by being innovative, by taking risks, by moving with the times, not holding on to the past, and most of all, by trusting in nature.

Despite all the technology invented by the British Victorians and improved on by the Dutch, and despite the GM technology and centuries of breeding, the key to tomato farming in Scotland, Holland or anywhere else in the world is bees. Thousands of bumblebees are buzzing around the flowers at the top of the canopy in Jim's greenhouse. The insects are brought in from Belgium, where the Biobest Group is now one of the biggest 'bio-control' companies in the world, supplying 700,000 bumblebees a week to greenhouses and breeding other insects to help protect fruits and vegetables against pests.

Like many childhood games, bumblebee racing was the best education Roland de Jonghe could have hoped for. The young veterinarian continued his hobby well into adulthood, breeding bees not only in the garage but in his living room, kitchen, backyard and attic. (Company legend has it that the only place without bumblebees was his bedroom because his wife 'didn't allow that'.) Yet it was only while watching a bumblebee pollinate a tomato that he had the 'eureka' moment that this strange hobby might be helpful in the greenhouses popping up all over Belgium.

Roland started to experiment with bumblebee nests in greenhouses in the early 1980s. He soon found that they worked. The greenhouses with his bumblebees supplied bigger and juicier fruit.[70] He started to sell the bumblebee colonies to farmers, and in 1987, he set up The Biobest Group. From 1980–96 in the Netherlands, physical yields of tomatoes increased by 97 per cent.[71] This increase was primarily thanks to improvements in glasshouse technology, but much of it was due to bees.

Bumblebees are vital to the tomato crop because they help to pollinate the fruit. All bees buzz when they fly,[72] but some buzz better than others. Bumblebees can also buzz their bodies when they hang on to a flower, which they do to dislodge the pollen. Although tomato plants are officially described as 'self-pollinators' because each flower has a male anther and a female stigma, they produce a lot more fruit if they are helped a little by insect pollinators. Ideally, the anther will be vibrated at around 400Hz.[73] Fortunately, bumblebees are very good at this, placing their upper body close to the anthers and then vibrating their hairy little bodies at a frequency of around 400Hz. These low vibrations, known as buzz pollination, shake free the pollen, allowing it to drop down onto the stigma so that fertilisation can occur. Blueberries, aubergines and kiwi fruit also have flowers structured so that buzz pollination will dislodge the pollen and allow fertilisation. Growers can even see where pollination has taken place because bumblebees will leave a small bite

---

[70] A subsequent study in the UK found that bumblebee-pollinated tomatoes were bigger than those pollinated by humans or honey bees (Banda and Paxton, 1991).

[71] Agricultural Economics Research Institute (LEI), The Hague.

[72] The buzzing sound we hear is because bees can flap their wings at a pretty impressive 230 beats per second.

[73] Interestingly, this is the same frequency as an ultrasonic toothbrush.

mark with their mandibles where they grab hold of the petals and vibrate their flight muscles at that magic number, 400Hz.

In the past, farmers have tried to imitate the bumblebee by using an artificial buzzer to pollinate the plants by hand. One brand of vibrating wand is known as an 'electric bee'. This is not only costly,[74] but it's also not that effective. No artificial pollination matches the efficiency of bumblebees buzzing from flower to flower.[75] The tomato will only release pollen for an hour a day. Only the bumblebee will find that flower and ensure they are pollinated, buzzing into four to six flowers every minute. The traditional name for a bumblebee is humblebee;[76] this is what Shakespeare calls the bumblebee in *A Midsummer Night's Dream*. I think it suits this hardworking insect, getting on with the job without fuss or much recognition.

Despite being key to pollinating a third of crops that require pollination[77] and providing honey and wax, honey bees are no good at this buzz pollination because they do not vibrate inside the flower. Also, honey bee hives are far too big to be contained in a greenhouse, unlike little bumblebee nests. Honey bees do not like living in greenhouses and will fly out to forage over a much wider area.

Since the Biobest Group – and, in its wake, several other companies – started breeding bumblebees for commercial use, the industry has exploded. Today around 2.5 million bumblebee colonies are reared artificially every year, and

---

[74] Mainly in terms of labour: it took one person per hectare to pollinate plants using the electric bee.

[75] Each commercial hive accounts for daily visits to half a million flowers, Koppert.

[76] Another traditional name is Dumbledore, which J. K. Rowling used for the Hogwarts headmaster in the *Harry Potter* book series.

[77] Apples and almonds are two key crops where honey bees are brought in for pollination.

they are used in over 30 countries on more than 25 crops. This has not come without problems, however.

Like humans and plants, bumblebees transfer disease. Non-native bumblebees can also outcompete native species. After being introduced for commercial use, the buff-tailed bumblebee (*Bombus terrestris*) has caused problems for native species in Japan and Chile. Breeders claim that bumblebees do not escape the greenhouses, but accidents happen. The only country that does not use bumblebees commercially is Australia because of the risks associated with introducing a non-native bee species. Currently, Australian tomato farmers use a vibrating wand and human labour to pollinate tomatoes, and they are experimenting with 'robot bees' to do the job. But they may do better to study the insects on their doorstep.

A study in the *Journal of Economic Entomology* in 2021 called for more research into (sub)species of buzz pollinators in different countries so native species could be used wherever possible. It pointed out there are 20,000 species of bees worldwide, each with unique flight patterns and body sizes to get into different flowers. It is crucial to preserve this diversity not only for rare flora but also for our food production. Biobest Group has introduced different species for various countries, including *Bombus impatiens* for North America (East Coast), *Bombus huntii* for North America (West Coast), *Bombus atratus* for South America, *Bombus ignitus* (Asia) and *Bombus terrestris audax* – a subspecies of the buff-tailed bumblebee – for the UK.

There is also concern about the treatment of the bees. They are bred in climate-controlled rooms stacked with cardboard boxes the same size as the rodent nests they would use in the wild. The bees are fed sugar water and mixed flower pollen and will die after one season, as they would in nature. This could be described as 'intensive' farming of a living species, and many feel uncomfortable with it. Many vegans exclude honey from their diets because it is a product made 'by bees for bees'. Avoiding fruits pollinated by commercially bred honey bees or bumblebees is harder for the vegan community to avoid, though the debate is ongoing. On the other hand, using bumblebees has meant significant progress in an area of horticulture important to the environment: a reduction in the use of pesticides.

Once you put bumblebees in a greenhouse, you cannot use pesticides because they will kill the bees. You have to think of more innovative ways to control pests. This has led to a growing area of agriculture called 'bio-control', in other words, controlling pests by using other organisms rather than chemical pesticides. Farmers have been doing this for generations. I remember my Uncle Kenneth keeping an empty jar in the combine harvester to fish out any ladybirds he found in the grain and return them to the field to eat aphids. A leading company in this area, Koppert, has a similarly interesting founding story to Biobest Group. Jan Koppert, a cucumber farmer, realised he was suffering from a rash caused by the pesticides he was using, so he started thinking of a way to try to control pests without using chemicals. Noticing that predatory mites got rid of spider mites, he developed a way to breed the insects so they could be released in greenhouses. Together, Koppert and Biobest Group are now two of the world's biggest companies producing 'bio-control solutions' for controlling pests in greenhouses. The companies list more than 50 'control agents' with names that sound like a roll call from the Marvel Cinematic Universe: 'Who is going to save the planet from blueberry aphid? Cryptobug or Ladybird?'

Even bumblebees have gotten in on the act. Bumblebees or 'flying doctors' leave the hive via an integrated dispenser system where they pick up biopesticides on their bodies; they then spread that onto flowers as they forage. This is an effective way to protect strawberries against grey mould, which tends to infect the berries through the flower. Bio-vectors, as the bumblebees are known, ensure only the targeted use of natural bio-control products.

Inside greenhouses, insects are more important than ever for pollination and to provide natural pest control. But outside, there has been a shocking decline in insect life. Globally, more than 40 per cent of insect species are declining, and a third are endangered. In the UK, a 2021 study that counted insect 'splats' on windscreens found the number of flying insects in the UK has plunged by almost 60 per cent since 2004. Scientists worldwide blame insect declines on habitat loss as we replace forests and other wild areas with buildings or monoculture farming. Another major contributor to insect declines has been the increasing use of pesticides. Like nitrogen fertilisers, pesticides were developed post-war by factories that had been producing weapons. Since the Second World War, the production of chemicals has increased worldwide to 3 million tonnes annually. Farmers claim they are reducing the use of pesticides, but campaign groups like the Soil Association and Pesticide Action Network say the pesticides still in use are more toxic. A key concern is neonicotinoids, which generally harm bees and insects.

The one area where pesticides are genuinely declining is in greenhouses, and increasingly, it is an inspiration to farmers growing crops outdoors. Organic farmers have always planted wildflowers and hedges near crops to allow 'beneficial predators' to thrive. Now 'conventional' farmers are getting on board. Beetle banks, wildflower meadows and just plain messy margins are actively encouraged under government subsidies to allow aphid- and fly-eating insects like ground beetles, spiders and wasps to thrive. Bumblebees have helped farmers realise how important insect life is.

A few months after my first visit, I get in touch again with Jim Shanks, the dairy and tomato farmer. He has terrible news: the dairy is closing down. The pandemic was brutal, he says. At one point, when all the staff had Covid-19

– including him – he had to 'crawl into the milking parlour' twice a day. It was just not worth it for the paltry amount the milk was earning him. Jim is sad to be 'the one who let it happen on his watch' but grateful that he had time to diversify into a crop that is making him money.

The tomatoes are thriving, supermarkets want to stock 'Scottish tomatoes' in their 'local aisle', Jim's wife has started making tomato wine,[78] and school trips all want to know about the bees buzzing around in the canopy. In a way, the insects have become Jim's livestock, working with him to produce food. It is not the same as a cattle herd built up over five generations, but Jim does seem fond of them. Touring the greenhouse, he bends down to show me a little cardboard box like the ones invented by Roland de Jonghe for breeding 'race' bumblebees. It looks like an ordinary shoebox and smells faintly of old socks[79] – industrious humblebees buzz in and out of the holes.

For all the talk of ionised glass, renewable electricity, genome editing and precision agriculture, there is one thing that this glasshouse cannot do without: 75 hives from Belgium every year.

'That's it,' says Jim. 'No bees, no food.'

Further reading

Not on the Label: What Really Goes into the Food on Your Plate by Felicity Lawrence (Penguin, 2004)

Tomatoland: How Modern Industrial Agriculture Destroyed Our Most Alluring Fruit by Barry Estabrook (Andrews McMeel Publishing, 2012)

A Sting in the Tale by Dave Goulson (Vintage, 2013)

'Seeding Controversy: Did Israel Invent the Cherry Tomato?', Anna Wexler, *Gastronomica*, 2016

---

[78] Apparently, it tastes just like good white wine.

[79] Bumblebee nests are surprisingly smelly. Dave Goulson, the author of *A Sting in the Tale*, told me they sometimes smell of Christmas cake.

Honey-roast tomatoes on toast

Like the bees that make it and the people who eat it, every jar of honey is different. Lined up on David Wainwright's desk, they range in colour from the palest lime cordial to a rich caramel. Each jar is from a different apiary, or group of hives, managed by David and his team at Wainwright's Bee Farm. The bees will forage depending on the landscape, the weather and the season. The colour and flavour will reflect the nectar and pollen collected by the bees, so the honey from Essex borage is the colour of Chardonnay and tastes of vanilla and cucumber. In contrast, the honey from Welsh mountain heather is a deep ruby port and tastes almost smoky, and the ivy honey from Wiltshire looks like apricot jam and tastes like fudge.

Most bee farms mix honeys, so they have one generic colour and flavour. David can appreciate all these colours because he collects 'single-estate honey'. Keeping the honey from different apiaries separate means their flavour and colour can stand out, just like single-malt whisky. It also means we can connect the honey back to the farm where it was collected. In partnership with Marks & Spencer, David has started a 'Select Farm' honeys range that namechecks the bee farmer and the farmer where the apiary is located. Many of David's hives are on fruit and vegetable farms where bees are essential to pollinating crops like strawberries, broad beans, apples, plums and raspberries. When I meet David to check hives on an apiary in Wiltshire, the honey dripping off the comb glints daffodil-yellow in the sunshine and tastes of cinnamon and hay. This is from nectar collected from the wild sainfoin flowers (or holy hay, as the pink spiked flowers are known on Salisbury Plain).

Speaking to David, it is clear he has a relationship with his bees. The label on each jar describes the harvest that year, the weather and how the bees responded or how they were 'feeling'. He describes his job as 'husbandry', providing the bees with a suitable home in clean, dry hives, feeding them over the winter and ensuring a home for the next generation so that a sort of 'trust' builds up. As a result, the yields generally improve as 'farmer and livestock', or 'parent and children', get to know each other better.

I am a little nervous around the bees on the edge of Salisbury Plain, even wearing a suit. When we are leaving the apiary, I am stung on the finger (when I carelessly take my gloves off too soon), and it's then that David says: 'You are a proper beekeeper now.' I certainly better appreciate where my honey comes from now.

We all eat, so we all have a relationship with insects, whether honey bees made the honey we put on our toast or bumblebees pollinated the tomatoes in our salad. This recipe brings out the sweetness in the tomatoes and reminds us of bees' role in producing both the honey and the tomatoes. It is an excellent savoury-ish breakfast.

- 4–8 whole tomatoes (I find vine tomatoes work best)
- A glug of olive oil
- 1 tbsp of runny honey
- rosemary (or other herbs you have available such as thyme)
- salt and pepper

1. Preheat the oven to 200°C.
2. Place some tomatoes in a roasting tin, and drizzle olive oil and a good spoonful of honey over them. (I use around one teaspoon per medium-sized tomato.)
3. Sprinkle the tomatoes with salt and pepper, and tuck in a few sprigs of rosemary or other herbs around them.
4. Cook smaller tomatoes for 10 minutes and larger ones for 20 minutes, or until their skins begin to crack and the tomatoes look like miniature volcanoes.
5. Remove the roasted tomatoes from the roasting tin, squash them onto buttered toast and drizzle over the juices.

CHAPTER SIX

Nightingale Farm

UK-grown lettuce: 0.6kg CO_2e per kg
Lettuce driven from Spain: 1.8kg CO_2e per kg[80]

'Thou wast not born for death, immortal Bird!'
John Keats, 'Ode to a Nightingale'

On a cool spring evening in the 1920s, the cellist Beatrice
Harrison was practising Elgar in her Surrey garden when a
nightingale joined in. The melodious birdsong, designed to
impress female nightingales, was more than a match for the
world-famous musician. Sensing an equal, Harrison played
Dvořák and Delius and still the nightingale would come,
showing off his range from high peel to low rasp with every
note in between.[81] The pair began to play together regularly,
filling the darkening sky with the most exquisite music of man
and beast. Soon, the nightingale joined her so frequently that

---

[80] Mike Berners Lee, Lancaster University.

[81] Studies of nightingales have identified more than 250 different phrases
compiled from a repertoire of some 600 sounds (British Trust for
Ornithology).

Harrison decided to phone her friend Sir John Reith, the
founder of the BBC, and suggest the 'duet' be recorded. At
first, the broadcaster rejected the idea, dismissing nightingales
as 'prima donnas' too unpredictable for live radio, but eventually,
he was persuaded. The first of the 'Nightingale Broadcasts'[82]
was aired on 19 May 1924 and proved to be an instant hit,
reportedly listened to by more than a million people. The
public was so enchanted by the sound that the BBC continued
to record in the Foyle Riding garden every summer, despite
interruptions from other birds, whirring insects and even
squirrels nibbling at the wires. Sir John himself was converted,
admitting birdsong was something that 'all of us in this busy
world unconsciously crave and urgently need'.

The BBC continued to record nightingales in the garden
each spring until 19 May 1942, when the birdsong was
interrupted by 197 Wellington and Lancaster bombers flying
over on a bombing raid on Mannheim, Germany.[83] The
broadcast ended abruptly, but the historic recording continued
thanks to a quick-thinking sound engineer. Strangely, the
poignant sound of a nightingale singing to the drone of
bombers flying overhead became even more famous than the
nightingale duet with the cello.

I first heard the 'Nightingale and Bombers' recording on
BBC Radio 4 when it was chosen by the author Vikram Seth
as one of his Desert Island Discs, and I have listened to it
many times since. It sends a chill down my spine every time,
the purity and innocence of nature against the sinister sound
of humans at war. In a sign of the world in which I grew up,
and continue to live, it is what comes to mind when I think
of a nightingale singing. I have never heard one in the wild.

The song of the nightingale has intrigued us for
generations. The birds are the most versified in the world,
from John Keats's 'Ode to a Nightingale' to 'A Nightingale

---

[82] It was also the first natural outside broadcast by the BBC.

[83] 11 fewer came back from the raid.

Sang in Berkeley Square'. Yet few of us will have seen or heard one in the UK. Over the last 50 years, the UK population of the songbird has declined by 90 per cent to just a few thousand pairs. Where once it was the sound of summer in southern England over the six weeks from April to June, it is now only heard at a few sites. The nightingale was recently added to the UK's Conservation Red List, meaning it is in danger of extinction.

Nightingales migrate to the UK every year from Africa, where their overwintering grounds are increasingly threatened by deforestation. But it is most likely the change of land use in the UK, where they breed, that has impacted the population. The birds nest not far from the ground and rely on hedgerows, which have mostly been grubbed out since the war,[84] and scrub that has been developed into housing. They feed on insects, especially beetles and larvae, that have decreased with the use of pesticides. The fall in numbers is likely connected to the transition of farming to larger fields with no hedges and monoculture crops with fewer insects. More recent studies have suggested that the increase in deer numbers has exacerbated the problem by removing more low bushes through browsing pressure.

A key element transforming our farming landscape, which links back to the 'Nightingale and Bombers' recording, is the nitrates in the bombs those 197 Lancaster and Wellington bombers carried. The weapons were manufactured in part thanks to the Haber–Bosch process, which turned nitrogen in the air into ammonia that could be used to produce explosives. The controversial process also created a form of nitrogen that farmers could spread on crops. By the end of the Second World War, the same factories manufacturing weapons produced more artificial nitrogen fertiliser than the world had ever seen. The use of artificial nitrogen fertiliser

---

[84] Between the Second World War and the 1990s, we lost 75,000 miles of hedgerows in the UK.

allowed for a massive explosion in the population (two-fifths of humanity are alive today because of the Haber–Bosch process), but it also led to monoculture crops.

Arguably, the use of nitrogen fertiliser, which allowed the intensification of farming, also led to the reduction in farmland biodiversity. Farmland birds have declined more sharply than birds in any other type of habitat, their populations plummeting by more than half in just 30 years.[85] Where there are bigger fields, fewer hedgerows and one crop, there tend to be fewer grey partridges, fewer sparrows – and fewer nightingales.

Where nightingales do survive, they are sought out by members of the public keen to hear the extraordinary song that has inspired poets and musicians. 'Nightingale walks', on which it's possible to listen to a nightingale in the wild, attract hundreds of enthusiasts and are massively oversubscribed. Just as Sir John Reith discovered, the sound of birdsong – particularly this beautiful birdsong – is something we crave deeply. Maybe this is why, or perhaps because of the image of England nightingales conjure up, Tesco decided to call their bags of salad Nightingale Farm.

❧

Tesco launched Nightingale Farm lettuce and salad vegetables in 2016 as part of several 'Farm Brands' replacing their 'Everyday Value' brand. There was also Willow Farms whole chicken, Boswell Farms diced beef, and Rosedene Farms blueberries. They all sounded perfectly charming, and for a while, consumers were quite pleased to find themselves eating food from all these lovely little family farms in the British countryside. But then the actual farmers found out, and they weren't pleased. *Farmers Weekly*, a trade magazine,

---

[85] *Rooted: Stories of Life, Land and a Farming Revolution* by Sarah Langford (Viking, 2022).

did a spot check at Acre Lane Tesco in Brixton and discovered that many of the products under 'Farm Brands' were not even British, never mind from these idyllic-sounding farms. Boswell beef was from Ireland, Rosedene blueberries were from Chile, and Nightingale Farm celery was from Spain. All of them were essentially made-up farms, invented to sell an image of food produced in a version of the UK we lost long ago. There was an outcry, but Tesco did not seem very sorry about it and, to date, is still doing it. When I phone to ask why they are still doing it, Tesco remain unapologetic.

The fact is that British-sounding names and rural, historical or natural references are reassuring to shoppers and remain popular. Everyone is at it. Aldi has used Ashfield Farm for certain lines of meat, while Lidl has opted for Birchwood Farm and Strathvale Farm. Marks & Spencer has been criticised in the past for using Lochmuir as the catch-all name for its salmon and Oakham for its fresh chicken. Campaign groups see this as another way to befuddle the consumer and trick them into buying food out of season or imported from abroad, and farmers remain resolutely furious. But although stories emerge every so often in the media about 'fake farms', the fact is shoppers rather like this trend. Retail analysts have said there is an element of hypocrisy in people's behaviour. While surveys suggest 70 per cent of people are outraged at the idea of fake farms,[86] buying behaviour shows the opposite. We favour a phoney but pretty name over 'Everyday Value'.

Nightingale Farm strikes me as a particularly evocative name. I want to know what inspired it, who came up with it and whether there are any nightingales. And, since Tesco won't talk to me, I decide to go straight to where most of our salad is grown.

[86] Morrisons survey, 2017.

If you have ever taken the train from Edinburgh to Peterborough and on to Cambridge, as I often do, you will gaze at the Fens, an expanse of black soil, lines of ditches reflecting the big sky and rows and rows of perfect vegetables. The 400,000-hectare area, stretching from the Wash in the north to the River Ouse in the south, was once marshland regularly flooded by a network of rivers. I remember learning about the Fenmen with their webbed feet and houses on stilts in school. The frogs were so plentiful they were known as 'Fen nightingales'. But, although the folklore still exists, the Fenmen – and women – are long gone. Since the seventeenth century, when we learned from the Dutch how to straighten the rivers and drain the marshes, the wild black Fens has been slowly neatened up and straightened out. It is now a convenient grid landscape containing our most productive farmland (90 per cent of the land is grade 1 or 2, meaning it is the best agricultural soil in England). Roads have been built across the flat fields to large packing houses and beyond to the motorway and the ports. Thanks to the rich peat soil and the infrastructure to pack and transport veg, the Fens has become the key to our self-sufficiency in horticulture, producing 40 per cent of the vegetables grown in the open in England. It seems like the perfect place to search for Nightingale Farm. Yet, when I arrive at Ely Station, I am not taken to a family farm but to a supermarket.

'This is all ours,' says Anthony Gardiner, the Marketing Director at G's Fresh, sweeping a hand across the cornucopia of fresh salads in a modern supermarket: beetroot, spring onions, radish, celery, lettuce and baby leaves. The original G, Guy Shropshire, set up G's Fresh in the 1950s when he started selling bushel boxes of celery peppered in that lovely black Fenland soil to local shops. It was the era of farmland expansion. Post Second World War, the use of artificial fertiliser and the introduction of much more powerful farm machinery allowed farmers to produce many more vegetables on the fertile land of the Fens. Like my grandfather George Gray, who was doing the same in Scotland, Guy was part of this 'productionist' model, producing more to feed the growing population. Guy was also smart enough to present the vegetables differently. He realised sooner than most that modern shoppers did not want to see evidence of the black soil; they wanted the clean-cut celery we find on the shelves today. He was one of the first farmers to not only grow the veg but to process, package and transport it. Gradually, he set up a network of small family farms to supply the new supermarkets; in fact, Rosedene and Redmere farms are all genuine farms in the area that inspired the 'Farm Brands' at Tesco. Nightingale Farm was also one of the original G's Fresh farms, but it looks very different today than when it first grew salad.

Nightingale Farm – or at least where some of the Nightingale Farm salads are produced – is as far away from a quaint English farm as you could get. It is one of the most intensive outdoor horticulture systems in the UK. As we drive out into the Fenlands of Norfolk, towards an almost endless horizon of green fields divided by ditches, I comment on how flat it is compared to Scotland. 'It's not just flat,' Anthony explains. 'It is laser flat.' Inspired by farming in Florida, G's Fresh has laser-levelled fields so that sub-irrigation systems can retain just the right amount of water beneath the surface without creating pools or dry patches. The design means that water requirement is reduced by 50 per cent compared to overhead irrigation, where water will evaporate. Fungicide use is also reduced as the plant canopy does not get wet. The fields, with rows of bright green lettuce, look almost unreal – it is as green and flat as a bowling green.

The futuristic theme continues at the glasshouse, where we meet Charles Shropshire, the managing director of G's Fresh Cambs and grandson of Guy Shropshire. His family have come a long way from selling bushel boxes of unwashed celery. Today the firm, which is still family-owned, encompasses 20,000 hectares and brings in veg from the UK, Poland, Spain and even Senegal to supply food to supermarkets across the country. Charles is now helping to run a £500-million business sending veg around the world and is managing 10 times as much land as his grandfather. Nightingale Farm has become part of a sophisticated food production system that ensures we have lettuce leaves all year round.

Charles is an energetic young man, in the modern farmer's uniform of smart checked shirt and gilet, keen to make me understand the realities of growing lettuce. He explains that it is a sector with very slim profit margins, just 1.5 to 4 per cent, and therefore relies on high volumes to make it viable. The lettuce has to be perfect; it has to be consistent, and it has to be affordable. Over the last 20 years, the cost of a lettuce has halved – from £1 in 1992 to 50p now. In the UK, we eat 10–15 million heads of lettuce per week, of which G's Fresh produce 65 per cent, at a lower relative cost than the original G ever could.

Charles is a man in a hurry. He drives fast, he talks fast and in a way, he farms fast. He has to. We are starting in a state-of-the-art greenhouse where 135 million lettuce seedlings are grown annually. From February, the seeds, mainly from the US or Netherlands, are planted in peat plugs by machines that scatter just the right numbers of seeds. They are then left for a few weeks to mature in a greenhouse controlled by computers to supply the right amount of water and spray just the right amount of fungicide and insecticides from sprayers attached to the ceiling. I can see vast trays waiting to be moved by robotic arms to the next stage, where they are hardened off in a slightly cooler area of the greenhouse. During that time, the seedlings will rarely be touched by a human as most of the process is robotic. Even the planting barely requires a human hand. The lettuce plugs are planted by a machine driven by a GPS computer to ensure the lines are straight (although workers still have to follow closely behind the tractor to make up for any missed patches). One to two months later, depending on the season, and after more sprays of pesticides and regular irrigation, they harvest the lettuces.

His grandfather focused on growth, but Charles talks non-stop about cuts. Cutting costs, cutting labour, cutting nitrogen, cutting water, cutting pesticides and ultimately, cutting carbon. His grandfather had to think constantly about the 'productionist' model; Charles has to think about 'climate-smart farming' and producing more with less. The artificial nitrogen fertiliser that his grandfather could spread like sugar and made the expansion of agriculture possible has been identified as a significant source of greenhouse gases and water pollution, so Charles has to limit amounts according to government guidance.[87] While his grandfather could plough the land, Charles uses 'min-till', planting lettuce plugs directly into the ground to avoid releasing carbon dioxide. And while his grandfather could rely on soil almost as a never-ending resource, Charles is aware of its fragility, especially in the Fens, where the precious peat is eroding at a rate of around 1.5cm a year and up to 2cm a year in some areas.[88] For the first time all afternoon, he stops suddenly and bends down to pick up a handful of soil.

'This is carbon,' he says. 'And somehow, we *have* to keep it in the soil.'

Back in the pick-up, we are soon driving at some speed to see lettuce being harvested. The harvesting 'rig' looks like a wedding marquee hovering over the field. Inside, workers[89]

---

[87] Much of the Fens is in a Nitrate Vulnerable Zone, meaning guidelines on the amounts of artificial nitrogen and application should be followed.

[88] An estimate of peat reserves and loss, RSPB, 2009.

[89] Like a lot of the horticulture business of the Fens, G's Fresh relies heavily on labour from Eastern Europe. Since Brexit, the company has moved much of its production to Poland.

cut lettuce, take off the outer leaves and throw the heads onto a machine that will bag the product. As predicted, each lettuce comes out looking perfect. In the future, even these humans will be replaced by robots.

Charles takes a lettuce in his hand. 'The supermarket wants perfect,' he says. 'This is how you make the perfect lettuce.'

It is indeed a perfect iceberg lettuce, the kind that is filmed being chopped in two in slow motion for a fast-food advert. It is exactly the kind of lettuce consumers want on top of their burgers. Yet I have a question: if this is Nightingale Farm, or at least what is left of it, where are all the nightingales?

'Oh, you wanted to see the nightingales?' says Charles, jumping back in the pick-up. 'You should have said …'

We drive just as fast along even bumpier roads to see how G's Fresh encourages wildlife on the farms. Charles has moved from talking about cuts to talking about boosting nature, boosting carbon sequestration, boosting biodiversity. His energy is infectious as he takes me to see one of the characteristic Fenland arable ditches. Aquatic weeds sway in the clear water, and bulrushes dance in the breeze. Peering in, I notice a water boatman rowing slowly across the surface of the water and think of Ratty, the water vole in *The Wind in the Willows*, a species that I know is doing well in the Fens.

Despite being an intensive agricultural landscape, the Fens is also an important area for wildlife in the UK. The stereotype of the Fens is of flat, 'boring' fields, but there are 2,865km of ditches and 435km of hedgerows. A recent biodiversity audit identified more than 13,000 species here, including 1,932 priority species. Endangered creatures include Ratty (water vole), fen violet, reed bunting, marsh harrier and great crested newt. But somehow, Great Crested Newt Farm Salad does not sound as good.

The farm that G's Fresh is perhaps most proud of is at Wissington, where they produce most of the country's

Romaine lettuce and have one of the densest breeding populations of nightingales in the country. Every morning, Martin Hammond, the farm manager, walks his dog around the reservoir, spotting sedge warblers, reed bunting and reed warbler. Migrants include chiffchaff, blackcaps and garden warbler. Birds of prey spotted are hen harrier, marsh harrier and peregrine.

Martin describes himself as a 'wildlife fanatic', but he is also a practical farmer. When he walks me through the life cycle of his lettuce, he is clear about the use of pesticides. Aside from the fungicides applied in the greenhouse and the 'pre-emergent' herbicides, insecticides may have to be applied against aphids and herbicides against weeds like groundsel. He insists that attention to detail has meant that the use of chemicals is less than it used to be. Martin has been with G's Fresh for 34 years and has seen the transition from a production focus to a much slicker farming operation. Perhaps this is why they have survived. 'Precision farming' using satellite data from drones means fertiliser is applied where it is most needed; seedlings are planted closer together, meaning greater efficiency of inputs; and constant sampling of soil and lettuce leaves in the in-house lab means any disease is spotted early.

Humanity's manipulation of the landscape has not necessarily been a bad thing for all wildlife. The 80km of dykes on the farm to irrigate the fields means 80km of willow and alder hedgerow to harbour wildlife such as the nightingale. Keeping the peat wet means less carbon dioxide is lost to oxidisation of carbon on the surface. Reservoirs collect water outside peak-use times, providing a wildlife sanctuary the rest of the time.

As for the nightingales, why have they survived? Ornithologists remain surprised. It was always thought that the species preferred dry scrub, but in recent years they have been found more in wet areas, and they are thriving in some areas of Fenland. The birds could benefit from the insect life near the water and the low-growing shrubs and hedgerows. A 2005 paper in the journal *Ibis* found that 5 per cent of UK breeding nightingales are in south-east East Anglia, with the highest density on 'humus-rich soils', where there tends to be rich invertebrate life – and horticulture. The best theory is that nightingales always liked wetland but inhabited dry scrub when their numbers were greater. Now there is such a small population that they stick to optimal habitat.[90]

Martin has worked with the British Trust for Ornithology for years to count the nightingales on the farm. When I ask him if he has heard one, he describes the melodious song in reverent tones, and then he goes very quiet before saying, 'Once, I held one in my hand.'

The reason 'Nightingale Farm' is on our salad is that the idea of wildlife on farms sells food. We like the idea of nightingales and other birds flitting around the farms where our food is grown. The question is whether we can have affordable food and still have wildlife on farms. There are two schools of thought on how we answer this question: Land Sharing or Land Sparing. The Land Sparing model is inspired by the American biologist E. O. Wilson. In 2017, he wrote *Half-Earth*, a book proposing that we should leave half the planet as a nature reserve. He argues that, in the face of mass extinction, the only way to protect ecosystems is to leave enough land for wildlife to thrive without the interference of humans. He argues that we are more than capable of growing the food we need intensively on land or in laboratories. Many biologists agree that this model could work and would make the world more pleasant for all of us since the half dedicated to nature would also ensure clean air and water.

The Land Sharing model argues wildlife is better protected when we share the land with other species and all thrive. This model is known by several names, including

---

[90] British Trust for Ornithology.

'high nature value farming' and 'agroecological farming'; some argue it should be *all* farming. Organic farms can use agroecological methods but do not necessarily need to. The critical takeaway from this model is that nature can survive where we grow our food. Farming with nature in mind generally means more diverse crops, hedgerows being allowed to grow wild, some land being left fallow for long periods, using less chemicals and planting trees.

But which model would be best for nightingales?

In the UK, there are only two sites where nightingale numbers are increasing rather than decreasing. One, in Lodge Hill in Kent, is the site of an ongoing battle between the RSPB and Medway council to stop housing development encroaching on woodland.[91] The other, Knepp Estate in Sussex, is the UK's first major lowland rewilding project. The 1,415-hectare Knepp estate, just south of Horsham, was run like most farming projects post-war: widening fields, trimming hedges, buying bigger tractors, throwing on cheaper, plentiful, artificial nitrogen fertiliser. That is, until the 1980s when current owners Charlie Burrell and Isabella Tree took over. At first, they followed the herd, updating machinery, squeezing margins and pushing the soil and the animals as hard as possible. But by 2000, they were done with that.

'We kept buying bigger machines, throwing more pesticides, more fertilizer, more nitrates [at it],'[92] Tree later said. But the farm was sinking in the thick Sussex clay. The returns did not justify the inputs. So, they took an extraordinary decision – a decision no farmer had taken for thousands of years. They let go. They took down the fences, released livestock that could survive all year round without

---

[91] Although Homes England have revised their plans for Lodge Hill from 2,000 to 500 houses, following the #SaveLodgeHill campaign, the RSPB remains concerned about development in the area.

[92] *The World*, public radio programme, December 2018.

intervention, such as Old English Longhorn cattle, Exmoor ponies and Tamworth pigs, and let the hedges run wild.

At first, it was a mess. Their neighbours complained, the weeds went wild, and the animals went feral. But then something even more extraordinary happened: the wildlife returned, and conservationists realised that 'a mess' was just what nature needed. The purple emperor butterfly returned to lay their eggs on sallow scrub, 23 species of dung beetle were found in one cowpat, and the nightingales returned to live in the hedgerows.

In her 2018 book, *Wilding*, Tree describes the hedgerows that had been flailed every autumn before the ground was too wet for the hedge-cutter, depriving birds of the vital resource of winter berries, 'exploding like a dowager liberated from her stays'. The hedges grew out to a depth of 7–12 metres, providing the perfect habitat for nightingales. Like the understorey of woodland, hedges offer cover from predators, nesting sites a few feet from the ground and plenty of insects in the leaf litter.

A study by Imperial College London found that Knepp went from only nine nightingale territories in 1999 to 34 in 2012 and 42 in 2013, almost 1 per cent of the UK population. Isabella and Charlie started to have 'nightingale dinner parties' where they could invite their guests to come out and hear the nightingales sing after petits fours and coffee. Today, you can go on a 'safari' across the estate in the hope of hearing the birds sing. From being a nuisance to neighbouring farms, Charlie and Isabella have become the 'king and queen of rewilding'.

If more land rewilds, though, where do we grow our food? The answer, of course, is underground. When we leave the land for wildlife, we have to think more creatively about where we grow our food, like under Clapham North station in central London. It is a place I remember vaguely from my 20s, stumbling out of underground nightclubs onto sticky pavements in the company of sweaty Australians. I don't remember seeing any vegetables, though – how things have changed. This time, I am going underground to inspect a 'farm' that produces 60 harvests of leafy greens a year.

Growing Underground is 10 metres underground in bunkers built to protect Londoners from bombs in the Second World War. Coming out of the caged lift, the 'farm' smells like a chlorinated swimming pool and does look slightly like a nightclub, with its purple UV lights and low, curved ceilings. Stretched out in front of me are shelves of pea shoots, chives, red mustard, wasabi and coriander growing under LED lights.

Hydroponics does away with the need for soil by providing the plant with everything it needs through a human-made structure. The plants are grown in coconut fibre and fed just the right amount of water and nutrients through drip irrigation. Computers control the whole thing, ensuring the atmosphere is at the right temperature and humidity, and there is even a bit of breeze to strengthen the stems. Artificial intelligence ensures each crop receives precisely the right amount of light, water and nutrients. Salads can be grown from seedlings in as little as a week and are then transported in electric vans to restaurants around the city. The only old-school instrument Growing Underground employs is at the processing stage when they use a huge kebab knife to chop off the stems.

There are no pesticides because insect life is uncommon given the controlled environment and quick plant life cycles. Water use is kept low by recycling it as part of the hydroponic system. And because they use renewable energy to power the lights and the transport, this salad is entirely carbon neutral. Similar vertical farms are already popping up in cities worldwide to feed local populations on a low-carbon footprint.

By growing salad in the heart of the city, Growing Underground is part of the intensive food production on the 'human half' of the world that allows other land, such as

Knepp, to be the 'wild half' for nature like nightingales. It is an example of how Land Sparing *could* work. So, how does Land Sharing work?

Down the road from G's Fresh is an agroecological farm called Straight from the Field. Here Kirstie Perfitt grows lettuce without any fertilisers or pesticides or computers. She leaves patches of nettles so that beneficial insects eat the aphids. She uses mushroom compost and locally-sourced manure rather than fertiliser and grows different types of lettuce, so at least some are resistant to disease. She hand-harvests her lettuces so she can carefully remove any damage. Some days, she cannot hear herself think because of the birdsong.

Straight from the Field is an example of an agroecological farm that encourages wildlife on the farms where we grow our food. In general, organic farms are better at doing this. A British Trust for Ornithology study found more biodiversity on organic farms compared to conventional, including 85 per cent more types of plant species, 5 per cent more birds and 33 per cent more bats.[93] Some species don't just thrive; in certain parts of the country, certain species have lived side by side with humans for generations, evolving to rely on agricultural practices. For example, skylarks flourish on farms that practise crop rotations, foraging in high cereal stubbles in the winter and lower and less dense crops for spring and the summer breeding season. Bird experts[94] have suggested that the nightingale should be a farmland bird since it now relies more on hedgerows in places like Wissington in the Fens or the overgrown hedges on Knepp Estate rather than our diminishing woodlands. As a whole, 50 per cent of European species depend on farmland. If that is the case, we need much more agroecological farming to protect wildlife. We don't just need Nightingale Farm. We need Skylark Farm

---

[93] *Biology Letters*, 2005.

[94] The Imperial College study of the Knepp Estate nightingales.

and Grey Partridge Farm and Water Milfoil Beetle Farm. However, this could mean those farms produce less food. One study found that, although organic farms are more environmentally friendly, their yields are 10 per cent lower than equivalent non-organic farms. Less intensive farming models also need more land to produce as much food. Could there be an argument that a combination of the Land Sharing and Land Sparing models would work?

Currently, in the UK, most conservationists feel they have to take sides in the Land Sparing versus Land Sharing debate, but there is an argument that you could – and should – have both. This approach is called the Three Compartment Model. It means leaving some land to rewild for nature, allowing some land to be intensively farmed for food and also leaving some land to be cultivated in an agroecological manner that benefits certain species.

A 2019 study involving the RSPB and the University of Cambridge published in *Conservation Biology* argued that this could be the best way forward. Researchers studied the population levels of almost 200 bird species – in the Fenlands of eastern England, where G's Fresh is based, and on Salisbury Plain, another agriculturally productive area – to gauge how well the various species seemed to fare under different models. The study also noted the food produced under the three models. The Land Sparing model boosted the numbers of species that struggle to survive under agriculture, while the Land Sharing model favoured species like the skylark. But overall, for all species, the Three Compartment Model was often the best option. And under this model, there was also adequate food produced.

The 'National Food Strategy' published in 2021 argues that the Three Compartment Model could offer a way forward for species, like the nightingale, that appear to thrive on both rewilded land and managed hedgerows. The report maintains that if the least productive land were left to wildlife, it would only reduce the calories farms produce by

3 per cent. That would also align with the '30x30' pledge the government has made to protect 30 per cent of land for nature by 2030. In the meantime, some of the money spent on farming subsidies (which have been around £2 billion per annum in recent decades and should continue at about 10 per cent of the Defra budget) could be spent helping ordinary farmers introduce more agroecological measures such as allowing wild hedgerows. Intensive systems like Growing Underground and some of the most productive land – such as parts of the Fens – could compensate for some Land Sparing with high returns.

I like the Three Compartment model; it reminds me of the old woodcuts of the British countryside showing a mosaic of small fields, each with its own purpose: growing food, leaving land for wildlife, and some doing a little bit of both.

Nightingales were still heard in the Home Counties when Beatrice Harrison was playing her cello. England was still a patchwork of fields. After the war, when those bombers' work was done, England's landscape began to change irrevocably. Fields became bigger, the woods retreated, hedges were grubbed up, and the same nitrogen in those bombs was spread on the land and led to a revolution in how we eat. We pushed that brave little nightingale who sang in the face of the bombers out to the margins.

If we want any nightingales to survive, we have to squeeze in just a bit of that 'old England' somewhere, whether on intensive farms like Wissington, through rewilding on places like Knepp or agroecological farms like Straight from the Field. I would argue we need all three. A 'mosaic model' might not bring back the kind of England where a nightingale sang all night in a Surrey garden, but it might mean an England where the 'Nightingale Farm' brand has even more truth to the name.

I have been wondering where the nightingales that once sang with Beatrice Harrison have gone. After a bit of digging, I manage to find the phone number of the current resident of the house, who was kind enough to speak to me.[95] The recordings of the nightingales remain. The music room where Beatrice Harrison played remains; a piano in the corner and artefacts from her bohemian life with her sisters remain. But the nightingales? The nightingales are long gone.

Further reading

The Omnivore's Dilemma: A Natural History of Four Meals by Michael Pollan (Penguin, 2006)

'Managing Scrub for Nightingales', British Trust for Ornithology, 2015

'State of Nature 2019', State of Nature partnership

Wilding: The Return of Nature to a British Farm by Isabella Tree (Picador, 2019)

'The National Food Strategy' 2021, an independent review for Government

---

[95] With thanks to Sandee Brown of the Old Barn, Foyle Riding.

Hedgerow salad

When I was little, my favourite den was in the hedgerows that had grown up by the old railway line. The outside was a thick wall of blackthorn and dog rose. But once you were inside the hedge, it was like a cathedral arching over your head, letting in chinks of green light onto the dirt floor like a stained-glass window.

As an adult, I can't fit inside the hedge any more, but I can forage for hedgerow salad. As well as being good for wildlife like nightingales, hedges are nature's supermarket. In autumn, there are sloes and haws and brambles to pick. In spring, there is jack in the hedge or 'bread and cheese' (as hawthorn leaves were known to children in the past) to nibble on as a snack. There is also sticky willy, rosebay willowherb, ground elder, dandelion leaves and lime leaves growing nearby. Jack in the hedge is more like a mustard leaf, and dandelion leaves are very bitter, although they can taste delicious mixed in with other milder greens like spinach or lettuce.

Foraging from hedgerows is a way of eating healthy green leaves[96] and celebrating hedgerows. The 'stitching' that holds the British Isles' mosaic of fields together is fragile in many places. Since the Second World War, we have lost half our hedgerows; of those we have left, 60 per cent are in bad condition.[97] The hedgerows are not only key to our cultural history but, as managed trees, they could help us in the fight against climate change. The Climate Change Committee has advised that the UK needs to increase our hedgerows by 40 per cent to meet our 2050 net-zero target, which means planting 200,000km of new hedgerows, the equivalent of half the length of the UK's road network. Hedgelink, a group of charities working together to conserve hedgerows, points out that, as well as absorbing carbon, hedgerows are

---

[96] See chapter nine on foraging for the health benefits of wild foods.

[97] Hedgelink.

the largest wildlife habitat in the UK. Some 2,000 species, including dormice, hedgehogs and nightingales, make their homes inside the 'cathedral' that is a hedgerow.

This recipe is a 'hedgerow' salad I made in Scotland in June using edible leaves I could find in and around my house in Edinburgh. You can add any leafy greens to your salad, as long as you are confident they are edible and are careful to avoid dog-walking routes. This is a great way to pep up shop-bought salad leaves in spring.

Before the 1990s, bagged salad did not exist; you either had to buy whole lettuce or grow your own. Now, thanks to Modified Atmosphere Packaging (MAP), we can purchase what looks like fresh salad on supermarket shelves. It may look green and freshly picked, but according to Joanna Blythman in *Swallow This*, your salad leaves can be up to ten days old by the time you eat them. Packaged salad leaves are often washed in chlorinated water before they are packed in bags. The bags are then 'gas flushed' with carbon dioxide to push out oxygen and stop bacteria from growing, which is why everything slightly wilts when you open the bag. A good tip for whole lettuce is to sit the stem in a glass of water, which helps keep it fresh for longer.

Lettuce is often one of the foods on the Pesticide Action Network's (PAN) list of the Dirty Dozen fruit and vegetables with the most pesticide residue. The charity collates the figures from the UK Government's pesticide residue monitoring programme. While the Government will only test the safety levels of individual pesticides, PAN looks at the combined pesticide residue on each food. PAN claims that the 'cocktail effect' of combined pesticide residues could be hazardous to human health and encourages consumers to buy organic fruit and vegetable options. The UK Government insist there is no evidence of dangerous pesticide residue levels on our fruit and vegetables. While the debate over the long-term effect of pesticide residues on human health continues, the science on the benefits of eating fruit and vegetables remains clear: eating plenty of greens is good for you.

- mild leaves from wherever you like to buy or pick your salad
- ground elder
- lime leaves
- jack in the hedge
- rosebay willowherb leaves
- dandelion leaves
- dandelion petals
- dressing of your choice – my grandfather always used two parts oil to one part vinegar, a clove of garlic to infuse flavour, a blob of honey, a blob of mustard, salt and pepper

1. Walk along a hedgerow and enjoy the birdsong. Pick whatever plants you can safely recognise as edible. (Refer to a guide, if you can, and don't take any risks.)
2. Wash the plants thoroughly before adding them to some home-grown or shop-bought salad leaves.
3. Put the ingredients for your preferred dressing into a jam jar and shake, then use it to dress your salad leaves.

CHAPTER SEVEN

The Taste of Summer

Scottish-grown strawberries: 1.7kg CO_2e per kg
Strawberries driven from Spain: 1.8kg CO_2e per kg[98]

*'Let us learn to appreciate there will be times when the trees will
be bare, and look forward to the time when we may pick the fruit.'*
Anton Chekhov

Everyone has a happy memory of eating a strawberry in
summer. Here is mine: I am lying in a huge marble bathroom
somewhere in West London, laughing my head off because
my sister has just vomited strawberries into the most
enormous toilet bowl I have ever seen. The marble floor is
cooling my sunburnt skin, and my stomach feels distended
from eating so much fruit. Still, I cannot stop laughing or
singing 'Strawberry Fields Forever'.

My sister Anna, our friend Hauwa and I had spent the
day at a pick-your-own farm in Essex, loudly singing
Beatles songs and eating more strawberries than we picked.
We were in our early teens, released from our all-girls

---

[98] Mike Berners-Lee, Lancaster University.

school for the weekend and excited to be going to stay with Hauwa in the Big City after visiting the farm. But once we got to London, I'm not sure we ever left that marble bathroom.

It is not the most appetising food memory. Of course, I have more romantic recollections of eating seasonal berries: my granny's famous fatless sponge filled with whipped cream and strawberries and wheeled out on the squeaky brass tea trolley for any summer birthday; eating raspberries and cream in the back of a Vauxhall Corsa in Monaco before being smuggled (under-age) into a casino; a blackcurrant binge hidden in the fragrant leaves at the bottom of the fruit cage; picking sour cherries with my nephews before the birds get them. But the 'Strawberry Fields' memory is my favourite. It says so much about the greed of little girls and the unexpected messiness of friendship and joy.

Repeatedly in literature, summer fruit triggers memories of lost youth and happiness. In *The Cherry Orchard*, Anton Chekhov's last play, a disintegrating family of spoilt Russian aristocrats take a last sentimental tour of an estate they can no longer afford without the abolished system of serfdom. In the final act, as the sound of the axes hitting the cherry trees reverberates, Madame Ranevskaya, the profligate aristocrat who has lost the family seat, also mourns the loss of the fruit that reminded her of happier times: 'Oh my darling, my precious, my beautiful orchard! My life, my youth, my happiness … good-bye! … Good-bye!'

A bowl of cherries or fresh strawberries is still the food memory many of us associate with the summers of our 'youth and happiness'. Ever since Marcel Proust dunked a madeleine cake into his tea and ate it, triggering a rush of childhood memories – and a novel in seven volumes – the world of literature has accepted the 'Proustian' idea that the taste of food is linked to memory. It is also proved by science.

Taste[99] is not determined by the taste buds on your tongue but by the smells of the food in your nose. When these signals from the mouth and the nose combine in the orbitofrontal cortex, just behind the eyes, our brain registers 'taste'. This is also the area that lights up on a brain scan when memory or emotions are triggered. We see that the two are linked when we bite into a strawberry and remember a moment from summers past, like the mushy strawberries soaked in Pimm's and too much mint that always remind me of drunken backyard barbecues. US writer Molly Birnbaum proved the theory when she lost her sense of taste after a car accident. Her sense of disorientation was profound, not only because food she ate tasted bland but because she had lost the ability to trigger precious memories. (When her sense of taste finally returned, it was from chocolate and rosemary first and came with memories of her youth.) In recent years, many more people have had this experience after suffering from Covid-19 and, as a result, losing their sense of smell, even temporarily.

Professor Charles Spence at the University of Oxford, a leading advocate for taking a 'multisensory' approach to food, understands the importance of taste to our emotional life better than anyone. He has proved that taste is not only about the sensations on your tongue or even the smells in your nose but also the appearance of the food, the environment you are eating it in, and the emotion you experience while eating. Experiments cited in his theory of 'gastronomics' include proving crisps taste better when you can hear the crunch, hot chocolate tasting better drunk from a brightly coloured cup, blue and green room lighting

[99] In scientific terms, taste refers to saltiness, sweetness, *etc*. The combination of the experience of taste, smell and expectation is known as 'flavour'. However, for this book, I will use the more common usage of taste as this is what I think most people understand when we talk about the full combined effect scientists would technically call flavour.

making wine taste spicier, and water tasting sweeter when we think of love.

A ripe strawberry – or one that looks perfectly ripe – is one of the best examples of how experiences come together to make 'taste'. When you bite into it, you enjoy the natural sweetness of the fruit and the juicy texture. But you also enjoy the fragrance that reminds you of summers past. Put that all together in the orbitofrontal cortex, and you have the 'taste' of strawberries.

In the modern age, this complex understanding of taste is increasingly helping restaurateurs and food companies to sell their produce. Heston Blumenthal plays the sound of the sea to his clients as they eat seafood to help them conjure happy memories of the seaside. Junk-food companies try to 'hook' young children with cartoon characters and colourful branding in the knowledge that childhood memories will mean a food 'tastes' better for life.

Most of us know instinctively that 'taste' is more complex than sour, sweet, salty, bitter and umami. We 'know' what tastes better in the right circumstances: *glühwein* on a cold day, home-made lemonade on a hot day, sandy sandwiches on the beach, Kendal Mint Cake on top of a mountain, strawberries in summer. When I started writing this book, sticking to seasons was one of the subjects that people were most passionate about: 'Oh, people who eat strawberries in January. What are they thinking? They taste like carrots! I only eat strawberries in July, you know.'

Strawberries do taste good with all those summer memories attached. But does that mean that out-of-season strawberries always taste bad?

Wild strawberries are perhaps the sweetest example of seasonal fruit. Their pretty white flowers brighten up the forest floor in spring, hence the botanical description 'June bearer', before the fruit emerges for a few weeks from June into July – if you can get them before the birds. Since Roman times,[100] in Europe, we have enjoyed these wild strawberries (*Fragaria vesca*), often called woodland strawberries because they thrive in shady spots under trees. The wild species is smaller than the commercial strawberries we know today and has a much more intense flavour and fragrance. Gradually, humans have transplanted the fruit from the woodland into our gardens. Monks in medieval times used strawberries to treat depressive illnesses, and the court of King Henry VIII went mad for strawberries and cream. Cardinal Thomas Wolsey, a powerful figure in the court, is credited with 'inventing' strawberries and cream. But although kings and princes enjoyed strawberries and peasants plucked them from the hedgerows, the strawberry did not take off as a cultivated fruit in Europe until larger varieties were introduced from the New World.

Two strawberry species quietly cultivated by indigenous people in Virginia in North America and Chile in South America, that were both bigger and juicier than the wild European strawberry, made their way to Europe and the gardens of the strawberry-loving aristocracy. In the process, the two different species spontaneously cross-bred and created a new version of the summer fruit, *Fragaria X ananassa*,[101] which tasted almost as good as the tart little woodland strawberry but was bigger and fatter and easier to cultivate.

Around the same time, in the eighteenth century, the Europeans noted that plants could produce male-only or female-only flowers. By identifying male and female flowers across different varieties and using a paintbrush to imitate an insect, it was possible to cross-pollinate and create new varieties. Strawberries turned out to be a perfect plant for experimenting with this exciting new science. Soon hundreds of strawberries were emerging to meet our hunger for bigger,

---

[100] The Roman poets Virgil and Ovid mention the strawberry.

[101] So-called because it smelled and tasted of *ananas* (pineapples).

smaller, sweeter or more aromatic strawberries. Sadly, because strawberries are so prone to disease, we have also lost more old varieties of strawberries than any other kind of fruit.

But even after all that fiddling around with breeding, the strawberry was still a seasonal fruit, prized for its short season during the summer. It was only in the 1970s that Californian breeders finally bred a new strawberry variety that went on fruiting as long as it was warm and light, rather than producing fruit only in the summer. It was described as a 'day neutral', and its arrival meant the short season of the strawberry was over (at least in California and the Mediterranean, where it was warm and light much of the year). There was only one problem: they didn't taste very nice.

Extending strawberry season has been a significant motivation for breeders since discovering the 'day neutral'. If they could only combine the flavour of traditional varieties with the constant fruiting ability of the new 'day neutral' plants, then we could all enjoy strawberries over a much longer season. This initially started happening in the 1980s; then, in the 1990s, new varieties began emerging from a most surprising place: the east coast of Scotland.

Despite its cool climate, Scotland has always been famous for its strawberries because long Scottish summer days allow the flavour to build up slowly. I am told the best-tasting strawberries served at Wimbledon are traditionally from Scotland since the tournament happens quite late in the English strawberry season. Scotland also breeds a particular type of farmer who does not give up easily.

Angus Soft Fruits has been producing berries since the 1960s, sending their fruit down from the north-east to Rankins' in Edinburgh and Covent Garden Market in London. In the 1990s, this family firm started to invest in breeding research. Speaking from his current laboratory

David Griffiths (head of research and one of the company's founders) explains his 'breakthrough moment'. He realised if he could create the conditions of the Mediterranean and California, he could grow the 'ever-bearing' day neutral strawberry in Scotland. At the same time, if he could add traits from the 'June-bearing' strawberries, so they build up flavour during the long Scottish summer evenings, he would have the 'perfect strawberry'. Working with Scottish farmers, he helped develop polytunnels that could create the perfect climate for strawberries at a relatively northern latitude. In tandem, he constantly experimented to find a variety that would also allow the slow build-up of flavour. Eventually, he was rewarded with tasty strawberries that continued to fruit in the warm polytunnels. He was among the first to cross 'June bearer' and 'day neutral' strawberries to develop varieties like AVA.

Today, Dr Griffiths continues to develop more varieties, crossing thousands of strawberry plants, still using a little paintbrush, and watching carefully for the characteristics the industry currently values to emerge. A larger size makes the strawberry more efficient to harvest. It must also be resistant to disease, firm enough to withstand transportation and display the fresh red colour consumers expect. Most importantly, it must taste sweet and retain that quintessential 'British strawberry' flavour. Once a successful strawberry is developed, it will effectively 'clone' itself by putting out runners, making the reproduction process relatively easy. From cross-pollinating to getting a new variety on the shelf usually takes about seven years.

At the same time, polytunnel technology is constantly developing, making it easier to grow new varieties on a large scale. Instead of being grown on straw[102] to suffocate

---

[102] Contrary to popular belief, strawberries are not called 'strawberries' because they used to be grown under straw, but from an Old English word meaning 'to strew' because the plant's runners stray in all directions and look as if they are strewn on the ground.

weeds and keep the strawberry plants above damp ground, modern strawberries are often grown on the ground under plastic. More recently, they are grown on raised tables to make it easier to pick the fruit and grow hydroponically. The so-called Seaton System, again led by Angus Soft Fruits, grows strawberries in a bed of composite, such as coconut coir, on raised tables. Tubes fed into the beds irrigate the crop 12 to 18 times a day. This system saves pickers' backs and allows a central computer system to monitor exactly how much water and fertiliser the plants need over a particular growing period. Crucially, this approach has allowed growers to extend the season by enabling the new breeds of strawberry with the heavy fruiting characteristics of 'day neutral' plants to grow in places like Scotland.

When Dr Griffiths started out in the 1990s, the strawberry season was a short-and-sweet six weeks, from June into July. Now, thanks to a combination of breeding and technology, the UK strawberry season lasts from May to September. If you include strawberries grown in English glasshouses, it extends from March to December. And if you import them from Spain, Egypt, Israel and Morocco, you have strawberries all year round.

Now that growers have developed a perfect Scottish summer strawberry, the current competition is who can breed a tasty strawberry grown in a polytunnel in Spain or Morocco over the winter. The challenge is concentrating flavour into the strawberry over the short winter days to prevent them from tasting like 'carrots' and making sure the fruit still tastes sweet when it is a little unripe (as it must be picked hard to withstand transportation). Already, Dr Griffiths reckons they are improving: 'There is no doubt the flavour profile coming in from abroad is getting better and better.'

Lochy Porter (the current managing director of Angus Soft Fruits) claims strawberries can be sweet even in winter: 'I think strawberries have hugely improved all year round compared to what they used to be.' He must be right, since the British public has readily bought into having strawberries out of season, despite the claim by most of us to prefer eating them only in summer. Since the 1990s, the number of strawberries produced in the UK has risen from 50,000 tonnes to more than 120,000 tonnes per year, supplying almost all the required fruit for the country. This increase is driven largely by demand from children – or at least their parents – as the berries are more appealing than eating apples or other bigger fruit. As Lochy says, 'do we really want to turn back the clock on this healthy habit by only eating strawberries in June and July?'

Other companies are also developing strawberry varieties, creating a highly competitive industry that is arguably working in the consumer's favour by cultivating better and better strawberries out of season. NIAB in East Malling, Kent, claim to have bred a variety that tastes like the best British strawberries served at Wimbledon but is available almost all year round – the appropriately-named 'Malling ACE'.

When I visit Angus Soft Fruits at their headquarters north of Arbroath, they are tasting their latest batch of experimental strawberries. Chemical sugar-analysis tests for sweetness and penetrometers test for firmness, but humans still do the ultimate taste test. Every day, punnets of new varieties are laid out to be tested by experts, and I am invited to help myself. The strawberries are all firm, red and sweet – and before I know it, I have eaten more than a dozen. The professional tasters carefully note down the 'sugar content' and describe the 'fragrance' of each different variety on special spreadsheets. When asked which tastes best, I choose a huge juicy strawberry but struggle to explain why except that 'it tastes like summer'.

The challenge for growers like Angus Soft Fruits is no longer the season but finding people to pick and pack their strawberries. Since the industry started expanding quickly in the 1990s, it has relied on an imported workforce. Initially, this was through the Seasonal Agricultural Workers Scheme (SAWS), which allowed in students from Eastern Europe, and then as a result of the free movement of people as new countries joined the EU. Brexit cut off this 'lifeline' for the industry, and it was only after lobbying by farmers like Angus Soft Fruits that the government re-established the SAWS so that workers could come in from Eastern Europe again. At the time of writing, there are plans to continue allowing in workers from Eastern Europe and beyond, but also concern from the industry that the numbers are not large enough. Although the government promises to invest in technology and training local labour, every year, at least 29,000 seasonal workers are required in the UK to satisfy our new-found taste in year-round berries. Without a significant change in robotics or UK demographics, that will not change. If anything, demand will likely grow.

Considering the size of the human operation, we rarely notice the strawberry fields in Britain. Most farms are hidden behind banks of willow trees in valleys in Kent or on the east coast of Scotland. The workers' accommodation is in caravan parks further into the farm. When I visit Angus Soft Fruits' farm perched on the cliffs just north of Arbroath, it is at the height of the season in the run-up to Wimbledon. Picking starts at 3.30 a.m. with teams trailing in from the workers' caravan park or the nearby town. On a morning like this, up to 800 people could be picking across the farm at any one time. Some are wearing their pyjamas or tracksuit bottoms or leggings with comfy T-shirts and woolly hats. We are all rubbing sleep out of our eyes. We are divided into groups and spaced between the polytunnels with two or three people per row. The dew still clings to the roof of the tunnel, though inside, it is warm and fragrant.

I trail behind a trolley with Lyuben 'Lubo' Gayev, one of the few people who speak English. He is jolly and friendly and shows me how to pick the strawberries at the stalk to avoid damaging the fruit. The best strawberries are put into the punnets for more high-end supermarkets, while smaller, less perfect-looking fruit is picked for discount lines. The pickers are expected to achieve a certain quality and volume checked by the supervisors. I watch pickers hauled up for a thumbprint on a strawberry or a smaller fruit ending up in a high-end box. Lubo has been coming for four years, supplementing his income as a mechanic in Bulgaria and building up some cash to establish a business. He is one of the best pickers and can pick 72kg of strawberries per day. He thinks this will probably be his last year. It is a fairly typical story. Most of the other workers I speak to in broken English are here temporarily to earn money to take back home. Some younger workers who speak better English have established themselves and their families here, pre-Brexit, finding other jobs out of season and putting their children into Scottish schools. The nearby town of Arbroath has an Eastern European supermarket selling Polish bread and Bulgarian cheeses. As a community with an ageing population, locals have broadly welcomed the influx of young, employed people.

At the 7 a.m. and 10 a.m. breaks, like most human groups, we split up into our respective tribes. We separate not just into the smokers and the non-smokers but urban and rural. I watch as women from villages in Bulgaria, wearing headscarves and long skirts, huddle in family groups while younger men, perhaps with more experience in the towns, trade jokes wearing baseball caps and tracksuit bottoms. The demographic has changed in recent years as new workers come in from more remote areas of Bulgaria and Romania to make up for the shortfall in demand. Lined up under the hedge, many of us on our haunches, squinting into the sun, we look like images you see of old agricultural workers in places like Kent. I guess not much has changed except the countries people come from and the portable loo at the end of the hedge.

I tentatively ask the workers about Brexit. Most nod their heads: yes, it has had an impact. But they shrug and tell me that if the UK really does not want them any more, they will find work elsewhere. Demand for seasonal workers is a Europe-wide market; if the UK no longer needs pickers from Bulgaria and Romania, then Germany and even the growing strawberry industry in Poland will. The person most worried about immigrant labour drying up and the industry in the area closing down is the farm manager, Allen Innes: 'What about *my* job? What will *I* do?'

The pickers are paid £7.50 an hour, plus National Insurance and overtime, so it ends up around £9.56 an hour and can be up to £14 an hour. It is expensive, admits Allen, but he thinks replacing seasonal pickers with robots is some decades off, and in any case, soft fruit will always need a certain amount of human labour.

By midday, the sun is high, and a skylark is singing above the tatty rigs beyond the polytunnels. We troop to the next picking job of the day, the raspberries. The plants are grown in pots of coconut fibre on the ground,[103] and the whole polytunnel smells like my grandmother's fruit cage, where blackcurrants and redcurrants were grown under a cage of netting large enough to allow humans to come and pick. The varieties developed over the last few years have fewer thorns; even so, they still scratch your wrists and hands when you reach in and pick the fruit.

At the end of a long day, at around 3.30 p.m., I accompany Atushe Hadzhieminova back to her caravan for a cup of Bulgarian coffee – sugared so heavily I could stand a spoon in it – accompanied by a selection of biscuits from Aldi. Six workers live in this small space. They say it is comfortable,

---

[103] Few farms are able to grow raspberries in the soil because of a disease known as raspberry rot.

with a shower, a large television on which they watch Bulgarian soap operas and a computer to Skype home. Atushe is a 23-year-old law student working during her summer break with her boyfriend, her mother and father and two cousins. She grew up in a village in rural Bulgaria, and her English is basic, but she is clearly bright and hard-working. Whichever way she has to do it, I have no doubt she will help pull her family up to the next rung of the ladder. Already her family is negotiating the shift from an isolated rural way of life to a lifestyle influenced by digital and economic connections with the rest of the world. She is part of a new European generation of Bulgarians educated in languages, economics and travel.

It is a sunny evening now, and pickers are lying out on the grass, socialising, preparing barbecues or fishing rods to take down to the beach. Few will leave the farm except to go for a weekly shop. It is difficult to see these people as any threat to the lifestyle or employment of the local population. However, in areas with a lot of seasonal workers, such as Boston in Lincolnshire, votes in favour of Brexit were high. It is a measure of resentment at the influx of people moving into the UK. Yet these areas would surely struggle to survive without seasonal workers. The idea that British people will pick our soft fruits is a big ask; even if all 1,500 people registered unemployed in Angus started picking strawberries tomorrow, they couldn't replace the 8,000 seasonal workers the industry needs in this county alone.

In the packing house, the strawberries picked that day are cooled down for a couple of hours before being sealed in a plastic punnet. I watch as the strawberries I have just picked trundle along a conveyor belt. Each punnet is stamped with a proud Saltire and labelled as Scottish strawberries. The soft fruits from Perthshire and Angus have always been famous, thanks to the climate and the soil. But nowadays, 'Perthshire' and 'Angus' strawberries are grown in Sri Lankan coir rather than Scottish soil. The young plants are brought over from the Netherlands, methods first used by the Israelis inspired the irrigation system, the fertiliser is manufactured in North Africa, and the fungicide and herbicide – if any are used – come from an American company. The fruit is picked and packed by people from Eastern Europe, and the plastic punnets are made in China. How Scottish are these strawberries, really? Like our idea of seasonality, our notion of Scottishness is becoming less relevant. Yes, they are produced by a Scottish company, and the climate of Scotland does grow better strawberries, but that is about it. Like most food-manufacturing businesses, strawberries are an international business.

The Scottish strawberry industry may have a sentimental idea at its heart, but the reality is perhaps an even more wonderful feat of technology and people power. Around 30,000 tonnes of strawberries are grown annually on 1,000 hectares, mostly under polytunnels. The wider British industry is concentrated around the Midlands and Kent and grows around another 100,000 tonnes. Altogether, it is a £3 billion industry and growing.

So, next time you eat a British strawberry, remember it is not only memories of summer that make it taste so delicious; that sweet taste is also thanks to technology and innovation and the hard work of people like Remiziye, Myumyun, Atushe, Angel, Bozhidar, Irina, Setso, Catalin, Lyuben, Ivan, Alia and Gyuten who picked that strawberry for you.

There is nothing wrong with eating seasonally. Fresh fruit does indeed taste better when it is given the time to mature and is picked fresh. Pick-your-own strawberries in July will always taste better than the supermarket version bought in January. As the British food writer Patience Gray wrote, it makes you appreciate food more to wait for the appropriate season: 'Once we lose touch with the spendthrift aspect of nature's provisions epitomised in the raising of a crop, we are in danger of losing touch with life itself.'

In this age of instant gratification, perhaps it is more important than ever that we appreciate the fleeting joy of English asparagus in June, apples in October and Pakistani honey mangos in July. One of the first things my daughter brought home from nursery was a clay pot she had painted with a strawberry planted in it. After a few weeks, we have two measly strawberries we nibble before the birds get them. It does give me a sense of the summer arriving and makes me appreciate how difficult it is to grow a whole crop. I intend to take her to the pick-your-own once she is old enough. I want her to get a sense of strawberries as a treat for summer, and we will eat more over the summer months because they taste so good.

But, like most readers of this book, I sometimes eat straw-berries out of the traditional season. Fruit like strawberries will be grown in the same way on the British Isles, whether you eat them in May or September, with similar demand for irrigation, chemicals and labour. There is no reason not to enjoy the fruit for an extended period. And if we understood the impressive scale and growth of the industry that provides us with this fruit for five months of the year, we might better appreciate the people who pick it for us.

Yes, children need to understand the seasons by growing their own fruit and veg, but it is also important they know how that fruit is grown for them out of season – and that they continue to eat fruit all year round. In the same way, adults must understand there is an added carbon footprint when they eat strawberries from Spain in January. If we want to eat seasonal fruit all year round, we must accept changes to our countryside, the wider global environment and population makeup. But those changes are not necessarily bad: children are eating more fruit, we have a thriving soft fruit industry in the British Isles, and the migrant workforce is bringing new life to many rural British areas.

Amid all the tragedy of *The Cherry Orchard*, one character – Ania, the daughter of Madame Ranevskaya – influenced by the radical politics of the time, believes in a better future. Even as the cherry trees fall, she reminds the audience that the loss of the old ways of doing things does not need to mean the end. It can be the beginning of making new worlds and memories and a 'better life!' Chekhov is pointing out that, while the season is fleeting, which can be painful, time also moves on.

I contacted Hauwa to tell her I was writing about our 'Strawberry Fields Forever' experience. She lives in Nigeria now. She tells me strawberries in Nigeria come into season at the same time as mangos. I would like to visit her one day with my sister, so we can taste a Nigerian strawberry and mango smoothie, sing Beatles songs and make new memories.

Further reading

The Cherry Orchard by Anton Chekhov (1904)

Season to Taste: How I Lost My Sense of Smell and Found My Way by Molly Birnbaum (Granta, 2011)

Summers Under the Tamarind Tree: Recipes and memories from Pakistan by Sumayya Usmani (Frances Lincoln, 2016)

Gastrophysics: The New Science of Eating by Charles Spence (Penguin, 2017)

'Government Food Strategy 2022: The UK as part of a global food system', Defra

Seasonal fruit chaat

Seasonal fruit means different things to different people. For me, it means summer pudding made by women with scratches on their arms from picking the raspberries and served with single cream on a cool summer evening. It means cousins gathered around my granny's mahogany dining table and a particular Presbyterian enjoyment of food that is sharp and filling but not necessarily sweet.

For my friend Sumayya Usmani, it is peeling a mango in front of the air conditioning at her granny's house in the Sindh province of Pakistan on a sweltering June afternoon. The famous 'Sindhri' or honey mango is known for its golden skin and aromatic flesh. Sumayya recalls waiting all summer for the mangos to ripen, watching as the teardrop-shaped fruit would droop 'slowly, slowly' to the ground, and her granny would scold her from the door 'not yet, not yet'. Finally, the day would come when they could pick the sun-warmed fruit and run inside to put them in the fridge to cool before 'finally, finally' they would gorge on mangos in front of the TV.

Every summer, from late June to early July, 'mango mania' hits Karachi for a few weeks. Vendors push wooden carts towering with tens of varieties of mangos from around the country, mango lassi drinks are sold on the streets, and children queue for mango ice creams.

As an adult in rainy Glasgow, Sumayya can still smell the mangos when they come into her local Asian supermarket in late June, and she can never resist buying a crate. As a bonus, she can also buy in-season strawberries in Scotland then. In Pakistan, strawberries come from the Swat region in the north of the country and are in season in the winter, so it is impossible to eat the two fruits together. But in Scotland, we can mix the two flavours when the strawberries are in season and imported Sindhri mangos are also available. For Sumayya, it is an opportunity to combine precious memories from different times in her life into a cross-continent taste experience.

This recipe recommended by Sumayya mixes seasonality from two different countries and brings out the flavour of both fruits with spices. You can buy honey mangos at your local Asian supermarket or greengrocers in late June or early July. Chaat masala is also available in big supermarkets or Asian shops. My version uses a teaspoon of sugar as a base, toasted ground cumin seeds that add texture and flavour and then a little cinnamon and chilli for warmth. But you can add other store cupboard spices, such as ground coriander and ginger. You can also use this spice mix on other fruits. Allow about one teaspoonful of it for a pudding bowl of fruit salad.

For the mixed fruit

- 2 Sindhri mangos
- 1 400g punnet of Scottish strawberries

For the chaat masala

- 1 tsp of white granulated sugar
- 1 tsp toasted and ground cumin seeds
- 1 tsp cinnamon
- A pinch of chilli
- A pinch of salt
- A good grind of pepper

1. Cut the mango flesh into cubes.
2. Remove the hulls, then cut the strawberries into quarters.
3. Add a squeeze of lemon or lime juice to keep the fruit fresh.
4. Mix the fruits and spices, then let it all sit for five minutes before serving – this allows the flavours to blend and creates a delicious fruit juice.

CHAPTER EIGHT

The Space Zucchini

UK-grown courgettes: 0.7kg CO_2e per kg[104]

'Perhaps if he got a great deal of fresh air and saw things growing, he might not think so much about dying.'
Frances Hodgson Burnett, *The Secret Garden*

At last, it is my moment: my allotment has erupted. Yes, there are weeds – there are always weeds – but I have also grown a giant beetroot, courgettes the size of shoes (OK, marrows), flowering runner beans, mutant carrots, loads of different varieties of potatoes, cavolo nero, seeded cabbages, bitter lettuce and tiny tomatoes. Everything is the wrong shape or the wrong size or just plain weird. A parsnip comes up curled in a ball, a cucumber grows spikes, and you know what wonky home-grown carrots are like. But it is, miraculously, alive. Best of all, carried home in a muddy carrier bag, washed in the sink and shared with friends, it tastes wonderful.

---

[104] Mike Berners-Lee, Lancaster University.

Growing my own food while writing this book seemed like a fitting companion project. I took on a share of a plot on my local allotments at Inverleith Park and got stuck in, digging over the soil and planting seeds in the greenhouse. I thought I could add details of my gardening epiphany over the growing year, but life gets in the way: a baby and a global pandemic and most of all, I am a bit useless at gardening. Don't get me wrong; I enjoy sitting in the allotment and listening to the bees, startling the fox or being startled by the heron. But in terms of producing actual food? It is very slow. For much of the time, I don't know what to do. When do I plant? What does a weed look like? And why won't anything grow? I feel frustrated and a little disappointed not to feel immediately at one with the earth simply by digging my hands into the soil. But when August comes around, and I have an oddball harvest to show for my efforts, I start to get the bug. Perhaps, I realise, this is something to learn over a lifetime, not a one-off project to show off about on social media.

Courgettes, in particular, make everything better. If I can grow a vegetable of this size, perhaps I am not so bad at it after all? When the annual show comes around, I enter my marrow into the Vegetable Monster category. I decorate my prize vegetable carefully with a squashy tomato nose, runner-bean smile and raspberries skewered in with cocktail sticks for eyes. I am beaten by a seven-year-old.

It is a fun day full of pride and laughter. Friends I have made over the year are all showing off their prize fruits, flowers and vegetables. Stewart, who always lectures everyone about the importance of growing food on an allotment, displays his fabulous gladioli. Cathy wins for her delicate little wildflowers. Marjorie has accidentally grown a giant squash, and Maggie and Ian present their prize-winning pears from a tree they brought back to life through something as simple as cleaning it with soap and water. Crisp purple apples, juicy blackberries, carrots grown in orange cartons to keep them straight, and perfect pink rhubarb all win awards. All day, we nibble on fruit and vegetables and congratulate ourselves on the fact they taste better than anything in the shops. But I don't think any of us are here to compare vegetables.

I'm here for this cosy feeling of eating home-made, home-grown apple pie while giggling at the wonky carrots, debating potato varieties and perhaps bitching a little bit about certain plots of perfect asparagus. I haven't excelled in gardening, but I've made friends and learned a few lessons about growing food. In a year that hasn't been that easy, I feel loved and nourished and hopeful. I think that is why people usually come to the allotment, isn't it?

We think of allotments as a rather quaint part of British life, a backwater where retirees can poke around in their sheds and compete to grow an enormous leek. There is an element of truth to this comfortable vision. Wander around any allotment, and you will find pigeon lofts, prize roses and show leeks. But you will also find food. Allotments exist for a much more radical reason than leisure gardening: they were created to help us grow food, and in a future of climate change and megacities, allotments have the potential to be radical once again.

Arguably, the first stirrings about allotments began as early as the Diggers in 1649, planting carrots on a bit of wasteland in Surrey in protest at the enclosure of common land. In the years that followed, the Levellers, the Luddites and the Tolpuddle Martyrs all rose up in protest against essentially the same thing: concentrating the power to grow food in the hands of a few landowners. The Enclosure Acts of the eighteenth century enclosed common land used by rural communities to grow food and used it for large-scale agriculture, leaving many families angry – and hungry. But it was only in the nineteenth century, perhaps prompted by the French Revolution across the Channel, that the British authorities officially decided to do something about the demand for land for the poor to grow food. The first recorded allotment in England was set up in Great Somerford, Wiltshire, in 1809, after the socially conscientious Reverend Stephen Demainbray petitioned King George III for six acres for the poor to grow food. The idea of paying a peppercorn rent for a small amount of land to help alleviate hunger took off. In 1819, the Poor Relief Act empowered church wardens or overseers to hire or buy land for allotments 'to be let out to the poor and unemployed'. In 1845, one of the final Enclosure Acts required that when land in England and Wales was being enclosed, 'allotment provision must be made for the labouring poor'. Finally, in 1887, the Allotments Act made it a right for the 'labouring population' to be able to rent land to grow food.

As the Industrial Revolution drove more people into cities, allotments – or cottage gardens – became more popular, and mill owners and local authorities provided land. In 1908, the Allotments Act was updated so that if six registered voters requested allotments, the local authority had a duty to respond. It was a great idea but largely ignored. It was not until the First World War that local authorities saw how useful it could be if people could grow some of their food. As German U-boats blockaded the seas around the British Isles, we had to learn to grow more of our own food, and allotments came into their own. Between 1914 and 1918, the number of allotments in the UK rose from 470,000 to 1.4 million.

During the interwar years, with poverty caused by stock market crashes, requests for allotments continued to rise – though less new land was made available for allotments, and some were even taken away. Again, it was only when war struck again that the provision of land was taken seriously by the authorities. Getting Britons to grow their own food was essential to ensure there was enough food to last us through the war. In August 1939, the government announced the Grow More Food Campaign, subtitled Dig for Victory.

Wasteland was requisitioned, and parks and games pitches were ploughed to make way for growing food. The number of plots rose to 1.75 million, and by 1945, around 11 per cent of fruit and veg was home-grown. In London, Selfridge's department store even used its roof garden to grow lettuces, radishes, cabbages, French beans and tomatoes.

During the post-war years, many of these new allotments disappeared when the land was needed for social housing and schools, while the end of rationing in 1954 and the rise of the supermarket and convenience foods meant demand for allotments began to drop off. People no longer needed to grow to eat, and gradually the perceived role of the allotment changed from a means to alleviate poverty and provide food in times of need to a mere recreational pursuit. Except for a tiny blip in interest in the 1970s, prompted by Barbara and Tom in *The Good Life*, demand for allotments continued to drop as we approached the Millennium. Councils only too happy to snap up land for housing development allowed the number of plots to fall, while campaign groups struggled to convince the public that growing food in and around cities was relevant in the twenty-first century.

It is only in recent years, with concern over the chemicals used in foods and a fashion for more outdoor pursuits, that the National Allotment Society (NAS) has recorded an increase in membership. The average age of the allotment holder has changed from 60-somethings to 50-somethings as older allotmenteers are balanced out by younger families signing up for plots. But that does not mean councils are taking demand seriously. The NAS estimates that more than 120,000 people in the UK are on a waiting list for one of just 330,000 allotments. Since the start of the pandemic, demand has risen even more. The Association of Public Sector Excellence estimates the average waiting time for an allotment is 18 months, with waiting lists of up to 400 people in some areas. In Scotland, there are 4,600 people on waiting lists in the four main cities. In Edinburgh, the wait time is particularly bad. Inverleith Allotments has 800 people on the waiting list for just 72 plots, meaning at the current turnover rate, you could be waiting for a hundred years. I only managed to temporarily take on a share of a plot while its owner was undergoing a hip operation. To get my own plot in Edinburgh, I face a wait of at least 10 years, just like everybody else.

As in the past, the government has created legislation that gives people rights to allotments. In 2011, the Community Right to Reclaim Land gave communities the power to take on land for allotments in England. In 2015 in Scotland, the Community Empowerment Act gave communities the right to demand land to grow food. Unfortunately, as before, the legislation is being largely ignored. As a priority, the NAS focuses on protecting existing allotments by urging plot holders to list their allotment as an Asset of Community Value. Doing this means that if the land is put up for sale, local community groups can 'pause' the sale for six months while they raise funds to bid to buy it.

The problem is that we have forgotten the history of allotments. Our traditional view of allotments as a cosy place to grow prize vegetables is a little outdated; they are much more important than that. We are not at war, but there is a food crisis. People want to reconnect to the land; they need to understand it, and they need to eat. New studies of the potential in urban soils show how vital – and how radical – growing food on an allotment could be.

My allotment in Edinburgh is part of one such study. On an overcast day in June, when the flowering onions stand out against a glowering sky, Roscoe Blevins of Sheffield University takes a barefoot inventory of the soils in each plot. First, he inspects each owner's planting plan for that year's vegetable rotation. My allotment neighbour Kathy's no-dig plot looks like a city-state divided into more than a hundred different growing areas: pretty yellow and white flowers, or poached egg plants, are a 'break crop' to improve fertility, marigolds at the end of a row of strawberries attract pollinators, and garlic planted among the lettuce deters pests. There are multiple layers of mulching and compost, and the earth seems to stir with life.

In comparison, my plot looks military and monotonous: tatties, brassicas, leeks, onions, runner beans. I designed it using the most basic rotation advised in an old 'Dig for Victory' gardening book I found in Oxfam (which also suggested multiple chemical applications). It seems a bit old-fashioned compared to the agroforestry going on next door. I feel sheepish as Roscoe tests the dry, cracked soil around my drooping runner beans.

Despite my embarrassment, it feels good to be part of something bigger. Roscoe's is the first study since the Second World War to estimate the value of allotments for growing food. Roscoe and the team have been touring the country to assess the soil so that it can be taken into account when they come to measure the harvest. Allotmenteers themselves will input the year's output into a website, MYHarvest, so that it is possible to see how much is being grown around the country. The idea is to get a more accurate picture of our growing potential. We know from the government's Family Food Survey that in 1947 when people were much better at growing than I am, 11 per cent of our fruit and veg was home-grown. Today it is estimated to be more like 3 per cent, but no one knows how accurate that figure is. If studies prove that allotments make a valuable contribution, there will be a much better argument for protecting and indeed creating more of them.

A few months later, Roscoe is in prison for protesting against fracking, so I have to rely on his mentor to give me the update on MYHarvest. Dr Jill Edmondson has spent the last decade investigating the carbon storage potential of the typical allotment. In a landmark study, she found that the soil is better on allotments than on conventional farmland. Jill took soil samples from allotment sites, local parks and gardens across the city of Leicester and compared them to the surrounding agricultural land. She found allotment soil had 32 per cent more organic carbon, 36 per cent higher carbon:nitrogen ratios and 25 per cent higher nitrogen – all measures used to assess the health of the soil. It was also significantly less compacted.

At a presentation I attend in Edinburgh with my fellow allotment holders, she shows a familiar picture of the Fens in England, where so much of our veg is grown. Billowing out into the coastal waters off eastern England, you can see a line of brown before the sea turns turquoise-green and then blue. The brown area is caused by all that lovely light agricultural land, perfect for growing carrots, running off our fields into the sea. Jill explained that, in many parts of the country, ploughing causes soil to erode into rivers and waterways. At the same time, nutrients are being lost from the soil by repeated cropping, whereas allotment soil is often fed every year with home-made compost, building up organic carbon.

'The soil in your allotments could be in a much better state than a neighbouring farm,' she says.

For the next stage in her studies, Jill wanted to know the contribution all this soil could make to our food system, so she looked at her home city of Sheffield. She calculated that if just 10 per cent of the available green space in the city was used to grow food, then it could feed 90,000 people, or 15 per cent of the population, five portions of fruit and veg a day.

Another study by Lancaster University scaled up the calculations to determine how much could be produced UK-wide if all urban green spaces were used to grow food. The first nationwide study of urban growing potential found the UK could grow 40 per cent of our own fruits and vegetables, including those we currently import from abroad.

Clearly, we are not going to start digging up parks and recreation grounds, like we did during the Second World War, but the study shows the huge potential for urban growing. Imagine: raspberries on the verge on the way to school; apple trees around the park, and a veg box scheme taking over the wasteland behind the hospital. The study concluded that government policy should encourage more growing in urban spaces to boost consumption of fresh fruit and veg, strengthening self-sufficiency and cutting food miles.

It is not a new idea. Cities have always needed agriculture close by; some archaeologists argue that farming only began because of cities, or at least dense tool-making settlements that evolved into cities. In her book, *Hungry City: How Food Shapes Our Lives*, Carolyn Steel argues that cities and agriculture co-evolved in the Fertile Crescent 10,000 years ago when human beings stopped hunting and gathering and settled down. As we began to farm the land, it gave more time for 'civilisation' and the development of urban life. Cities became bigger based on how much food could be brought in from the surrounding countryside or produced inside the city walls. Most of us can see evidence of this in the cities we live in today. I am sitting in Stockbridge in Edinburgh, where vendors brought timber and livestock over the Water of Leith into the city. Down the road are Cowgate, Grassmarket and Fruitmarket. The Shambles in York is named from the Anglo-Saxon *Fleshammels* (meaning 'flesh-shelves'), the word for the shelves on which butchers used to display their meat. Mill Lane, Bread Street, Pudding Lane, Frying Pan Alley – we all know city streets named for food, but few will still be used for the activities that gave them their names. As cities have developed, the agriculture that made them possible has been pushed further and further out until only the names remain. Since the Industrial Revolution and the speeding-up of transport, we urban-dwellers have become decoupled from the food brought into the city, sometimes from thousands of miles away, arriving in neat little packages, convenient, clean and fleshless.

The industrialisation of food production and the speed at which it can be transported has allowed cities to grow into the sprawling metropolises we know today. However, it has also led to problems – not just because we still long for the sight and smell of food in our streets, but because it is dangerous to rely on getting our food from the other side of the world. Ancient Rome learned the hard way that depending on a sprawling empire for food will leave you very vulnerable when those supply lines start to dry up because of war and pestilence. Climate change could mean we find our supplies running out, too, as other parts of the world become impossible to farm because of floods and drought. With the global population expected to grow to 9 billion by 2050 and most of those living in towns and cities, our reliance on a reliable supply of food coming from outside urban areas makes us more vulnerable than ever. Somehow, we have to start learning to grow food in cities again.

Allotments are only part of the answer. Modern growing methods – hydroponics, vertical farms and subterranean gardens – will free up even more space for urban agriculture. In 2018, a study by researchers at five universities in the US and China, as well as Google, made the first attempt to predict the potential for urban agriculture through analysis of satellite imaging and population and weather data. They estimated that growing on roofs, in parks and underground car parks could produce up to 180 million tonnes of food each year – about 10 per cent of the world's pulses, roots and vegetables. Rooftop gardens could also reduce flooding and provide insulation that keeps buildings cooler without air conditioning. Already commercial operations are growing strawberries on rooftops in Paris, lettuce in an underground air-raid shelter in London, Chinese cabbage in vertical farms in Singapore, and herbs in hydroponic shipping containers in Dubai. Perhaps in time, we will see names emerging again like Aeroponics Bridge, Salad High Rise and Cabbage Patch Towers?

In her conclusion to *Hungry City* and her next book, *Sitopia*, Carolyn Steel suggests that urban food growing, including in allotments, must be taken into account in future urban development. She cites fresh food markets, commonly-owned forest gardens, community compost and city farms as other ways to bring food production into urban areas. Just as cities in the past understood the need for residents to be connected to the food they ate, we need to rediscover how we can plan our conurbations around the sustenance we all need. Gardens in cities have always been here. They should be here again – and not just for food.

Gardens in cities are also important for mental health. In my home city of Edinburgh, the Royal Edinburgh Hospital has a garden as part of its care for patients. The Royal, as it is known in the city, was part of the 'lunacy reform' of the 1800s that hoped to improve conditions for mental health patients. Originally called the Edinburgh Lunatic Asylum, the hospital opened in 1813 in response to the death of the poet Robert Fergusson. His friends were appalled at the conditions in which they found this great poet and inspiration to Robert Burns. They vowed to create a hospital with greater dignity and respect for mental health patients, whoever they were. From the beginning, patients were encouraged to be active, using any existing skills such as sewing, carpentry or gardening.

In the 150 years since, we have allowed the concept of gardening for our mental health and well-being to be lost in the more urgent demands of modern medicine. But, unlike a lot of hospitals, the Royal managed to retain some of its seventeenth-century buildings and green space. Driven by NHS doctors keen to help their patients get outside, a tender was put out to charitable groups to create a community garden for the hospital. In 2010, the Edinburgh

Cyrenians, a Scottish social welfare and environmental charity, set up the growing space. Initially on the outskirts of the hospital grounds, it has recently been moved into the centre so patients can visit the garden whenever they like. The 1.2-hectare site is maintained entirely by volunteers and used as a place for courses, therapy and simple relaxation.

Doctors have known the benefits of gardening to our mental health since the time of the poet Robert Fergusson. Voltaire wrote about the joy of planting trees, and Freud found the flowers in his garden restful. But only in recent years have peer-reviewed studies proven the health benefits of gardening. In the first formal statistical assessment of the best evidence to date by universities in Japan and the UK, it was found that gardening positively affects human health. The meta-analysis[105] looked at more than 20 articles published in the last 20 years on gardening and mental health. The articles included studies of patients with dementia, recovering from heart attacks or suffering from depression. The positive impacts included reductions in depression and anxiety symptoms and stress. Patients also experienced increased quality of life and gained a sense of community.

True to its founding principle, the Royal is one of the many hospitals using this kind of research to help patients. Squashed between the original yellow sandstone buildings and in front of the new 1960s tower blocks and ongoing development, the community garden is treated as a crucial part of the hospital, though it can be challenging to find in such a packed NHS campus. On the day I arrive, it is raining, and I get lost in the labyrinth of buildings. By the time I arrive at the garden, I am out of breath and close to tears. Lucy Holyrood, the garden manager, sits me down in a Portacabin smelling of soup and biscuits and gives me a

---

[105] Preventative Medicine Reports, 2017.

cup of tea. She offers me a brief history of the garden and politely asks me not to ask anyone any questions.

'People come here to get away from being assessed,' she says. 'You can ask about the garden. Just don't ask anyone if they are a patient, a member of staff or a volunteer.'

We agree, and I venture into the outdoor kitchen. Like all gardens, this one looks a little shabbier in the rain. The microfleece tunnels are sagging, a few marigold petals adorn the mud, and the neat lawn is soggy. But the rosehip hedgerows that edge the site are full of birdsong and the winter purslane, spinach and chard present an enticing green.

Around half a dozen people are milling about under the corrugated-iron shelter. Soon I am chopping leeks while my feet turn to ice and a drip forms on the end of my nose. People gradually open up as we chop. We talk about why gardening can help you feel better.

'It is an opportunity to use the senses to notice the seasons, hear the birdsong, smell the herbs.'

'You are told you are crazy and cannot do anything. But perhaps you can rake a piece of soil or water a flower bed.'

'It is an opportunity to give something back. We all need to do that.'

'You lose your self-confidence inside. Here, you are outside.'

'It does not smell of antiseptic.'

No one knows precisely why gardening helps our minds, but there are a few theories. The first, biophilia, suggests there is a genetic basis for our love of nature. In the 1980s, E. O. Wilson proposed that human evolution had predisposed us to find enjoyment in nature since it provides our sustenance. Today, we still find joy in nature and should sustain that to drive conservation. The second is the Attention Restoration Theory, popularised by Stephen and Rachel Kaplan in the late 1990s. This theory suggests the human mind is capable of different types of attention. Focusing on a busy task, or 'hard attention', can be stressful. But when we use 'soft attention' on something repetitive in a known environment, such as gardening, it can be restorative. The third, Stress Reduction Theory, is based on a famous study that found patients recovered better from an operation when they could look at a tree out the window rather than a brick wall.[106] It states that simply looking at scenery containing natural elements like greenery or water creates positive emotions and feelings like interest, pleasure and calm and has a therapeutic effect.

By the time lunch comes, I have given up being a stressed-out journalist. Whether it's thanks to evolution, soft attention or the scenery, I feel calmer. I enjoy the soup with crispy kale and potatoes and the chat. The food is simply prepared from fresh vegetables grown here. And like all food eaten outside, especially in the cold, it tastes good.

'How delicious compared to the hospital food you get by ticking a box on a sheet,' says one of my fellow sous chefs.

Studies show that it is not only being in nature and gardening that help our mental health but specifically the growing and gathering of food on allotments. Back at Sheffield University, another study involving Dr Jill Edmondson found that allotments boost a feeling of well-being. The researchers asked 163 people to keep allotment diaries and found evidence of mental health benefits. The diarists noted the sharing of surplus food and knowledge, awareness and interaction with wildlife and time spent outside as ways in which the allotment made them feel good. Participants also noted benefits to physical health from working outside and were more likely than the rest of the population to eat the recommended five fruits and vegetables a day. Another study by the University of Cardiff found that allotment gardeners over 50 had significantly lower perceived stress levels compared to adults of similar ages who were active in other outdoor and indoor activities.

---

[106] Ulrich, 1984.

After lunch, I am taken on a tour of the compost heap. None of us is wearing jackets, though the rain is still falling. We stick our fingers into the heat to feel the warmth as we discuss the scandal of plastic in tea bags. Then we retire to a garden shed to make Christmas wreaths and talk about mindfulness. I'm never sure what mindfulness is, but as I twist holly and ivy together using my best 'soft attention', it strikes me that my mind is quieter now. I feel less alone and a little more hopeful.

'We'll see you again,' says one of my fellow leek choppers. It is not a question.

If you are in any doubt about the importance of plants to human beings, ask an astronaut. Don Pettit has spent over a year on the International Space Station, in six-month stints, and each time he goes into space, he takes a pot plant. This keen gardener and chemical engineer was not doing scientific experiments or following the captain's orders; he simply wanted to look at a living plant from back home.

'I just wanted some green in this electro-mechanical environment we live in for months at a time,' he tells me on a call from the United States. 'I wanted to work out how to have a potted plant in the corner without having to use millions of dollars of facilities.'

He chose a zucchini – or courgette, as we call them in the UK – because the seed sprout is strong enough to cope with the stress of floating around in space. He created a mini aeroponic chamber with a bit of water in a resealable bag. The plant was fed by siphoning off a liquid from composting food waste, and light was provided by shuttling the bag between space station windows.

'I got a lot of enjoyment out of watching the shades of green and putting my nose to something that smelled alive, that smelled green,' he says.

The zucchini not only survived but sprouted leaves and eventually a flower.

Don started to write a blog called 'Diary of a Space Zucchini' about the adventures of the first courgette in space. Soon his 'pot plant' had more followers on Twitter than he did. The blog told the story of life on the space station, including Don's offer of the Space Zucchini flower to his wife on Valentine's Day. Back down on Earth, it took off, perhaps offering a glimpse of a more sentimental side to the engineers in space. There was even hope that little Space Zucchinis might appear until Don realised that, like the rest of this particular crew, all the flowers were male.

Don noticed that other astronauts would also come to be around a living plant, even offering to do mundane tasks such as vacuuming in return for five minutes with their noses next to the 'green smell' of the zucchini.

The experiment may not have been an official NASA project, but it led to other astronauts taking plants into space, and Don intends to bring plants on his future space missions. He admits that remembering Earth and growing – or even just making the 'home' space more comfortable with plants – is good for mental health on the space station.

'I think somewhere in the human subconscious, we have a visceral understanding that plants are important, and being around them makes us feel relaxed,' he says.

NASA may not publish his findings, but you never know, Don's efforts could lead to the first allotment in space.

Further reading

Hungry City: How Food Shapes Our Lives by Carolyn Steel (Chatto & Windus, 2008)

Seeds to Solutions: The power of small actions by Pam Warhurst, CBE (SP Square, 2011)

Growing Space: A History of the Allotment Movement by Lesley Acton (Five Leaves Publications, 2015)

'My little piece of the planet: the multiplicity of well-being benefits from allotment gardening', J. Edmondson *et al.*, *British Journal of Nutrition*, 2020

'An assessment of urban horticulture soil quality in the United Kingdom and its contribution to carbon storage', J. Edmondson *et al.*, *Science of the Total Environment*, 2021

'Potential of urban green spaces for supporting horticultural production', *Environmental Research Letters*, 2022

The Guerrilla Gardening Home Page: To find out more information about Guerrilla Gardening visit guerrillagardening.org

Guerrilla courgettes

I first understood the power of a courgette when I saw one growing at a bus stop. The town of Todmorden in Yorkshire has rhubarb sprouting out of the roundabouts and herbs lining the pavements. There is an orchard outside the doctor's surgery and sweetcorn plants sheltering the police station. This is an 'edible landscape' created by the local community to provide food, boost mental health and fight back against vandalism.

The greening of the town began 10 years ago when a group of friends sitting around a kitchen table decided to do something about the petty crime and litter on their streets. Frustrated with the state of their town and the apathy of people towards the wider global environment, they asked: what one thing motivates people? What one thing unites everyone across culture, language, age? The answer, of course, was food. So why not make the landscape edible and see whether people take notice?

These were not ladies who asked anyone's permission. They dug up their own front gardens and planted fruit and vegetables for others to help themselves. Then they dug up land in front of the railway station, the mayor's office and the school. People took notice, and volunteers joined in. Suddenly, it was possible to pick raspberries at the bus stop, pluck a courgette at the cemetery and munch on a strawberry while waiting for a train. Todmorden transformed itself from a lesser-known Yorkshire market town into an 'Incredible Edible' landscape.

Local produce began to sell better at the market, boosting the income of small farmers and producers. A box scheme now delivers local fruit and veg to households. The high school started growing fruits and vegetables. 'Vegetable tourists' came from around the world to see how reconnecting people to local food can transform a community. The future King, HRH Prince Charles came to poke around the raised beds. Vandalism was down and not just because the police officers were busy gardening. Other local towns set up their own Incredible Edible landscapes, followed by towns and cities across the UK and eventually the globe, from Saudi Arabia to New Zealand.

One of the founders, Pam Warhurst – who has gone on to do TED Talks that more than a million people have watched, calls it 'propaganda planting'. In her view, the best way to get vegetables growing in a city or town is to do it yourself. Another name is 'Guerrilla Gardening', which is taking off worldwide. Activists share tips online and encourage others to plant up public spaces wherever they can, sometimes under cover of darkness, to bring back colour, life and food to urban areas. Sunflowers have been planted in Brussels, tulips outside the Elephant and Castle tube stop in London and banana trees in South Central Los Angeles. Why not do your own guerrilla gardening in your local urban space and see what could grow?

- One packet of courgette seeds
- Empty yoghurt pot
- Compost and soil

1. Buy some courgette seeds or ask around at your local community garden to see if anyone has some to share.
2. Punch some holes in an empty yoghurt pot and fill it with compost. (You can use a big or small yoghurt pot, depending on what you have.)
3. Make an indent with your finger around 1cm deep, place the seed on its edge, not flat, and cover with soil.
4. Place on the windowsill and keep the soil moist with regular watering.
5. Once the seed has germinated and grown a few leaves, it is ready to plant out, as long as it is big enough to handle and the last frost has passed.

6. Choose a sunny spot with enough soil to dig a hole and where you can regularly visit to ensure the plant is watered.

7. Carefully take the seedling out of the pot and plant it in the soil. Cut the bottom off the yoghurt pot and place it over the plant to protect it from slugs.

8. Once the plant starts to flower, you can add a little tomato feed to the water once a week.

9. Harvest the vegetables once they reach 10cm and share with friends and neighbours.

CHAPTER NINE

Magic Berries

UK berries, foraged: 0kg CO_2e

'Hunting and gathering isn't about survival at all:
it's about freedom and bliss.'
Ffyona Campbell, *The Hunter-Gatherer Way*

It is the autumn equinox, the start of winter. One minute I am dressed in shorts and tights and a warm jacket, the next, I have my jacket and jumper tied bulkily around my waist as I wade into a rose bush, my tights catching on thorns. The air is changing from cold to warm and back again, clouds chasing away the last of the season. The smells are changing too, from the sweet scent of late summer to a musky, appley mould as all that fruit drops to the earth.

Ostensibly, I am picking rosehips to make syrup, but something in me wants to change too. I want to shake off the glumness of these woolly clothes tied around my waist. It is the end of summer, a summer many of us hardly noticed because we were locked down. I am not looking forward to retreating indoors again with the cold weather – and possibly more lockdowns. I want the fruits I'm picking today to do more than add a bit of vitamin C to my life. I want them to remind me of summer, of what it is like to be outdoors and free. I want them to conjure magic. As my basket fills with russet gems and my fingers begin to itch, I start to feel better. I notice the woodpigeon crashing around in the tree nearby, the soft dust from the recently harvested field settling on my upper lip and the smell of warm straw. Later, I note in my diary that I feel 'alive', 'connected'.

I feel ridiculous writing these things and even more ridiculous attempting to publish them. I went for a walk in the countryside and picked some wild food. Big deal! But foraging does have a reputation for 'the other'. Women, in particular, who go foraging in the countryside for materials they later claim as medicine or simply nutritious food are treated with suspicion.

A few miles from where I am picking my rosehips, there are signs of other people who once found magic in the hedgerows. The Green Man is difficult to find amid the upstanding Presbyterian headstones of St Mary's Kirk in Haddington, but once you see him, you wonder how you missed him. He looks so oddly familiar. With his living crown and leafy moustache, the Green Man recalls our pre-Christian past, when we worshipped plant life and its potential properties. For centuries – even long since paganism was 'purged' from Scotland – this symbol of growth and renewal has continued to appear in art.

The inhabitants of East Lothian may have been mostly Christian for a long time – I should know, being descended from a daughter of the Manse myself – but as the Green Men dotted around kirkyards and window mantles in the area attest, there have always been lingering pagan beliefs. In the seventeenth century, the power of these beliefs in plant magic and a fear of what they could do – especially in the hands of women – came to the fore in the 'burning times'. Between the end of the sixteenth century and the mid-seventeenth century in Scotland, thousands of men and women were persecuted and put to death for being 'witches and warlocks'. Scotland carried out five times more executions per capita than the European average. One of the most famous 'witches', Agnes Sampson, would have foraged ingredients not far from where I am picking wild food today. She was described as an 'elderly' widow, so she was probably about the same age as me. As a midwife and herbalist, she would almost certainly have used plants as part of her healing process. Reports of the time claim the 'Wise Wife of Keith' was able to soothe the pain of childbirth through her powers and cure illness. She was sent for by the poor and the gentry alike and was well known in the district for the colourful incantations she used as part of the healing process. In the eyes of the kirk, however, her powers were suspicious. In 1589, she was investigated by the Church of Scotland Synod for 'devilish activities', including the usual accusations of dissatisfied patients and disgruntled neighbours.

It might have ended there, but the investigation into Agnes coincided with the King of Scotland, James VI's pathological interest in witchcraft. It also appears to have been sexed up by the media of the time in an English pamphlet, 'Newes from Scotland'. The reports claim that at the trial, Agnes admitted to attending a witches' convent at which corpses were dug up to make powders and the Devil preached a sermon, sticking his bare backside over the pulpit at the end for the congregation to kiss. Agnes was shaved to show a 'devil's mark' on her private parts and forced to wear the 'witch's bridle', an iron headdress with four metal spikes inserted into her mouth so that speaking pierced her tongue and cheeks. After several days of torture, Agnes admitted to raising storms at sea off the east coast of Scotland. She was brought before the King, a man so obsessed with the occult he later wrote a textbook on how to hunt witches. At a sensational trial at Holyrood Palace, she confessed to working with the Devil to impede the journey of the King in his voyages to Scandinavia to marry his beloved Anne of Denmark.

On 27 January 1591, Agnes was found guilty of 54 charges of witchcraft and burned at the stake on Castlehill Edinburgh using 10 loads of coal, two bundles of heather, a pile of broom, six tar barrels and two dry barrels. As the historian David Robertson noted, 'It is probably worth emphasising that in Scotland, witches were not burned alive, as is commonly supposed, but were strangled to death before their corpses were consumed by the flames'. So that's all right then.

To modern ears, such persecution of mostly poor widows seems like a combination of mass hysteria, repressed sexual tension and pure misogyny. Indeed, academics have noted that the persecution of witches coincides with a shift in medicine from a predominantly female world of plant-based herbalism to a medical science dominated by men. We look at these supposedly learned men and wonder how they could have believed that an old(ish) lady administering herbs, inciting rhymes and, yes, occasionally cursing neighbours could conjure powers to threaten a so-called all-powerful king. But this was when people believed fully in the power of traditional medicine and in the Church. Today the power of the Church has faded – particularly the more misogynistic 'religious' treatises of people like James VI – but I'm not so sure we have let the power of traditional magic go altogether. The Green Man is still peeking out from gravestones, and I am still foraging in hedges. Sure enough, when I give people my rosehip syrup, the colour of stained-glass windows, there is something in their eyes, a spark of 'belief', not just in the power of vitamin C to cure a cold, but in something else, too – in magic.

Professor Wendy Russell is not a witch. She is possibly the most sensible, down-to-earth person you could hope to encounter. We meet at the Rowett Institute in Aberdeen, a world-renowned centre for nutrition research that was recently moved into a brand-new building. From the outside, it looks rather clinical, with its concrete façade and slit windows. Inside though, it is light and airy, with a floating staircase rising through a central atrium, modern art on the walls and just the occasional glimpse of white coats swishing between labs to remind you of what is going on behind closed doors. Wendy ushers me into her book-lined office and closes the door.

'Oh, I always wanted to be a witch when I was a wee girl!' she exclaims when I tell her about my foraging exploits so far. 'These women who were burned at the stake were doing exactly the same thing as the learned men in the city – harvesting plants to try to heal others – except they were rural and poor and doing it for free. In a sense, we are still doing it today; most of the drugs we use in medicine are derived from plants.' Thankfully, however, we celebrate witches rather than burning them these days.[107]

Wendy moved on from making 'potions' in the garden as a little girl to becoming a chemist studying how the properties in plants can help our health. Unlike her predecessors – those 'witches' using plants to ease pain in childbirth or cure a sick child – Wendy's focus has been on more 'modern' non-communicable diseases like diabetes, heart disease and cancer. For Wendy, the key to healing these diseases is to look at our food system.

'Food used to be the thing that kept us healthy,' she says. 'Now food is the thing that is giving us all the non-communicable diseases. So, what has gone wrong?'

---

[107] Nicola Sturgeon has issued a posthumous apology to the thousands of people in Scotland persecuted as witches, including Agnes Sampson, and there is an ongoing campaign to officially pardon the more than 4,000 people in Scotland who were accused, convicted and often executed under the Witchcraft Act of 1563.

Pouring me a herbal tea, Wendy returns to a time before modern agriculture to explain where the problems may have begun. In the past, she says, humans relied on wild plants, foraging a diverse variety from their local area. However, as farming spread, we began to rely more on domesticated varieties bred to grow fast and taste good. This shift accelerated with the advent of modern agriculture and artificial fertiliser, allowing us to create efficient monocultures and a ready supply of affordable food. It undoubtedly led to a bigger and better-fed population. But it also led to many of the health problems of the modern age, such as heart disease and diabetes. As medicine grapples with the massive problem of tackling these diseases, a crucial question for scientists like Wendy is 'was there something in those wild plants that we have lost that was protecting us from disease?'

It is well known that certain wild plants contain more vitamins. For example, rosehips are packed with vitamin C. But Wendy thinks something more interesting – or magical – is happening in wild plants that we don't even know about and could hold the key to a much healthier population. The secret ingredients are known as phytochemicals. While science has identified 13 vitamins and minerals essential to our health, there are between 2 and 4 million phytochemicals in plants that could be at least as beneficial to our health, most of which we have not yet identified. For instance, carotenoids, which give carrots their bright orange colour, could inhibit cancer growth; isothiocyanates, which give Brussels sprouts their bitter taste, may help protect us against cancer, and sulphides in onions may help decrease cholesterol. Wendy thinks there are more phytochemicals in wild plants because the chemical compounds develop to protect the plant from pests and diseases in the environment or to help plants grow in harsh conditions. For instance, the Brussels sprout is bitter not only to torture school children but to dissuade herbivores from eating the plant. We have unwittingly bred out many of those phytochemicals to make vegetables more palatable and easier to grow.

'Today, we mollycoddle our plants,' she says. 'We put all the nutrients into the soil, so plants don't have to work hard to grow strong. We spray them with pesticides, so they don't have to fend for themselves any more. Whereas all those plants growing on the hills in Scotland don't have any nutrients in the soil, they don't have any spraying to kill the insects, and they are protecting themselves perfectly well. So we know these plants must contain key chemical compounds as part of that protection mechanism. The question is: could those phytochemicals protect our health as well? We need the evidence, but that is what we are working towards.'

To test her thesis, Wendy recently conducted a study in Scotland comparing the levels of phytochemicals in wild plants to domesticated plant breeds. The Really Wild Veg project took five sites in Scotland and planted cabbage, beets and radishes. For each vegetable, they chose a wild variety, a heritage variety and a modern hybrid variety grown to suit today's tastes and farming techniques. The results showed that the wild varieties of all vegetables contained more phytochemicals; consuming those varieties could, therefore, improve our health.

Popping into the Royal Botanic Gardens in Edinburgh earlier in the summer, where the Really Wild Veg project continues to grow experimental crops, it is difficult to see evidence of phytochemicals in the slightly scraggy dark leaves of the wild cabbage compared to the neater (but also well-nibbled) leaves of the commercial variety. I wonder what powers Wendy has to help her see these mysterious chemical compounds. As if reading my mind, she takes me down a series of hidden staircases to the lab to see a mass spectrometer that analyses the phytochemicals in the plants. The clinical white machine looks like a Magnetic Resonance Imaging (MRI) machine used for human brain scans, except a little bit smaller and for plants. Specially prepared plant samples are fed under a powerful microscope, producing a read-out of the bioactive compounds on a linked computer. It is like a witch's cauldron, except instead of relying on magic, we are finally starting to understand the science behind what makes plants so powerful.

Wendy tells me that early research suggests at least some phytochemicals could help fight non-communicable diseases. One study by a PhD student she supported found that the 20 most-foraged plants in Scotland all contain high quantities of phytochemicals. That study found that common foods we forage, such as nettles, blackberries and elderberries, all boost health. It feels like a win-win situation, so why aren't we encouraging people to forage more wild food? Are we still frightened of being accused of witchcraft?

Wendy laughs as she loves to forage without fear of anyone judging but is realistic about the potential for the wider public to get those extra phytochemicals from a few brambles every autumn. Instead, she wants to see wild plants 'farmed' on marginal land that we aren't using for growing food already. Doing this would provide nutritious extra food without needing to bring more fertile land into production. Even plants that do not appear to be edible can be processed to extract protein and other nutrients. Gorse and bracken could be grown on wild land. Urban weeds like buddleia and fireweed could be grown on wasteland in cities to provide nutritious food and perhaps even a protein replacement for meat. It would also reduce our carbon footprint as these foods need less energy input from fertilisers and pesticides, creating a more 'carbon neutral' agriculture.

It is all very well asking people with the time and green space to go foraging, but what about those with less access to the countryside? Wendy thinks the answer is to try to get the nutrients from wild foods 'hidden' in processed foods. She envisages the food produced by these plants being used in processed food, such as a coating for chicken nuggets (or the vegan equivalent), providing an easy and affordable nutritious food.

'At the end of the day, people who are foraging are healthy,' she says. 'We need to get the harder-to-reach demographic – people who buy chicken nuggets from Iceland – if we are going to change anything. We will never be able to go back. Foraging is a lovely idea for a very few people. What we really need to change is our food, particularly our fruits and vegetables, and we need to change them, so they contain the nutrients our foods contained long ago.'

The properties of wild plants that can help protect us against conditions like cardiovascular disease could be bred back into domestic plants. Wendy explains that most varieties we consume now have had the bitterness bred out of them, as well as any spikes or discolouration. However, the phytochemicals that cause bitterness and often protect the plants from pests and diseases are also those that could protect us from human disease. Already, plant breeders are looking to bring back these ancient properties.

The only problem is the taste, although that may not be a problem after all. At a public event explaining the Really Wild Veg project in the Botanic Gardens Edinburgh, where I first met Wendy, I tasted the wild cabbage versus the commercial varieties. In my opinion (possibly influenced by the recent fashion for kale), the more bitter wild cabbage had a more interesting flavour than the watery white commercial variety. The rest of the public seemed to agree with me. Though it was not an official science experiment, it could point to more acceptance of some bitterness in our foods, especially if people understand it is good for them. Most of us are keen to know about the 'magic' in wild plants, especially if scientists like Wendy back it up. If the phytochemicals in plants could be identified and affordably brought into our foods, it could benefit our health and the wider environment.

As I leave the Rowett Institute, I notice the wild plants are already beginning to creep into the new car park, the nettles and rosebay willowherb, buddleia and pineapple weed these scientists are studying upstairs in their white coats. I pluck a blackberry off a bush and pop it into my mouth. I feel a bit witchier already, and that is always a good thing.

Brambling in Edinburgh a few days after meeting Wendy, I am struck by the berries' gorgeous gothic colour that stains my fingers purple and persists beneath the cuticles on my nails for days to come, like ink from a leaky pen. I have done my research, and sure enough, brambles are packed with phytochemicals. The best known is anthocyanin, meaning 'flower blue' in Greek. You may have read about it recently as the latest antioxidant 'cure' for everything from cancer to heart disease, and it has been labelled as a superfood. Scientists are even trying to inject it into tomatoes to make them more 'super'.[108] As Wendy has pointed out, those anti-inflammatory properties are often part of the plant's defence mechanism to withstand inflammation and disease. In the same way, when humans digest anthocyanin, it may help us boost our own system in fighting disease.

In Scotland, at this time of year, we collect blaeberries (you might call them bilberries), which have even more anthocyanin. I love picking them from the blooming heather as I walk the hills in the summer. Unlike shop-bought berries, which are only blue on the outside and yellow on the inside, blaeberries are blue all the way through, suggesting even more anthocyanin is present. Indeed, a study by the Rowett Institute recently found up to five times more anthocyanin in wild blaeberries than in the cultivated varieties.

---

[108] The purple GM tomatoes mentioned in chapter five have been modified to contain more anthocyanin.

Back in Edinburgh, the anthocyanin has stained my fingers and my shirt, and I am beginning to thoroughly enjoy myself. I am brambling with the Willow Gardening Group from the Health Agency in Wester Hailes, who meet here every week to tend the garden and forage in the hedgerows. The community group, part-funded by the NHS, is prescribed by GPs in the area as a 'green prescription'. Participants may come to get fit after a heart operation or as part of a programme to try to ease depression. I am aware that this is a safe space for people to recover from trauma, and so instead of being nosy for once, I concentrate on the job of picking. Before long, we are in rhythm, quietly filling up our baskets with squishy berries as swans glide by us on the canal, and the air fills with the scent of marzipan from brushing past all the frothy meadowsweet.

Afterwards, we retire to the hut for a cup of 'communitea' brewed from herbs the group grew, picked and dried. Hanging from the ceiling are drying racks filled with bright orange calendula petals and yellow St John's-wort. The punnets of blackberries glitter alongside hawthorn berries we have brought in from outside. A witch hunter from the age of James VI would take these as signs of 'devilish activities', but in this little hut, they feel more like signs of healing.

Ally and Soraya, who invited me to join the group, gently explain the properties of the herbs drying on a rack. St John's-wort is used as an antidepressant. Calendula flowers, or the sunshine herb, are yet another 'mood lifter' and an effective antifungal treatment for athlete's foot. The pair, both in their early 30s, are not witches but radical herbalists and health activists working in Wester Hailes to try to tackle ill health in a historically deprived area. They run a herbal clinic at a nearby health centre, the first in Scotland to offer alternative healing alongside the NHS. Patients are not only prescribed herbal remedies but also the action of foraging and making their own teas and tinctures.

Like Wendy, Ally is passionate about the health benefits of wild plants. She shows me a well-known German study from the Aid Infodienst, a German nutrition information service funded by the government, that found wild foods are higher in protein, vitamins and minerals. For example, red clover has almost 10 times as much vitamin A as lettuce, ground elder has more than six times more protein than leeks, and stinging nettles have six times more calcium than swiss chard.

'If this were in the supermarket, they would call it a superfood,' she says, popping a blackberry in her mouth.

I can't help thinking of Wendy's ideas to get just some of these proteins in common mallow or fat hen into the processed food in the supermarket. But for Ally and Soraya, foraging is not only about boosting our physical health but our mental health, too. On rainy days, groups prescribed gardening time can sit in the hut and pluck the seeds off nettles to make a delicious nettle salt or boil up birch polypore to make a tea to boost the immune system. Dressed in Dr. Martens and anoraks, showing off a glimpse of a bee tattoo and an undercut, Ally and Soraya look trendy enough to appeal to a mixed-up teenager or a grandmother looking to spend time in the garden.

Ally believes simple foraging skills connect us to our past hunting and gathering – skills we may have forgotten in the digital age – and says, 'It is about learning to use your hands and knowledge of the countryside.' Soraya, who is also a community gardener, says foraging can connect a community with their landscape – not only by getting people outside but also by empowering them to understand their local environment and potentially feeding and healing themselves. In the last hour, we found hawthorn berries for curing colds, nettle seeds for protein, dandelion leaves for lowering blood pressure, and meadowsweet for a sore tummy. As Soraya says, 'Food and medicine cannot be separated.'

Once again, science backs up Ally and Soraya's work. Many studies show how the mere act of being outside can improve mental health. One study by the University of Oregon put participants through an MRI scanner as they looked at fractal shapes found in nature. The results showed that shapes like snowflakes and flowers brought on a relaxed, focused state that could reduce stress levels. Why not shapes like the sepals of a rosehip or seeds of a blackberry? Colours in nature are already well known to soothe. Why do you think Farrow & Ball have so many colours named after natural phenomena such as lichen, wet sand, sap green or snow white?

Natural smells can also ease our minds. Australian scientists have found that the scent of the earth after rain – or petrichor (a delicious word in itself) – can relieve stress. Is there any better smell than wild garlic in the spring or elderflowers in the summer? And don't worry if you consume dirt from the fruits and vegetables you forage, as research at the University of Bristol found bacteria in the soil can work as an antidepressant and could also boost your gut bacteria. Finally, to bring it all together, in Japan, the Nippon Medical School's study of forest-bathing or *shinrin-yoku* – the process of taking a mindful, multi-sensory walk in the woods – found this simple act can reduce stress, anxiety, symptoms of depression, fatigue and confusion while increasing vigour and energy levels.

Even in the short time I was out picking blackberries, I noticed myself using my senses to smell the earthy blackberries like old textbooks, feel the seeds in my teeth, spot the juiciest berries, touch the rough leaves, hear the rustle of wind and, of course, taste their bitter flavour at the back of the tongue. And yes, I did feel better for it. Emma Mitchell, who trained as a molecular cell biologist, says we have evolved to get a hit from foraging. Writing about her recovery from depression in her book, *Wild Remedy*, she says there are 'ancient foraging pathways' in our brains that reward us for using our senses to identify good things to eat in nature. Seeing or smelling the fruit or berry or the action of picking the fruit can trigger this 'harvest high': 'The moment we discover a beautiful snail shell or the perfect cluster of hawthorn berries, our brains produce a burst of the neurotransmitter dopamine,' she writes.

It appears plenty of scientific studies can point to why foraging is good for our mental health and can potentially protect us from disease, as Wendy explained. But the objective evidence for me is how popular it has become in the last few years among everyone from radio DJs to cordon bleu chefs. Fancy restaurants advertise foraged dishes, celebrity chefs like Hugh Fearnley-Whittingstall publish recipes for hedgerow jam using foraged ingredients, and newspapers publish foraging guides. René Redzepi, founder of Noma in Denmark and possibly one of the world's most influential chefs, encourages people to forage for 'survival, flavour and the thrill of discovery and experimentation'. He has launched an app, WildMad, to help people in Denmark find their own wild food. Even the Forestry Commission has picked up on it, launching campaigns to promote wild foods and information to ensure people forage responsibly. It is estimated that wild harvesting, including harvesting lichens and mosses for natural remedies and horticulture, is worth as much as £21 million a year in Scotland. In recent years, tourism bodies in Scotland have arranged a Foraging Fortnight in September to cash in on the enthusiasm for hunting around in hedgerows.

Of course, foraging does come with its problems. Firstly, you have to know what you are doing. Instagram 'influencers' have come under fire for recommending recipes that could cause an upset stomach,[109] but I think it goes without saying

---

[109] In 2018, Johnna Holmgren had her first cookbook pulled from shelves after readers warned its recipes contained potentially toxic and dangerous ingredients that could make people sick.

that you must be sure of a plant or fungus before eating it. There have also been concerns that foraging is dangerous, not because of witchcraft but because of the impact on precious biodiversity. This has certainly been a problem in the past: Epping Forest in Essex, on the outskirts of London, has had to ban mushroom foragers because commercial pickers have damaged the ancient woodland by taking too many. But most foragers argue they are guardians of the environment, foraging just for personal use and taking only what nature can afford to give. They point out that enjoying wild food encourages people to protect the landscape for the bounty it offers and that eating food produced locally is better for our carbon footprint. Ally and Soraya preach 'ecologically sound wild harvesting' that takes only what nature can spare – for example, leaving enough blackberries for the birds and other wildlife. They advise only taking from abundant common plants, and just 10 per cent from a native plant community and 20 per cent from a naturalised plant community.

I have watched many of my friends catch the foraging bug. It starts with blackberries and soon ramps up to elderflowers, rosehips, wild garlic and – when they get confident enough – mushrooms. Guidebooks, podcasts and recipe books all start with an explanation of what is readily available and how to ensure you are being a responsible forager and know what you are doing. Mushrooms, in particular, can be fatally poisonous if you choose the wrong one (which is why I stick to plants, flowers and fungi that I know).

On social media, foraging is now one of the most popular food searches, alongside avocados. Take a quick look on Instagram, and you will discover a wealth of accounts full of gorgeous photographs of beautiful people wielding Opinel knives and wading into the undergrowth to cut down Japanese knotweed or whipping up canapés from Alaskan sea kelp. Why are so many people following these accounts, signing up for their courses and attempting to make dandelion wine at home? I don't think it is just fashion. I think it's because they crave those connections that the science hints at and nature's colours, shapes and smells. There is a sense of belonging in understanding what season it is and what will be in flower in your neighbourhood, a sense of belonging many young people struggle to find in busy urban lives. In foraging our own food, there is also a sense of freedom from the supermarkets that dominate our lives. Some social anthropologists have suggested witch hunts can be sparked by a society struggling to come to terms with a huge change from a hunter-gatherer society to an industrialised society;[110] maybe our response to foraging says something about our response to the high-tech world we are living in and our need to return to nature. There are periods in history when we go mad and burn witches, and there are periods in history when we go mad and put our photos on Instagram instead.

I take the blackberries home, make blackberry and apple crumble and post a photo on Instagram. Ping, ping, ping goes my phone with likes, another happy feeling from the 'dangerous' act of picking fruit from the hedgerow.

Towards the end of the month, I go foraging for a more unusual berry, sea buckthorn. It appears to be the most 'super' of superfoods around, and is also associated with mental health benefits. Yet most people would not recognise the berry, and in many areas where it grows most prolifically, it is considered a pest and cleared by the council.

I first tried it mixed with vodka in a Scottish twist on the Moscow mule. It smelled of vomit but tasted delicious. I

---

[110] I got a 2:1 Bachelor of Social Science degree in Social Anthropology from the University of Manchester. My dissertation compared the moral panic caused by Essex Girls in the 1980s to witch hunts in Papua New Guinea when female hunter-gatherers started earning cash.

was hooked. Kirstie Campbell, who fed me the cocktail, is happy to take me out the following weekend to forage for the berries on Gullane Bents in East Lothian. The coast could look wild at this time of year, with the white horses breaking on the sands, but there is something about the perfection of the golf courses that makes it all look a bit suburban. Wildness is allowed only on the edges, where sea buckthorn bushes proliferate. The large shrubs have silver-grey leaves and long spiky thorns. They were initially planted to stabilise the coastline and have since spread. From September, they are full of bright orange berries enjoyed by the birds[111] but largely ignored by humans – until now. Armed with secateurs and gardening gloves (I only have my Marigolds), Kirstie and I reach into the bushes to snap off bunches of the berries.

Kirstie first discovered sea buckthorn when spending time as a professional humanitarian worker for the World Food Programme following the floods in Pakistan in 2010. She noticed that the local people would forage for the berries as a supplement to the food provided by development organisations. When she came back to Scotland, exhausted and stressed, Kirstie noticed the plant growing at home. She began to forage for the berries, finding them delicious sprinkled in porridge or crushed into a juice and mixed with vodka. Each time she came home from missions in Syria, Libya and Palestine, she would pick the berries, and each time, she learned more about their health-giving properties. After coming home for good, following a diagnosis of post-traumatic stress disorder (PTSD), Kirstie spent time at Redhall Walled Garden learning about therapeutic gardening. But foraging for sea buckthorn took over her life – and maybe even saved her.

As she snaps off branches full of berries, her hair blowing in the wind, Kirstie understandably does not want to talk

---

[111] Migrants like fieldfares and redwings especially enjoy sea buckthorn.

about this period of her life too much. Instead, she talks incessantly about the many benefits of sea buckthorn. She claims Genghis Khan and Alexander the Great used it to fuel their armies and fed it to the horses to keep their coats shiny. More recently, Russian cosmonauts took it into space, and the Chinese Olympic team used it as their official drink in 2008 (before winning 51 medals). Like many wild berries, sea buckthorns are packed full of antioxidants and vitamins. The oil from its seeds contains high levels of Omega-3 fatty acids that are not only good for our skin but potentially for our brains, too. Like fellow witches Wendy, Ally and Soraya, Kirstie sees wild food as a possible way to tackle heart disease, diabetes, obesity and even mental health problems: 'the things that grow naturally, that we curse as weeds, are the plants that heal us,' she says.

As we circumvent the links, Kirstie urges me to munch the berries as we go along, crunching the seeds in my teeth to ensure I get the Omega-3 fatty acids. I have to admit there is something about the raw berries that wakes you up – they are so sour it makes you grimace – but it also makes you smack your lips and smile. There is only one small problem: they smell a little bit like vomit. To some people, it is just a whiff, but for others, it seems to be stronger. Perhaps this has stopped sea buckthorn from becoming a commercial hit in the West, and the fact that it is hard work processing the plant. I put them in the freezer first before knocking the berries off. The berries are then crushed and pushed through muslin to take out the seeds. It makes a bright orange juice that I freeze and serve as a mixer with prosecco for 'Seabucks Fizz' at Christmas. It divides the family between those who love it and those who can only smell vomit. It feels fun and a little provocative: a small pagan offering at what is, after all, a pagan feast.

The next time I go out foraging with Kirstie, around a year later, something has changed. She has turned her passion for sea buckthorn into a Community Interest Company, complete with official orange T-shirts. In September, volunteers fan over the East Lothian coast to help pick sea buckthorn, stopping to explain what they are doing to confused golfers and dog walkers. Charities helping vulnerable women are involved, and it is hoped even more of the community will volunteer in future. Kirstie has the use of huge freezers at a nearby farm and some large champagne bottles for 'bashing' the berries. She is making juice from the berries and oils from the seeds. Unlike many sea buckthorn producers, her juice includes the oils from the seeds, while she uses the pulp for other products, such as skincare. Meanwhile, Kirstie's under-utilised chemistry degree has, at last, become useful. She has established partnerships with Scottish Rural Colleges to develop sea buckthorn kefir and ginger beer and with Bangor University to create products from the pulp oil.

Kirstie has also changed: she seems more relaxed and at ease. Finally, she is ready to talk about what sea buckthorn might have done for her, as well as its potential to alleviate broader health problems in Scotland: 'when you are out in a group picking, it is hard work, but there is a feeling of acceptance that is rare to find in our lives nowadays. It is about reconnecting with something simple and natural that returns every year, and it gives you joy as well as purpose. There is a "peace" to it.'

I can't find any peer-reviewed studies that claim foraging can cure PTSD, though there are plenty that talk about the therapeutic benefits of gardening and being in nature. However, I do recognise the 'peace' Kirstie talks about in being out in nature and concentrating your mind on one simple thing – the act of picking food to share with others. Perhaps this is 'soft attention' again.

Kirstie has found something in foraging. Call it magic, call it hard science of human psychology through companionship, fresh air and purpose, but something is happening, and it is beyond our ken.

Further reading

Food for Free by Richard Mabey (HarperCollins, 1972)

The Hunter-Gatherer Way: Putting Back the Apple by Ffyona
    Campbell (Wild Publishing, 2012)

A Spell in the Wild: A Year (and Six Centuries) of Magic by
    Alice Tarbuck (Two Roads, 2020)

The Concise Foraging Guide by Tiffany Francis-Baker
    (Bloomsbury, 2021)

*Losing Eden: Our Fundamental Need for the Natural World and
    Its Ability to Heal Body and Soul* by Lucy Jones (Penguin,
    2021)

The Wheel: A Witch's Path Back to the Ancient Self by Jennifer
    Lane (September Publishing, 2021)

Witchy rosehip and blackberry syrup

Before picking brambles, or rosehips, you should ask permission first. Not from the landowner (it is legal in the UK to forage for berries as long as it is for personal use) but from the plant itself. Jennifer Lane, a 'green witch' and forager, likes to ask permission by incanting, 'I appreciate this has come from the Earth …' but I think I am happy with a whispered 'thank you'. Jennifer also likes to 'give something back' to nature by channelling her energy back to the plant or doing something as simple as feeding the birds. She has been described as a 'hot witch' on social media (where she writes as @thegreenwitchwriter), but she is more than that: she credits witchcraft with saving her from a mental health breakdown in her late 20s when she quit a job in communications, and she now practises her 'art' full time alongside work as a reiki practitioner.

Jennifer is one of many millennials practising a form of witchcraft expressed primarily through concocting 'potions' out of foraged plants, casting 'spells' like burning bad thoughts in a cauldron, and spiritual practices such as having an altar to Mother Earth and following the pagan cycles of the year. It is all based on a deep reverence for the Earth, and as far as I can see, it is perfectly harmless. Perhaps it comes from a childhood watching *Buffy the Vampire Slayer* or *Sabrina the Teenage Witch*. Or maybe it is because, for this generation, there is such a profound disconnect with nature that they need to perform some kind of ritual to make it their own once again.

'People are fed up of being inside their own heads, constantly online, on a screen, processing transient information on TikTok or Instagram,' she says. 'They want to put down roots, to reach out and feel nature, like the branches of a bramble bush.'

I can't claim to know any witchcraft, but I know that after I go foraging, I feel less anxious, and when I share what I have made with others, it works a kind of magic into the meal.

'Witchcraft today is not necessarily about magic and ritual and concocting potions,' says Jennifer. 'It is about being out in nature, understanding the seasons, knowing your landscape and the plants in it, and that feeling of connection. That is the really magical thing about it.'

This recipe, passed to me by the green witch, combines the 'power' of the vitamin C in rosehip with the flavour of the brambles to create a truly 'magical' potion.

- 500g of rosehips, picked whole
- 350g of blackberries, picked whole
- 1 tbsp of lemon juice
- 500g of sugar
- 1 litre of water
- 2 muslin cloths or some old tights

Ask permission of both the bramble bush and rose before you pick.

Rosehip preparation

1. For soft ripe fruit, pick your rosehips after the first frost of the season or pop them in the freezer for 24 hours. Allow them to defrost before use.
2. Blend the defrosted rosehips or chop them into a pulp. Add them to a saucepan of 750ml tap water. Bring to the boil, leaving the pot uncovered, and simmer for 20 minutes.
3. Slowly strain this pulp through a muslin cloth into a bowl. This removes any of the hairs left from inside the rosehip casing, which can irritate the gut.
4. Set aside for later.

Blackberry preparation

5. Add the blackberries, lemon juice and a small amount of cold tap water to a pan and bring to a boil, stirring occasionally. Boil for 10 to 15 minutes until the berries are soft and mushy (if you get impatient, you can always squash them with the back of a fork).
6. Strain the pulp through a muslin cloth.

Mixing juices

7. Combine the two juices in a saucepan and keep warm.
8. Add the sugar gradually, along with a small amount of water. Once all the sugar has dissolved into the juices, you have your syrup.
9. Bottle it in a sterilised jar and keep it for winter.

This syrup is delicious drizzled on porridge, and it is an excellent potion for building the immune system in autumn/ winter and fighting off colds.

CHAPTER TEN

The Orchard

UK-grown apples: 0.3kg CO_2e per kg
Apples shipped from New Zealand: 0.6kg CO_2e per kg[112]

'Humanity will be renewed in the Orchard, and the
Orchard will restore it.'

Fyodor Dostoevsky

I come from a long line of women who eat their apple cores. Even before I knew my mother ate the whole apple, I had developed a taste for the core. One of my first memories of primary school was meeting my best friend, Gemma Peardon, in the 'safe' corner of the playground. She noticed my unusual habit and suggested I could eat her apple cores if she could eat my mini Mars bars at break time. I felt this was a reasonable deal for gaining the protection of the fiercest girl in the class – and I needed protection. I had NHS glasses that were invariably repaired with gaffer tape, an extraordinary 1980s haircut, and I wore my cousins' hand-me-downs. We didn't have anyone else in our gang except Claire Goodchild, who

---

[112] Mike Berners-Lee, Lancaster University.

was painfully shy and had a haircut a bit like mine. Still, we were a gang, and that was the main thing. Gemma would get us into fights with people bigger than us, like Steven Smith, Wayne the Pain, and her even fiercer big sister, Katrina. We always lost. After school, we would cross the road and go into the churchyard where no one else played and where you could fill your pockets with the decorative glass chippings left on graves, which looked like precious stones. Through a gate at the bottom of the graveyard was the orchard by my house. The trees were all my friends, easy to climb, covered in lichen and soft moss, with rooms and corridors, pantries full of apples and ballrooms full of blossom. One was a spaceship, another a castle, another a very busy veterinary surgery treating talking wild animals. My friends and I could each sit in one for hours, creating our own strange little worlds, or leap between them to avoid the crocodiles in the treacherous sea beneath. For three little girls with few other friends, it was far safer and more fun than the corner of the playground watched over by the teachers.

Growing up, apples were a constant from August to Christmas and even beyond. First came the little pink Discovery apples, then tart Spartan, then Blenheim Oranges that taste like oranges but better and finally, soft D'Arcy Spice. Sometimes the fruit bowl was full, but more often than not, you just went outside and filled your pockets. Apples were stored in crates next to a burring freezer full of meat in an outhouse that smelled of sweetness and flesh. Apples, and peaches and raspberries in summer, were snacking fruit to be grazed on constantly. Nowadays, when I feel in need of comfort, I brush my teeth and then eat an apple to remind me of my granny's rather dentally misguided habit of feeding small children apples as she read them Bible stories at bedtime. My niece Stella's first word was 'apple'; as soon as she was able to reach the fruit bowl, you would find small indentations of tiny little teeth in each apple you picked out.

I consider an apple a day a ridiculous maxim when most people eat three … don't they? Especially the small British ones. Britain has at least 2,000 varieties of apples, glorious in their colour, taste and – best of all – their delicious names. Monikers like Bloody Ploughman, Sheep's Nose, Catshead, Golden Knob, Beauty of Bath, to name just a few. In 1739, a slightly befuddled Richard Bradley noted in his *New Improvements of Planting and Gardening, Both Physical and Practical* that 'to set down the several various names of apples would be a work almost impossible, seeing how many various kinds are yearly produced from kernels in almost every county in England and where they happen to prove good, either for making cider or table-use have names given to them according to the mind and person that raised them.' I feel his pain. There is the Irish Peach, the Keswick Codlin, the Newton Wonder. The list is endless. Each name hints at a story, rooted in place, weather, time, family. Each is different.

The original apple orchard would have been entirely different to the friendly orchards of my childhood. It was a densely tangled wild forest in the mountains of Asia prowled by wolves and bears. The apples themselves were tiny, bitter and probably toxic. But they had one advantage: no two apple seeds were the same. Whereas the seed from a tomato or a runner bean will usually produce the same variety of tomato or bean, an apple pip will create a new cultivar, as a cross between the two parent trees but different to both (a little like humans produce children different to themselves and their brothers and sisters). This genetic creativity, or 'extreme heterozygosity', is quite clever in terms of evolution since it means that different apples will pop up that can survive emerging diseases or changing environmental conditions. And so, different seeds grew into different trees that produced red apples, green apples, yellow apples, sweet, sour, bitter, big, small and all sorts of shapes and sizes in between. Eventually, an apple grew that tasted good to humans, and finally, a human picked it up and ate it.

Fortunately for that apple, its position in the Tian Shan mountains of Kazakhstan was on the Silk Road, so in time, it spread east along the old spice roads to China and west through Persia into Europe. Traders selected the sweetest apples, and they arrived in Europe around 11,000 years ago. At first, they continued to cross by accident. Apple trees grew from the imported seeds that had accidentally ended up in latrines or compost heaps and been pollinated by insects carrying pollen from indigenous crab apple trees, creating yet more variation. Officially, there are more than 7,500 varieties of apple in the world today. However, there will have been many more variations over the millennia, and there are probably far more that have simply not been named yet.

However, humans will only cope with uncertainty for so long. The second great advantage of apples is that, as well as being wonderfully diverse, they can also be exactly the same. Although humans have largely struggled to clone ourselves or our pets (except Dolly the Sheep, of course), we managed to clone apples very early on. As far back as 1000 BC, our ancestors realised that once you have a variety you like, it is relatively simple to clone it by 'grafting'. This means taking a cutting of the favoured variety and binding it to the rootstock of another healthy apple tree. Really, it's that simple. Binding the trunks together with a special kind of tree-friendly gaffer tape (in the old days, they used clay) will keep the moisture in, and the trunks will meld together and create a new tree producing the new variety. You can even graft multiple varieties onto one tree. Grafting allowed control of this delicious fruit and a proliferation of orchards.

It quickly became apparent that humans and apples went well together. The fruit was tasty and nutritious, there were plenty of varieties available, and cultivation was easy. The creation myths of many cultures, including Germanic paganism, Norse sagas and Greek mythology, all celebrate this most convenient of fruit and the orchards in which it is grown. The sacred island mentioned in the tales of King

Arthur, Avalon, translates as 'apple orchard'. The 'garden' of
Eden was not a garden at all, but an orchard 'planted with
every tree that is pleasant to the sight, and good for food'.

British culture, in particular, embraced the apple orchard.
For the industrious Victorians, the idea of a paradise where the
world was a better place – a garden of Eden perhaps – appealed.
Benjamin Disraeli spoke of 'ripe pears and famous pippins ...
and plums of every shape and hue', and Charlotte Brontë
extolled the 'blossom blanched orchard trees whose boughs
droop like white garlands', while Robert Browning longed to
be 'in England now' in April when 'the chaffinch sings on the
orchard bough'. Like the potato breeding craze, the Victorians
also delighted in discovering new apple varieties. Many of our
most famous English apples emerged in the 1800s, including
the Bramley and the Cox's Orange Pippin. Then, of course,
there were the recipes. Mrs Beeton included a recipe for apple
crumble in her *Book of Household Management*, Charles Dickens
mentions a semi-dried apple – the Norfolk Biffin – as a
Christmas delicacy, and Queen Victoria apparently loved
baked apples. Thanks to this enthusiasm – and possibly the fact
that you can also make cider out of apples – the garden of
England became an orchard. Every farm, country house and
suburban garden had a collection of apple trees. And then we
chopped them all down.

It is tempting to link the loss of apple orchards with the loss
of a more innocent time in England. Their demise began
with the First World War and the loss of young men to tend
the trees in those grand country houses. The head gardeners
at such country piles would traditionally vie for the best
apple varieties for show and table and to impress the guests
at those endless Edwardian house parties we still fantasise
about in TV programmes like *Downton Abbey*. But after 1914,
there was no one to tend to the trees, never mind show off

the different apple varieties. A graph in the House of Commons library shows the hectarage of orchards slowly climbing from just over 60,000 hectares in the Victorian heyday of 1875 to more than 100,000 in 1914. Then there is a sharp drop when all the young men went off to war. It climbs again slowly in the inter-war years back to 100,000, but by the end of the Second World War, the loss of men in another war and the industrialisation of agriculture meant the orchard heyday was over. Government figures show commercial orchards declined from 62,200 hectares in 1970 to 46,600 hectares in 1980. By 1997 there were just 22,400 hectares left, and by 2009, that figure was 22,000.

It is easy to see why orchards were cut down. Following the wars and the advent of cheap chemicals and machines, farmers began concentrating on a single crop, so they no longer needed orchards for livestock or income. Their land became far more valuable ploughed up and used to grow a cash crop like wheat or barley. Consequently, the workforce needed to run an apple orchard disappeared to the cities. Part of the problem was an incentive offered by the European Union in the late 1980s to grub up apple trees because of an oversupply in the wider European market, as imports of apples from other parts of the world meant that commercial apples were worth less. The Red Mac apples from Canada that my grandmother remembers so well were just the beginning; soon, there were Granny Smiths from Australia and Royal Gala from New Zealand, not to mention the Golden Delicious from France and Red Delicious from Italy. The English varieties we had taken so long to build up suddenly seemed rather small and scabby compared to the new imports. Supermarkets began to stock foreign varieties, and consumers got used to more uniform or 'perfect' cheap apples available all year round.

For most consumers, the decline of commercial orchards went unnoticed, just another part of the transformation of the British countryside, like the loss of dairy farms and haystacks. But for one group of people, apple orchards were too important to lose. In a small office in Covent Garden, a movement was growing in defiance of the 'dumbing down' of apples. Common Ground was set up in 1983 by the writer Roger Deakin, campaigner Sue Clifford and academic Angela King. All three had worked for Friends of the Earth in the previous decade during successful campaigns to Save the Whale and stop mining in national parks, but the trio felt the charity was concentrating too much on big political issues. They wanted to start a new kind of environmentalism that looked at the 'ordinary things' in your backyard, at saving 'the primrose bank, the millpond, the bluebell wood and the orchard'. Common Ground was set up to protect 'local distinctiveness' through education, art, music and film – and what could be more local and distinctive than an apple orchard?

The idea for Apple Day was sparked by the transformation of the apple market in Covent Garden (where my great-grandfather would have bought English apples to be transported to Edinburgh by train) into a shopping mall. The market is still there today, and one of the biggest shops in the area is – you guessed it – Apple. In the 1980s, this transformation represented the shift from fruit and veg markets in city centres to shopping malls selling global brands. For Common Ground, looking down from their tiny office, it was an aberration. So they decided to take action: on 21 October 1990, the first Apple Day returned the apple market to its original purpose for one day only, with traders from across England presenting different varieties of apples. Forty stalls were taken, selling various apples, cider, juice and saplings, while artists and illustrators sold pictures and books on apples. Grainy video shows customers tucking into a First and Last from Sussex or a Dog's Snout from Yorkshire and debating with great passion the different flavours and advantages of local varieties. Common Ground claimed thousands attended that first Apple Day, and they have helped to organise events on the day since. In 1991, there were 60 events around the country, 300 by 1997 and 600 in 1999. Sue and Angela published *The Apple Source Book*, with pages of activity ideas for the day, such as longest peel, apple bobbing, apple printing, poetry, songs and, of course, apple tasting and identification. It became so successful that it has now gone beyond Common Ground and become a fixed part of the British calendar. National Trust properties, Women's Institutes, nurseries, schools, horticultural societies, restaurants and farmers' markets will all celebrate the day. Over the years, I have been to a few, and I am always moved by the enthusiasm and joy people take in tasting new varieties of apples as if they have forgotten a fruit they eat every day could be so exciting and variable. At the Royal Botanic Gardens in Edinburgh, children can taste a James Grieve, discovered in the city but not available in most supermarkets. On National Trust properties, visitors are encouraged to try varieties with names like the Lemon Pippin, the Edward VII or the Peasgood Nonsuch. In Cornwall, they can sample the Cornish Gilly Flower, in Scotland, the Scotch Dumpling, and in Wales, the Pippin Bach Llydan. Each orchard has its own varieties, its own history and its own wildlife.

Some of the wildlife is so distinctive it is endangered. The People's Trust for Endangered Species (PTES) claims several species, including the wryneck bird, the mistletoe weevil and the orchard tooth fungus, all rely on orchards. Many species thrive in an orchard because of the mosaic of habitats. The dead wood is a haven for up to 400 species of insects, the meadow grassland is good for butterflies, bees use the flowers and the birds eat the fruit. Rare species that thrive in orchards include hedgehogs, woodpeckers and red squirrels. UK orchards have even been marked as a priority habitat in the UK's Biodiversity Action Plan.[113]

---

[113] Part of an international agreement to protect global biodiversity, the Convention on Biological Diversity (CBD).

The PTES began mapping orchards in 2007 to try to save the habitat of the endangered noble chafer beetle, a striking beetle with a metallic green body speckled white, which is only found in orchards. It soon became apparent that plenty of other rare and even endangered animals lived in orchards. So the tiny charity called for volunteers to register the traditional orchards (those grown at a low density and managed without chemicals) in their area. The feedback was overwhelming. Since 2007, more than 700 people have registered traditional orchards across England and Wales. So far, PTES has mapped 35,000 orchards in England and 7,000 in Wales, creating a valuable database on the condition of the trees and the state of the habitat. Unfortunately, in England, only 9 per cent of orchards are in excellent condition, 45 per cent are in good condition and 46 per cent are poor. The survey also showed the alarming loss of traditional orchards, revealing that 90 per cent have been lost since the 1950s to neglect, development or conversion to intensive modern orchards or housing.

PTES is now focusing on saving not just the noble chafer beetle, but the red belted clearwing, the European orchard bee and the shaggy bracket. And the only way to do this is to save all the orchards that are left by supporting communities to care for the trees and plant new ones. The charity also urges the public to help traditional orchards by buying local apples wherever possible and cider or juice made from old varieties of apples. I'm sure many of us do just that on the days following Apple Day, and whenever you find an Egremont Russet or a Discovery apple in your local greengrocers or farmers' market; the rest of the time, most of us buy apples in the supermarket.

I must admit that a few weeks after Apple Day, when my store of home-grown apples has finally run out, I find myself munching on a British Royal Gala, that garish commercial apple developed in New Zealand for its pleasingly unthreatening red and yellow and peach tones. They have lovely crunchable cores (unlike the Pink Lady, which is tooth-meltingly sweet but has a horrible, indigestible core). I know. It is wrong, and I should be denigrating these incomers and celebrating our precious heritage varieties. Or should I?

The modern Royal Gala orchard is not like the orchard of our *Downton Abbey* daydreams. The trees, while just as pretty bright with blossom or heavy with apples, are lined up in straight rows between tracks of mown grass like ranks of stiff-backed soldiers. Each one is planted 80cm apart using a global positioning system (GPS). A dwarf rootstock ensures the trees only grow to about 150cm tall. Look closely, and you can see posts holding up the dwarf trees that could otherwise fall over under the weight of so much fruit. Wires support the branches and ensure the apples are growing on a trellis. This post-and-wire system, a little like espalier, is easier for picking, spraying and pruning. It is not a new system – the Hanging Gardens of Babylon were supported by masonry walls – but it is relatively new to England. Today, most commercial orchards you see across the apple-growing counties of England, such as Kent, Herefordshire and Suffolk, will use a variation on post-and-wire. I think they can look a bit military compared to my childhood idyll, but when I suggest this to Ali Capper, the owner of a Royal Gala orchard, Stocks in Herefordshire, she is nonplussed. Ali is also chairwoman of English Apples and Pears and is in charge of promoting the industry in Britain. She sees the Royal Gala orchards not as an industrial orchard but as the saviour of the apple industry: 'this is where your apples come from,' she says. 'And if you want to buy British apples at a competitive price, then orchards have to be modern systems like this.'

When Ali got into the industry, English orchards were dying. For someone as passionate about Grimes Golden, King of the Pippins and Laxton's Superb as any Victorian apple taster, it was painful to watch. But with a background in advertising, she was unsentimental about why this was happening: people simply did not want knobbly English apples when given the option of bigger, juicier apples that they were used to eating all year round. As Ali says, 'People do buy with the eye.' The English apple industry had a choice: it could become a smaller industry, or it had to accept consumers' changing tastes and compete with the newcomers on their terms. 'If English growers want to make a living from apples,' she says, 'they have to grow the varieties that people want.' In other words, get big or go home.

Ali's Stocks Orchard became part of a vanguard of orchards growing new varieties like Royal Gala and Braeburn in Britain. It was a significant investment since apple orchards not only have to think about this year's orchard but also make enough profit to reinvest in the next orchard every eight to 10 years. The switch encouraged growers to move to more modern systems like post-and-wire and further streamline the processing and distribution of apples. Soon, British Gala appeared on supermarket shelves next to the imported apples. The funny thing was, they were better than the original New Zealand Royal Gala and Braeburns. The new varieties may have been developed in the New World, but the long days and cooler temperatures in the Old World meant that the apples built up sweetness and arguably tasted better when grown in Britain.

The British Gala fitted neatly into the supermarket model of filling the shelves with the same product all year round. Gala apples can be harvested in the UK from August and last through to the New Year when apples from Chile, South Africa and the Southern Hemisphere fill in the gap. The apples are all the same size, so they can be washed, polished and distributed in the same factories as the imported Royal Gala. The average shopper can fill their basket with the same 'brand' every day. Boring, some might say, but for the British apple industry, it has meant hope.

Slowly the British apple industry began to recover. With Ali at the helm, English Apples and Pears have watched as the British portion of the crop has grown from a third to just over 40 per cent. Much of that increase is due to the planting of new varieties like Braeburn and Gala. In Kent – still the centre of the British apple market – the main varieties are now Braeburn, Gala and Cox, making up 80 per cent of what we buy. Ali wants to increase the number of British apples we eat to 60 per cent by 2030, and it looks like she could be on track. This is a rare good-news story in British horticulture, yet we rarely celebrate it because it does not live up to our image of what orchards should be. For Ali, this is a point of frustration. In a world where not enough of us are eating our five-a-day, shouldn't we be supporting a home-grown industry that provides an affordable and sustainable source of fruit practically all year round?

Ali also claims commercial British apple orchards are environmentally friendly: 'you can never harm the environment too much because apples rely on pollination and pollination relies on bees, and bees need a healthy environment,' she says. 'For me, that is the measure of whether or not an orchard is healthy.'

Yes, the modern intensive apple orchard will be sprayed regularly with fungicides to stop mildew and scab, just like potatoes. There could also be three or four doses of insecticide to control pests like aphids and herbicides to prevent grass and weeds from growing at the base of the trees. However, there is a concerted effort to reduce the use of chemicals. For example, instead of insecticides, orchards use pheromone moth traps to stop 'maggoty' apples. These traps work by attracting the male codling moth with a female hormone. It reduces the breeding success of the females and, therefore, the caterpillars that bore into apples in late summer. Hedges around orchards and wildflower strips are a way to encourage predatory insects that kill aphids and other apple pests. Mulch at the bottom of the tree reduces the need for herbicides to kill weeds. Another way to reduce chemical use and water is by using drones to monitor the apple trees so that insecticides or fertilisers are only targeted at the trees showing problems.

Ali claims commercial apple orchards are still a haven for wildlife. OK, you may not get a wryneck or an orchard tooth fungus that relies on dead wood, but you will get hedgehogs, chaffinches and, most importantly, bees. She compares the environment to an intensively farmed wheat field where the land will be regularly ploughed to an orchard where hedges and grassland are maintained, and bees are encouraged by planting crab apple trees and wildflowers.

After speaking to Ali, I feel slightly better about my Royal Gala habit. Yes, the modern commercial orchards are pretty different to the traditional orchards that Common Ground and PTES are trying to save. They are undoubtedly different to the orchards of my childhood. But I do not think of them as a blight on the British countryside, and I want to support one of the few areas of horticulture in the UK that is holding up against the global competition. Gala and Braeburn are not bad to grow, and they are not bad to eat. The orchards are becoming more environmentally friendly, so why do we need the traditional orchards? Why do we need all this diversity?

The reason for diversity is not necessarily because of the taste or even those delicious names, but for survival. Like any other monoculture, an apple orchard of one variety faces annihilation if disease hits or conditions no longer suit that particular variety. With climate change on the horizon, the UK – and indeed every country – must preserve diversity to ensure some apples survive into the future.

Fortunately, in the UK, we have the world's most extensive collection of temperate fruit in one place from which to breed new varieties. The National Fruit Collection in Brogdale, Kent, has become a living gene collection of global importance. But when it was set up, it was for a very

different, very British reason: to stop amateur enthusiasts
from fighting. Hundreds of new varieties emerged during
the mania for apple breeding in the Victorian era, each a
potential goldmine for its 'inventor'. Is it any wonder that
canny nurserymen were wont to market hoary existing
varieties under a brand-new name or that entire counties
fought over whether an apple had been 'discovered' on their
patch or not? Eventually, the burgeoning Horticultural
Society, now the Royal Horticultural Society (RHS),
decided to get a handle on the situation by starting a
collection where the different varieties could be categorised
and preserved. By 1921, the collection had grown and was
moved to RHS Wisley, where it became a more scientific
collection designed to preserve as many varieties as possible
for the glory of the nation. The collection survived cuts by
Margaret Thatcher in the 1980s and a move to Brogdale
Farm in Kent, where there is less frost and more than 60
hectares to plant new trees. After much wrangling, its
management has been taken over recently by a private
company, the Fruit Advisory Services Team (FAST), in
collaboration with the University of Reading.

As one of the oldest fruit collections in existence, I
expected it to be a beautiful old orchard wreathed in lichen,
but in fact, the National Fruit Collection is more like a
modern orchard with strict lines of dwarf trees. There are
2,200 apple trees arranged in a grid formation, so if I want
to find Annie Elizabeth, I should head to row 45, tree 93.
Allens Everlasting? Row 31, tree 57. Orchard tours are
popular, especially when the trees are flowering or the apples
are falling, but this is also a working laboratory. The farm is
about science, not just about preventing horticultural
in-fighting. Tim Biddlecombe, chairman of FAST, explains
that the trees were recently grafted onto new rootstock to
keep the fruit healthy. The collection is not organic, and
apples are sprayed regularly to ensure the health of the fruit.
Unlike seed collections kept in 'stasis' in freezers, a living

collection of trees means the apples can be monitored, and breeders can take pollen for research.

Ongoing experiments using varieties from the orchard include the 'apples for a warmer world study', which is looking for apples that can withstand climate change. Temperatures in Kent have already reached above 38°C in the summer, and orchards are struggling. For the experiment, more than 15 varieties of apples are being studied in modified polytunnels where the temperature can be controlled for over 10 years. Common varieties like Golden Delicious that are not generally grown in the UK are being studied to see how they cope if we had hotter summers and warmer, wetter winters. The study is not only looking for varieties that better cope with higher temperatures but also ways to manage the crop to cope with new pests and diseases.

Then there is the original purpose of the collection, which is to categorise and preserve new emerging varieties – and to stop amateur enthusiasts from claiming they have found something that already exists. Since 2006, when the first apple DNA sequence was published, this process has gotten much quicker. (It also confirmed the apples do indeed descend from wild apples still found in the mountains of Tian Shan in south Kazakhstan.)[114] Previously, to identify apples, it took trawling through historical pictures and descriptions. The collection can now check samples against existing varieties or confirm if a new cultivar has just been discovered by looking for the unique DNA of an apple variety, just like a human fingerprint. It has meant a renaissance in the Victorian mania for finding new varieties – except this time, we are finding ones we have 'lost' rather than new ones grown from seed. So-called 'apple detectives' are browsing the countryside looking for apples developed

---

[114] *Malus sieversii*, the wild apple which is the primary ancestor of all our favourite apples, has been on the IUCN Red List of Threatened Species since 2007.

by their Victorian forebears or simply from the apple trees that used to be in every back garden. In Shropshire, a crop of bright yellow apples, first bred in the nineteenth century by horticulturist Thomas Andrew Knight and thought to be lost forever, was identified as a Bringewood Pippin. More than 60 varieties have been found growing on the Welsh border alone. As well as the 'lost' varieties, there are the new varieties that could be discovered by luck on the roadside. According to the Marcher Apple Network of apple enthusiasts, there could be hundreds more varieties that have not yet been registered at Brogdale. Just think of the potential new shapes, colours, textures – and, of course, the potentially charming names.

Diversity in wildlife habitats is essential for sustaining certain species, as orchards have shown. But humans also need it for our health and the fight against climate change. Even though more than 6,000 crops have been used for food historically, fewer than 200 are commonly used today and only nine account for nearly 70 per cent of all food produced.[115] That is a problem for our gut health. Diversity in the gut cultivates a healthy microbial community, which plays a vital role in digesting our food, regulating our hormone system and even our brain chemistry. Diversity in the crops we grow could save us from starving by preventing disease from wiping out species, as we saw with bananas in chapter two, and it could help us survive climate change, as the apples in a warmer world study shows. Lastly, diversity in flavour, appearance and texture is a boon to our mental health. Ultimately this joyful diversity, passed on to us by all those crazy Victorian amateur enthusiasts, could be critical to the apple's – and our own – survival.

---

[115] World Wide Fund for Nature (WWF).

Survival is not just about science and propagating your genes. It is about getting through every day, one step at a time. For some people, that can mean tending an orchard. When Dawn Adams's son Sam died, she planted apple trees at his school: one for his sister Olivia, one for his brother Joe and six in memory of Sam's age. Unlike a cemetery, with an orchard, Dawn found purpose in doing something positive, in pruning and tending to the trees. 'The grief and loss never go. I miss Sam every day,' she says, 'but the orchard is a positive place to come to. The trees are a constant I can always return to.'

Over the years, Dawn became more experienced and began teaching others. She became a 'grafter', teaching others how to graft apple trees onto rootstock. It was a way to connect, make friends and do something while always thinking of Sam. She is now a volunteer at the Orchard Project, the only national charity dedicated to creating, restoring and celebrating community orchards. While the PTES has been concentrating on maintaining and bringing back orchards in the countryside, the Orchard Project has focused more on city orchards. Their ultimate aim is for every household in the UK's towns and cities to be within walking distance of a productive, well-cared-for, community-run orchard.

This noble aim has surprisingly deep roots. Watching the industrialisation of the countryside in 1876, the Russian author Fyodor Dostoevsky called on every person to own an orchard: 'Think of my words in 100 years' time, and you will remember that I told you this,' he writes. 'Humanity will discover its better self through the orchard – that's the formula …'

Since 2009, the Orchard Project has planted and cared for more than 430 community orchards across England and Scotland. The charity points out that orchards can help mental well-being and connect people, as volunteers like Dawn have found. It also provides a source of organic fruit close to home.

In an era of climate change, orchards could contribute to tree coverage that cools the urban environment and prevents flooding, as well as providing low-carbon food. Again, these orchards will be different to some of the more romantic images we have of the orchard, though all are run and enjoyed by the community. Some are on the edge of housing estates or squeezed between tower blocks. Some are on derelict land or by the railway or on school grounds. As Dawn says, 'every orchard is different'. It is this diversity that is key.

Royal Gala may be easy to buy because they are a consistent shape, size, colour and brand – and it is OK to fill up your shopping basket with an affordable British product – but we also need to support the apple orchards growing all these different varieties of apples. I'm not saying we have to buy them every day, but we should at least buy them during the season if we can. What will happen to those diverse colours, flavours and names if we don't? What about the potential in these different varieties to resist disease or survive climate change? What about our childhood memories of playing in an orchard?

Further reading

The Common Ground Book of Orchards: Community, Conservation and Culture by the Common Ground Editorial Committee (Common Ground, 2000)

The Apple Orchard: The Story of Our Most English Fruit by Pete Brown (Penguin, 2016)

Eating to Extinction: The World's Rarest Foods and Why We Need to Save Them by Dan Saldino (Macmillan, 2021)

After-dinner apple diversity appreciation

A popular parlour game during the Victorian era was to appreciate and compare the different varieties of apple available in your local orchard. (In Britain, Victorians could have eaten an apple a day for four years and never eaten the same one twice.) The fruit was commonly eaten as pudding, and special cutlery and crockery – such as an apple corer, a fruit knife and fork and a custom fruit plate – were invented to eat apples. A Victorian etiquette book of 1880 advised: 'In eating pears or apples, they would be peeled and cut into halves and quarters with a fruit knife and fork.'

I'm afraid I don't have a fruit knife and fork, but I do enjoy an after-dinner apple tasting. It is a great way to share knowledge of your local area and appreciate the distinctive flavours available, especially when so many are under threat. Traditional varieties of apples are available from around August until the end of the year and after that from storage.

- Buy or pick some local apples. The Orchard Network has a regional directory online where you can find local shops that sell produce, orchards that allow the public to buy fruit, community orchards where you can visit or volunteer and nurseries that sell trees to plant yourself. The People's Trust for Endangered Species has an online search engine where you can find your local community orchard. The Orchard Project provides advice online about setting up your own community orchard.

1. Present the apples in a fruit bowl in the centre of the table.
2. Choose a few apples of different varieties, core and cut into quarters.
3. Share around the table, taking time to discuss the different flavours.

4. At my father's house in Scotland recently, we had a forthright discussion about the qualities of the apples in his garden. Ashmead's Kernel (which I always think of as Ashmead's Colonel – perhaps because of its no-nonsense khaki jacket and refreshing bite) is famous for storing well over winter. In contrast, the Katie is pretty and sweet but unremarkable, and the James Grieve is a satisfyingly sour Scottish apple.

5. Enjoy the different colours, textures and flavours, and most of all, argue about it.

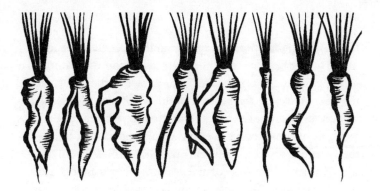

CHAPTER ELEVEN

Perfectly Imperfect

British-grown carrots: 0.3kg CO_2e per kg[116]

'Everything has beauty, but not everyone sees it.'
Confucius

The Kingdom of Fife makes perfect carrot country. The long summer days and sandy loam allow root vegetables to burrow deep into the soil and develop that sweet, earthy flavour. All down the east coast, the feathery fronds of carrot-tops are part of the crop rotation, allowing Scotland to produce half a million tonnes of the vegetables and export them to England and mainland Europe.

On a visit to one of the main farms in the area, Kettle Produce, I find myself wading through fields of carrots. You can't really go wrong with this crop in terms of climate change. They have a low carbon footprint, they can be produced year-round in the UK, they store well, and they help you see in the dark (more on that 'fact' later). There is only one problem: we waste an awful lot of them. Of this

---

[116] Mike Berners-Lee, Lancaster University.

field of carrots, 10 per cent are lost in the harvesting process,[117] up to 50 per cent are too big, too small or too ugly to make it into the shops as fresh produce,[118] and once in the supermarket, they may be left at the bottom of the heap until they are slimy and chucked away. Even if we buy them, we chop off the tops and tails of the ones we use, and we forget about a quarter of them until they are shrivelled up, then throw them in the bin.[119] Carrots are one of the top-10 most wasted foods in UK households. We waste 2.7 million whole carrots a year.

Food waste doesn't seem like too much of a problem as I stand here knee-deep in carrot-tops, listening to a quarrel of little brown birds twittering through the hedge. The hare I saw earlier lolloping across a ploughed field could munch on a carrot left in the field, and even if the vegetables are left to rot, they make good compost for the worms.

The problem is its impact on the other side of the world. On a global scale, we throw away a third of the food we produce.[120] That means we are ploughing fields in Scotland, chopping down rainforests in Indonesia and draining rivers in South America to grow food, a third of which we will never eat. If we planted trees on the land currently used to produce unnecessary food surplus, we could theoretically offset a maximum of 50–100 per cent of the world's greenhouse gas (GHG) emissions.[121] Even in Fife, it would mean more hedgerows for little brown birds.

According to Project Drawdown, reducing food waste is the number-one solution to the climate crisis – above

---

[117] WRAP report estimated that 3–10 per cent of fresh retail carrots are left in the field.

[118] Carrots face the highest losses for cosmetic imperfection at 24–50 per cent, University of Edinburgh.

[119] WRAP estimate that between a fifth and a quarter of food purchased for consumption is wasted.

[120] UN.

[121] *Waste: Uncovering the Global Food Scandal*, Tristram Stuart.

electric cars, solar power and plant-based diets. And that is not just because we burn fossil fuels to produce and transport food; when we don't eat food and instead leave it to rot in landfill, it produces methane, a particularly potent GHG that causes more warming than carbon dioxide in the short term. The UN estimates that up to 10 per cent of global GHG emissions are associated with the food we have not consumed.[122] If food waste were a country, it would be the world's third-biggest emitter, after the US and China.

However, there is an answer to this problem, and I have come here looking for it while doing a little 'gleaning'[123] for my supper. Carrying a tote bag, I randomly pluck carrots from the ground, occasionally cleaning one on my jeans and munching on it like Bugs Bunny. There are even different-coloured 'Imperator' carrots in purple, red and yellow to taste in the field. Eventually, I find one, or rather two coiled around each other like lovers. I brandish my prize. An aberration, an outcast, a freak. A wonky carrot. Some would call it food waste. I consider it a thing of great beauty.

I'd like to ask you to imagine an upside-down triangle – an unwonky carrot, if you will. This is the Food Waste Hierarchy, and UK environmental law requires us to consider the waste hierarchy when disposing of anything. At the top, we have the largest section: Prevention. Prevention is the most important part of the hierarchy and the key to reducing food waste. If we prevent food from going to waste in the first place, we not only avoid those emissions from landfill but also bring back

---

[122] In the UK, food waste accounts for between 6 and 7 per cent of total greenhouse gas emissions.

[123] The act of collecting leftover crops from farmers' fields after they have been commercially harvested. To join your local gleaning network, go to the Feedback online page.

the land used to grow that food, potentially for planting trees. On the moral side, it also means we can prevent food from going to waste that could feed other hungry humans.[124] Prevention includes on the farm, in shops and at home. Next is Redistribution, first to people, then to animals. The food you have no use for could feed a family or make a delicious chutney. Pigs or chickens have lived side by side with humans for millennia to share our scraps. Next is Recycling: turning the food waste into new materials, using it as compost or creating green energy through anaerobic digestion. As a last resort, there is Recovery of some of the energy lost through incineration, and finally, there is Landfill. The point of the upside-down triangle is the smallest part of the hierarchy, and the point is it shouldn't be there at all. I will take you through this hierarchy to prove that food waste does not really exist because there is always a use for food, even a wonky carrot.

If you have ever grown carrots from seed, you will know they are challenging to grow. Indeed, I have never managed anything beyond a few centimetres long with limbs twisting in several directions. The only person I know who does grow straight carrots grows them in old orange cartons dug into the soil with plenty of sand mixed in. So, it is no surprise that farmers do not grow a perfect field of carrots. However, to find that they have to reject up to 40 per cent on cosmetic grounds is a far larger proportion than I ever could have imagined. Researchers at the University of Edinburgh blamed government regulations, the 'gold-plated' standards of the supermarkets and the 'learned expectations' of modern consumers. The University's 2018 study found there were more conditions ascribed to the appearance of carrots than nutrition or food safety. The vegetables must be a specific

---

[124] All the world's nearly 1 billion hungry people could be fed on less than a quarter of the food that is wasted in the UK, US and Europe (Feedback).

size, colour, length and width and free of cracks, blemishes, bends or lumps. A Hollywood studio contract would have less stringent conditions. And before anyone complains that it is the European Union (pre-Brexit) insisting on perfect carrots and straight bananas, that is no longer true (if it ever was).[125] It is down to you, or at least to the supermarkets' interpretation of what you want.

Watching carrots fly through a photographic sensor machine at Kettle Produce, where the carrots from my field in Fife end up, I can see how such high expectations are kept. Automated optical graders measure the diameter of the carrot at the crown and the length and detect blemishes and kinks. Each carrot popping out the other side is a uniformly straight orange specimen that will fit neatly into a plastic supermarket bag. But I am more interested in the slightly less than perfect carrots rolling down a conveyer belt on the other side of the factory. Workers in hairnets and white coats are chopping them into neat carrot sticks. Kettle Produce proudly tells me they have managed to cut waste by redirecting wonky carrots into soups, pre-cut vegetables and baby food (though they pointedly refuse to tell me how much is still wasted).

Creating a new life for wonky carrots is an idea that has taken off in recent years, not so much thanks to a group of farmers but because of their wives. A group of women in Queensland, Australia, set up Just Veg. The slightly old-fashioned story, which makes up a lot of their marketing, is that a group of wives persuaded their farmer husbands to redirect the wonky carrots 'thrown out back' into the food chain by processing them into ready-cut veg. In fact, they are all high-powered women in banking, education, marketing and journalism who just happened to be married to farmers and saw a gap in the market. 'There is nothing

---

[125] Commission Regulation 2257/94 identifies certain restrictions for fruits that producers have to conform to to sell their produce within the EU. The regulation states that bananas must be 'free from malformation or abnormal curvature'. But it does not ban straight or very curved bananas.

wrong with a wonky carrot,' says Tracey Rieck, a banker. 'They still taste the same; they just do not look as pretty. Not everyone can be a supermodel.'

Along with five other women, Tracey developed the concept of pre-cut veg sticks that can be used as snacks or in cooking. As busy working women, they could see the advantages of a pre-packed vegetable. Yes, it comes in plastic, but it helps many people get one of their five fruit and veg a day. Just Veg was born in Australia and is now one of the country's most popular fresh veg 'snacking options'.

'The fact that we could turn something that would be thrown out the back or taken away as waste into something that would increase our return was amazing,' adds Tracey.

Oh, and their husbands? They made some carrot beer.

Pre-cut veg has helped cut food waste in the UK and Australia, where farmers are selling into packing houses with the facilities to process 'wonky' specimens. But where fruits and vegetables are expected to go straight to fresh produce, 'outsize' vegetables are still a problem. That is because most farmers in the UK are locked into contracts with the big five supermarkets. It means they are contracted to produce a certain amount of cosmetically perfect carrots and massively overproduce to meet the exacting criteria of those automated 'carrot cameras' I saw in the processing house. An ombudsman has been set up to try to force the supermarkets to relax standards, but this has had little impact so far. Farmers have been pushed out of business because they are forced to waste tonnes of 'wonky' vegetables that do not meet the supermarkets' exacting criteria. Every so often,[126] one dares to grass to the media, and there are photos of sobbing farmers next to a towering pile of perfectly edible 'wonky' parsnips or carrots destined for landfill.

---

[126] *Hugh's War on Waste* on BBC One featured Hugh Fearnley-Whittingstall interviewing a parsnip farmer who claimed she was forced out of business because of the supermarkets' exacting standards.

The supermarkets are saying they are doing something about it. Morrisons has a Naturally Wonky line, including a box of wonky veg for £3.50 that promises to feed a family of four for a week. Asda launched the Beautiful on the Inside range, Tesco has Perfectly Imperfect, Lidl has Too Good to Waste, Sainsbury's launched Imperfectly Tasty and Waitrose has A Little Less Than Perfect. These lines have at least raised awareness of wonky veg, but have they really stopped waste on the farm? Next time you see the 'wonky range' at a supermarket, look closely. Is it that wonky? The cosmetic standards are still so exacting that in most cases, it just means the fruit and veg are a little outsize. Piles and piles of carrots and onions and parsnips and potatoes are still rejected because they do not meet cosmetic standards, and with no television crew there to capture it, the supermarkets get away with it.

There is a lot that supermarkets can do, but the most significant area for preventing waste is in your own home. The government advisory body on waste, the Waste and Resources Action Programme (WRAP), estimates that we waste more food in our homes than is wasted at the harvesting and processing stage. After leaving the farm, household waste makes up 70 per cent of UK food waste, manufacturing 16 per cent, hospitality and food service 12 per cent and retail just 3 per cent. That does not include inedible parts like apple cores or potato peelings (unless you eat them, like me). To illustrate, the 4.5 million tonnes of food per year that could have been eaten would fill 90 Albert Halls or 3,600 Olympic-sized swimming pools. Home food waste creates 5.3 million tonnes of CO_2e a year – the same as 2.4 million cars driving on roads.

WRAP was set up in 2000 to try to tackle the problem, not least because the UK was running out of landfill,[127] and

---

[127] It has been reported the UK has less than six years' worth of landfill space left.

if waste continued to pile up, there would be nowhere to put it. The Love Food Hate Waste campaign highlighted the cost of food waste, as research showed this to be the primary motivating factor. It was claimed the average family of four could save a little over £60 per month, or £720 a year, by reducing their food waste. That could pay for all your streaming subscriptions and still leave you £300 for annual membership of the National Trust *and* English Heritage.

Much of the campaign's advice consisted of simple tips that most of us should know, but many of us don't, such as keeping your fridge at 5°C to keep food fresh, storing certain fruits and vegetables in the fridge, keeping bread in the freezer so you can toast it one slice at a time, tips on meal planning, and recipes from celebrity chefs on how to make the most of leftovers. A big part of the campaign focused on ending 'best before' dates on fruit and veg as this encouraged people to throw out good fruit and veg when it was still edible.[128] Supermarkets were also asked to clarify confusing 'use by' and 'best before' labelling systems. Most people assume they mean the same thing; in fact, 'use by' is a safety warning that a product could have expired or gone off by that date, whereas 'best before' is merely guidance, and we can often eat food well after that date. There was also a campaign to stop BOGOF (Buy One Get One Free) offers as they motivate people to buy more food than they need.

The campaigns had moderate success, reducing waste by 26 per cent between 2007 and 2018, from 6.1 million to 4.5 million tonnes. The amount of food saved would have filled 30 Royal Albert Halls or 1,300 Olympic-sized swimming pools. (They are fond of the Albert Hall at WRAP.) It was a start, but it's not nearly enough. There is only so much WRAP

---

[128] At the time of writing, many UK supermarkets, including Waitrose, Marks & Spencer, Co-op and Morrisons, are making efforts to remove 'best before' dates on fresh produce. Tesco led the way by removing 'best before' dates from fruit and vegetables in 2018.

could do by changing labels, offering advice and nudging buying habits; it was time for our attitude towards food to change. It was decided we needed a return to the mentality of our grandparents, to 'frugality' rather than behaving as though we live in a world of never-ending abundance.

In 2008, a campaign was fronted by the Green Party and the Tyndall Centre for Climate Research to tackle the problem, modelled on the last time the UK experienced great success in cutting food waste: during the Second World War. 'The New Home Front' compared the threat of climate change with the threat of war and called for a 'carbon army' to help reduce emissions. I remember going to the launch in the Imperial War Museum and admiring the 1940s-style posters of a woman in overalls showing her biceps and the words 'We can do it'. The report suggested working together, as we had in the 1940s, to save energy by setting up car shares, using public transport or switching off lights. It also suggested we could cut food waste.

Between 1939 and 1945, dependence on food imports halved, while at the same time, the nation's health improved. Rates of infant mortality, heart disease and diabetes all fell. One contributing factor was rationing, but another element was making more of the food we did have. By April 1943, 31,000 tonnes of kitchen waste were being saved every week – enough to feed 210,000 pigs, which is what they did to make the waste go even further.

How did they manage to persuade people to waste less? Much was thanks to authorities taking the 'stick' approach. Wasting food was illegal, and there were instances of people being fined. In 1942, *Good Housekeeping* suggested that people 'Learn to regard every type of waste as a crime.' But more powerful even than this was the 'carrot' approach: propaganda. In a precursor of the messages put out by WRAP today, the Ministry of Food claimed reducing food waste would cut your waist size and your bills and issued advice on storage, planning and cooking. 'Grow fit not fat on your war diet!' said Food Facts No.1, from the Ministry of Food in 1940. 'Make full use of the fruit and vegetables in season. Cut out "extras", cut out waste; don't eat more than you need. You'll save yourself money … and you'll feel fitter than you ever felt before.' Then there was Churchill's real secret weapon: the Women's Institute (WI), which set up 5,800 food-preservation centres where people learned to make pickles, jams and store food. The organisation secured precious sugar supplies from the Ministry of Food, and in their first wave of jam making, it is estimated they saved at least 450 tonnes of fruit from rotting.

Many of us will recognise this kind of frugality from older generations who remember the war. Indeed, 'The New Home Front' suggested speaking to people who lived through it. So, I talk to Eileen, my daughter's great-grandmother, who was born in 1922. Eileen was 16 when the Second World War broke out, and the war was a formative time for her; she went to work as a land girl and then a chemist, and she met her husband, Ted. Yes, she was hungry sometimes (she remembers pilfering dried apricots while working as a land girl), but everyone was. And she never felt particularly 'deprived'. I ask her if she thinks we need to repeat the exercise, and she pauses before replying: 'It was a different world.' People lived a simpler life; they were used to a certain level of deprivation. Everyone was in the same boat. 'Today, expectations are higher.'

I think she is right. You can't go back. 'The New Home Front' never really took off. In wartime, people put up with so much disruption and deprivation because they knew there was no alternative and believed society would emerge stronger in the end. It's harder to change for something that can seem as far away as climate change (though with record-breaking temperatures and rainfall hitting the UK, it feels closer every year), especially when we are used to relative luxury. The modern WI has taught us about planning our meals, but in an age where many families are juggling kids and busy jobs, this can seem like an impossible task. Instead, what is needed is a new campaign that encourages people to stop wasting food using the tools of the world we live in today.

We may not be as 'frugal' as we were in the past, but we can be engaged and connected like never before. Tessa Clarke, a farmer's daughter raised to hate waste, set up Olio in 2014 after the removal company told her the leftover food she had packed while moving house (six sweet potatoes, a white cabbage and some pots of yoghurt) had to be thrown away. Desperate for an app to help share her food rather than throw it away, the idea for Olio was born. Olio, meaning a miscellaneous collection of things, is a sharing app that allows you to post any surplus food you have so that your neighbours can pick it up. Since being set up in 2015, it has saved 17 million meals from going to waste and spawned multiple copycat apps. Others such as No Waste and Nosh allow you to log the weekly shop and scan receipts and barcodes to alert you when food is about to go off and help you plan meals better. Already, there are 'smart fridges' able to sync with apps to tell you when food should be eaten. All these apps talk about climate change and the moral case for fighting food waste in their mission statement, but they do it differently from the government-led wartime propaganda. The message is not overt but rather about being smart, saving money and even looking good. Maybe we should all be showing off about sharing our surplus food on an app or about eating #wonkycarrots on Instagram (as, indeed, many celebrity chefs already are).[129]

Another area where food citizens can cut waste is plastic. For many people, plastic packaging is a huge bugbear. Fresh

---

[129] Check out Melissa Hemsley, Hugh Fearnley-Whittingstall and Rachel Khoo on social media.

fruit and vegetables always used to be sold loose, so why can't they be sold that way now and avoid plastic that ends up in landfill or the ocean? Retailers claim that plastic can reduce carbon by cutting food waste, which is true in many cases. For example, cucumbers wrapped in plastic are likely to last longer, avoiding food waste that would generate more GHGs than the production of the plastic packaging. However, with consumer behaviour change, we could solve both problems. In 2020, Greenpeace published a report that found supermarkets could cut their usage of single-use plastics in half by 2025, and a significant area of change would be in the fruit and veg aisle. A fifth of all plastic in supermarkets (by sales units) is packaging for vegetables, salads and fruit, amounting to 38,000 tonnes. Worse, many of these prepared products are sold with two or three separate plastic components, some of which can be recycled via roadside collection and some of which cannot. The report found a 70 per cent reduction would be possible, saving over 30,000 tonnes. Already Morrisons have switched to more loose fruit and veg in store, with positive feedback from customers who can now choose to buy smaller amounts, saving them money and cutting back on waste at home. A separate trial selling loose fruit and veg in Waitrose stores found an initial increase in food waste because of the spoiling of fresh produce and a failure to predict what shoppers would choose. But once customers got used to bringing their own containers and handling the produce, volumes could be forecast more accurately, food waste dropped off quickly, and less plastic was used.

New technology like misting can also be used to keep fruit and vegetables from degrading while on display, helping to cut plastic waste. Cucumbers could be wrapped not in plastic but Apeel, a thin peel of edible plant material developed with a grant from the Bill & Melinda Gates Foundation. More loose fruit and veg means bringing our own containers to the shops. Still, with 2 million people signing the Greenpeace petition to cut plastics in supermarkets, it seems consumers are ready to make the change – if retailers are brave enough.

It is not only consumers and supermarkets that need to see food waste differently; the business world does too. That is exactly what many innovative young entrepreneurs are doing. Instead of seeing food waste as a problem, they see it as a resource with which to make another product that can be fed back into the economy. The approach, known as the circular economy, is gaining traction as concerns grow about climate change and resource depletion. The greatest advocate of the circular economy is Dame Ellen MacArthur. In 2005, she sailed around the world in a record-beating 71 days, 14 hours, 18 minutes and 33 seconds.[130] On reaching dry land, her great vow wasn't to never set foot on a boat again but to never throw anything in the bin again. There is not a lot of room on a boat, so you have to learn how not to waste things. After floating on the open seas for weeks, with no company except whales, albatrosses and lots and lots of plastic, most of all, Dame Ellen realised the world is a delicate system where everything has a purpose. As long as we think about the economy as linear, where resources are made, used and disposed of, the ocean and other areas of wilderness will carry on being our dumping grounds. But as soon as we start thinking about the economy as a circle, where surplus material is returned to continue regenerating the system, we can eliminate waste. The Ellen MacArthur Foundation has become the leading global charity helping businesses transition to a circular economy.

---

[130] At the time of writing, the record was held by Francis Joyon at 57 days, 13 hours, 34 minutes and 6 seconds.

One example of a circular business is Rubies in the Rubble, set up by Jenny Costa, another farmer's daughter, in response to seeing perfectly edible but unsold fruits and vegetables going in the bin at New Covent Garden Market. Taught from a young age to save fruit, she went home and made jams and chutneys from the 'waste' market fruit. They were so good she started a stall in Borough Market and now supplies Fortnum & Mason and Waitrose. To date, Rubies in the Rubble claims to have saved close to 4 million pieces of fruit and veg from rotting away to nothing. Another example is Toast Ale, which in 2015 was born from the shocking statistic that we throw away 24 million slices of bread every day. The company uses 30 per cent less malting barley than other breweries by using old buns and bread from bakeries and retailers in their open-source recipe. Another is the Craft Pickle Company, set up in Scotland by a couple of registered nutritionists, which uses surplus wonky veg to make sauerkrauts, kimchi and piccalilli. Like Olio, these companies see the usefulness or beauty in a wonky carrot or the 'rubies in the rubble'.

Sometimes, however, food waste cannot be prevented, so it moves to the next stage in the hierarchy: Redistribution. It seems like an obvious next step. If good food is available, then surely we should give it to those who need it rather than chucking it in the bin? This seemingly straightforward solution to food poverty became even more urgent during the global pandemic. Food piled up that could not be sold in restaurants or cafes, while families one street away went hungry because the principal earner could no longer work. Such inequality has always existed, but when the world stopped, it became impossible to look away. Even before the Covid-19 pandemic, according to the UN, 8 million people were experiencing food poverty in the UK. This worsened during the pandemic due to loss of income, loss of free school meals, difficulty accessing food during lockdowns and shortages in the shops. In Scotland, the need for food banks doubled in 2020, according to the Independent Food Aid Network.

Not all food banks use surplus food, but it is increasingly used as a stopgap for food poverty. FareShare, Britain's largest redistribution charity, trebled the amount of food it gave out between 2015 and 2021. That is not just driven by need; supermarkets are bowing to pressure from campaigners to redistribute food rather than let it go to waste.[131] FareShare collects surplus food from factories, farmers and retailers and redistributes the food through a network of warehouses to organisations like homeless shelters, community kitchens, food banks and community pantries. FareShare claims that for every tonne of food it redistributed in 2019–20, it prevented the waste of 1.6 tonnes of embedded CO_2e. The charity points out that 92 per cent of beneficiaries say the food they receive helps them stay healthy. For 29 per cent of the clientele, it's the only time they eat fruit and veg.

It seems like a better use for wonky carrots than going to landfill, yet there is pushback. Tim Lang, Emeritus Professor of Food Policy at City, University of London, thinks redistributing food to the poor creates cycles of dependence and takes the pressure off governments to do something more fundamental about poverty issues. He has a point; even the charities using food waste to feed hungry people don't think redistribution is the answer. The Trussell Trust, the UK's largest food bank provider, has campaigned for years for more government help so that people can feed themselves. It states its ultimate mission is not to exist at all because its users can feed themselves. But, while hunger from food poverty exists, it makes sense to redistribute food and allow someone to benefit from saving money – and all of us to benefit from reducing carbon.

Just down the road from me, in Granton, a charity called Empty Kitchens, Full Hearts (EKFH) is redistributing

---

[131] FareShare charges just £16 per tonne to redistribute food, which is a lot cheaper than landfill tax.

surplus food with the help of out-of-work chefs. EKFH was
started by a young chef named Lewis McLachlan as much as
to stop his friends in hospitality from getting bored and
depressed during the first lockdown as to use up surplus
food. It started as just five friends making soup for around
30 vulnerable people with food donated from local producers
and retailers. Within 14 months, the charity had cooked 1
million meals, and Lewis's little side hustle to stave off
loneliness had become a full-time job. By the time I visit in
2022, EKFH has morphed into a well known charity with
300 volunteers making meal packs out of food primarily
from FareShare, but also from the John Lewis Partnership, a
local organic farm and other retailers and producers. When I
arrive, the day's soup is in full swing and, of course, it
includes wonky carrots: 'there are always carrots,' says Dylan
Childs, the operations manager. 'There is a consistent supply
of root veg, and it usually ends up in the day's soup.' Though
recently, he also roasted wonky carrots with Caribbean
spices, which were apparently equally delicious.

Chefs from Michelin-starred kitchens and some of the
most prestigious hotels in the city volunteer at EKFH.
Dishes have included wagyu beef burgers, pork raclette and
kangaroo sausage stovies, though with a tonne of pasta to
go through every month, there is also a lot of tuna pasta
bake. The soup bubbling away in a 150-litre kettle, called
Big Bertha, does smell delicious, but so does the venison
ragout they are making for lunch and the roast vegetable
risotto for dinner. As an organisation set up by chefs, EKFH
prides itself on cooking 'proper' meals. They do not take
out-of-date processed foods from supermarkets; instead,
they concentrate on building nutritious meals from
wholesome ingredients. Fresh fruits and vegetables are
included in every meal pack. Feedback from service users
– who range from working families struggling to make
ends meet to those in homeless shelters or the isolated
elderly or disabled – is glowing: 'You are amazingly

awesome, treasures in this world,' wrote one. 'Once again, I eat a yummy meal and smile.'

Like other emergency food-provision charities, EKFH freely admits its end goal is not to exist at all. As Dylan says cheerfully, 'One of our primary goals is for us to be redundant.' EKFH is working with Edinburgh City Council and other charities to try to connect its service users to ways out of food poverty wherever they can through help with benefits, training and even cookery classes. But while there is a need, EKFH will continue to provide good food.

I think one of the reasons EKFH has worked is that it did not come out of pity for the people in food poverty; instead, the chefs did it for their mental health. It adds dignity to the service; this is about food, not charity. I notice that whenever I mention food waste, I am corrected: it is 'surplus' food or 'intercepted' food. It is nutrition, it is routine, it is a 'yummy meal', it is 'a smile'. It is never, ever waste.

If food waste cannot be fed to people, the next best thing is to feed it to animals. And you could not get more grateful recipients than the pigs at Monkton Wyld Court Farm. Basie and Bostic (named after the jazz musicians Count Basie and Earl Bostic) positively snort with delight when they are fed organic pizza crusts, wilted seasonal vegetables, the rinds of award-winning cheese and frothy carrot-tops. The pigs and their forebears are part of a well-established educational charity in rural Dorset. Their purpose is to demonstrate how livestock can be part of a regenerative farming system. By feeding food scraps to pigs, food waste is eliminated, then the pigs' manure fertilises more vegetables to cook in the kitchen, and at the end of their short but happy lives, the animals are made into sausages – a perfect circle.

Yet what the residents of Monkton Wyld Court are doing is highly illegal. Since 2001, it has been outlawed to feed 'slop' to pigs. After the foot-and-mouth disease outbreak, the government cracked down on feeding catering waste to livestock because of the risk of infected meat getting into the food chain. A year later, the rest of Europe followed suit. Even though the farm kitchen is strictly vegetarian (any pork resulting from the pigs is cooked in an outdoor oven), it is still considered a danger.[132] I suspect other smallholders around the country are merrily breaking the law on feeding scraps to pigs. There are undoubtedly many people angry at this 'ridiculous' law that prevents us from using one of the world's most efficient converters of food waste to turn a critical environmental problem into bacon. Pig farmers frustrated at the rising prices of feed and celebrity chefs and consumers who believe happy pigs fed on a varied diet just taste better have all campaigned against the law.

As a young man, Tristram Stuart earned his pocket money fattening pigs on the scraps from his primary school, and he has led the charge for the last decade. Through his food waste charity, Feedback, he set up The Pig Idea: a campaign to reverse the law so that pigs can be fed food waste again. He has commissioned reports to prove that feeding food waste to pigs can cut carbon and has travelled widely to show how it can work. He claims around 20 times more carbon dioxide can be saved by sending food waste for pig swill[133] rather than anaerobic digestion. That is mainly because the pigs are no longer fed GM soy imported from areas in the world suffering deforestation.

Feedback is confident that in the long run, politicians will see sense and allow biosecure food scraps to be fed to animals again, as it is in Japan and Taiwan, but the intensive-pork

---

[132] To date, no taxpayers' money has been wasted arresting the gentle souls of Monkton Wyld Court.

[133] A combined total of 2.5 million tonnes of surplus food from manufacturing, retail and commercial catering could potentially be fed to pigs – 20 per cent of the UK's total estimated food waste (Feedback).

industry remains sceptical. A more popular option among policymakers seems to be to feed food waste to insects and then feed the insect protein to pigs. Already, there is an industrial insect farm in the UK where black soldier flies are used to convert food waste from farms and factories into organic insect-based protein feed. The EU recently gave the regulatory go-ahead for insects to be used as food for pigs and poultry.[134] In the future, you may not be eating pork from animals fed organic carrot-tops, like at Monkton Wyld Court (unless you are lucky enough to visit), but you could eat pork from animals fed protein from insects fed on food waste. You never know, it may taste better as well as saving the planet.

Recycling is the next segment of the Food Waste Hierarchy, after Prevention and Redistribution. Even the most conscientious of us would struggle to find a use for carrot-tops[135] or potato peelings,[136] but that does not mean these 'scraps' should go to waste. As we have already seen, rotting food waste produces a GHG called methane. This gas can also be burned as a source of energy. It makes perfect sense, therefore, to capture the methane through a process known as anaerobic digestion (AD) and use it as 'renewable' energy.

Since the beginning of the twenty-first century, the UK government has encouraged councils to build AD plants to recycle food waste and contribute to cutting overall GHG emissions. Currently, UK-wide, AD powers more than 1 million homes. My council, Edinburgh, has an AD plant that now powers 3,500 homes in the Scottish capital. On a cold

---

[134] In 2021, WWF and Tesco claimed insect meal could replace one-fifth of the UK's projected soya imports.

[135] The chef Tom Hunt has an excellent recipe for making chimichurri using carrot-tops.

[136] See chapter three's recipe for my suggestion.

November day, I followed my food waste bin to an industrial estate on the outskirts of the city to watch my food scraps being dumped alongside thousands of other compostable plastic sacks in a vast holding bay. I can't say it was a pleasant smell – the nearest equivalent is pig slurry. Within minutes, a huge digger, called a tiger, had clawed away any packaging or plastic before the remaining gunk was scraped up by another front loader and sent to be 'digested' for 40 days in a giant silo. Inside the tank, the food waste is deprived of oxygen, allowing certain micro organisms to break down the organic matter and produce biogas (a mixture of methane and carbon dioxide). As the gases are created, the green gas bell gradually rises. At the bottom, the leftover digestate remains as fertiliser to be used on crops. Scott Hardingham, the general manager, describes it as an enormous stomach producing what most stomachs produce: biogas and fertiliser, otherwise known as farts and shit. It may sound like a disgusting process, but I love the idea that my carrot-tops are now lighting my home.

Yet not everyone recycles their food waste, even when given the opportunity. In the UK as a whole, only 50 per cent of the population recycles food waste, despite many more of us being offered the service. In some areas, the rate can be as low as 10 per cent. I don't mean to start an internecine battle in the genteel streets of Edinburgh, but not everyone uses their food bin. Why? Well, to be blunt, most of these people would identify as caring very much about the environment, but they are frightened of 'slop buckets'. Much of the blame relates to the fear of food caddies attracting flies and wasps. I understand this can be a problem, and it is especially frustrating if the council does not collect caddies on schedule. Even so, there are many ways to protect against vermin, such as using a caddy with a good seal, removing food waste regularly to a covered outside food bin or even smearing tea tree oil on the caddy lid to deter flies. What is worse? Allowing food to go to waste so that more GHGs are pumped into the atmosphere or using a 'slop bucket'?

I am not going to get involved in other people's bin collections. Read any local newspaper, and you will find it is a highly emotive subject. Some councils do not have an adequate system in place. But they should. Wales has proved it is possible. Unlike the rest of the UK, Wales recycles 99 per cent of its food waste, making it third in the world for household recycling, behind Germany and Taiwan. The majority is treated at AD units and turned into biogas and fertiliser. In Wales, it is just 'normal' to recycle food waste. To chuck something of value in the landfill bin would be strange, immoral even. Landfill is expensive and polluting; in any case, we don't have much land left to fill. Incidentally, that is why Taiwan is so good at feeding food waste to pigs: they simply ran out of landfill.

Food waste should not go to Landfill, the final segment of the Food Waste Hierarchy, because food is never a waste. A wonky carrot can be soup or veg sticks or food shared on an app or a meal for someone in need. It can be chutney or kimchi or a high-end pickle, or a way for us to show off on Instagram. It can be animal feed or compost, or green energy. When I get home and switch on the kettle – powered by the carrot peelings I put in the caddy a few months ago – I reflect that the Food Waste Hierarchy is wrong; it should not be an upside-down triangle after all, but a circle.

Further reading

'The New Home Front', Green Party (2011)
'Feeding food to pigs safely', Feedback
'How to build a circular economy', Ellen MacArthur
     Foundation
'Food surplus and waste in the UK – key facts', WRAP
'Eating for 2 degrees, new and updated Livewell Plates',
     WWF

'Circular' wartime carrot biscuits

During the war, carrots were promoted as an alternative to sugar for sweetening cakes and biscuits. The Ministry of Food disseminated recipes for carrot Christmas pudding, carrot cake and even carrot and chocolate pudding. Carrots were promoted because they could be home-grown and for the health benefits from all that vitamin A.

The idea that carrots help you see in the dark was also heavily promoted, although this was propaganda dreamed up by British Intelligence. They wanted people to believe that vitamin A gave British pilots the edge over the Luftwaffe during night missions, not the top-secret development of radar.

I based this recipe on a wartime recipe, adding apricots in homage to Eileen and all the land girls who kept Britain fed during the war. The biscuits are circular to remind you of the strength of the circular economy in powering your home with any leftovers put in the food waste caddy.

- 1 tbsp of butter, margarine or vegan spread
- 75g of sugar
- 1 tsp of vanilla essence
- 200g of self-raising flour (or 150g of self-raising flour and 50g of fava bean flour, if you have it)
- 1 wonky carrot (or two smaller wonky carrots), grated
- The zest of 1 orange
- 1–3 tbsp of water
- 50g (a handful) of dried apricots cut into raisin-sized cubes
- 1 tbsp demerara sugar (optional)
- A handful of dandelion petals (optional)

1. Pre-heat the oven to 200°C.
2. Cream the butter and sugar in a mixing bowl, then stir through the vanilla essence.

3. Mix in the grated carrot, chopped apricots and orange zest. You can also add the dandelion petals if you have them.

4. Fold in the flour and baking powder, adding water as it gets dry. The final mixture should be pretty wet.

5. Drop small spoonfuls onto a greased and lined tray and press down a little to form circular biscuits.

6. Sprinkle the tops with a little extra demerara or white sugar and bake in the oven for 10–15 minutes until the biscuits are golden brown. Cool on a rack and share with someone who can remember the war.

7. The biscuits should keep in a tin for a few days. If any are forgotten about and go stale, dispose of them in your food caddy.

CHAPTER TWELVE

Avocado Anxiety

Avocados shipped from Peru: 1.6kg CO_2e per kg[137]

*'Hello it is me, token millennial, and I love avocado toast more than
I love the idea of buying a home and filling a garage with junk.'*
@itstheannmarie, Twitter 2017

My name is Louise Gray, and I am addicted to Instagram. I like to post pictures of my breakfast, and I enjoy seeing what complete strangers are eating on the other side of the world. Sometimes, when my friends are talking to me (that is, my real friends sitting in the same room as me), I wish they would shut up so I can check on what my 'followers' are doing. I get a dopamine hit when someone 'likes' my photo – just a little hit, but enough that I want to feel it again and again and again.[138]

---

[137] Mike Berners-Lee, Lancaster University.

[138] In 2017, a survey found 89 per cent of social media users said that getting plenty of likes on their pictures and posts makes them feel happy, but for 40 per cent of them, the happiness stops when the likes do. Only around 10 per cent of people will carry that happiness for the whole day.

It's pathetic but frankly not abnormal. Social media apps like Instagram and Twitter have become ways to communicate with our 'followers' as well as our friends. They are a way of keeping up with news and fashion and whatever peculiar hobby you happen to be into. Increasingly, they are also about keeping up with food trends. Humans have evolved to be hunter-gatherers constantly on the lookout for what is edible. When we are not eating food, we generally like to talk about food or look at pictures of food. Lots of pictures of food. Of the millions of photos or videos shared on Instagram every day, one of the most common subjects is food. And the most popular fruit or veg? Avocado. It's a little bit greedy and a little bit needy, but I know that if I want to get plenty of likes, then all I need to do is post a picture of an avocado – though not just any avocado, the perfect avocado.

The first question I want to ask on my quest to find the perfect avocado is: where does it come from? How has this berry – yes, it is a berry – with an oversized seed and rough skin become the most Instagrammable fruit of all time? Well, technically, it should not be here at all, as it should have died out with the giant ground sloth. Around 60 million years ago, the avocado evolved with species that could eat the fruit whole, travel massive distances and then discard the seed out the other end. But when the megafauna went extinct, the avocado kept going. It is what is called an 'evolutionary anachronism'. Other animals and eventually humans took advantage of the tasty fruit and continued dispersing its seeds, this time without going through the digestive tract. The first archaeological evidence of humans consuming avocados is from around 10,000 years ago in South and Central America. A water jar shaped like an avocado, dating back to AD 900, was unearthed in the pre-Incan city of Chan Chan. When the Aztecs discovered the avocado, they named it *āhuacatl*, which translates as testicle, because of its shape, wrinkled texture and the way it hangs in pairs on the tree.

Despite the early adoption of the potato and the tomato – and despite the avocado's humorous shape – it took much longer for Europeans to appreciate this fruit. You could say it is only in the last century that it has genuinely conquered the Old World. Marks & Spencer claims to have introduced avocados to UK supermarkets when they stocked them in 1968, along with a leaflet explaining how to eat them. Indeed, my maternal grandmother remembers 'alligator pears' in Rankins', but they were sold as an exotic 'fruit'. I imagine my paternal grandmother would have had no idea whether to serve an avocado alongside the meatloaf or the fruit loaf.

If you grew up in the 1980s, avocado was the colour of a bathroom suite. I knew my mother loved them, but we barely ate them since they were usually out of season and expensive. One of the first avocados I ate was when I was aged 19 and on the Tazara train from Tanzania to Zambia. I bought it from a vendor through the train window and squashed it between warm white bread rolls. My friend Jade, who grew up in Scotland, ate her first avocado when she was 23 in Australia. Today our children eat avocados with their sweet potatoes and out-of-season strawberries.

The real increase in the Western consumption of avocados came in the 1990s when, thanks to imports from Mexico, it became a year-round food in the US. Marketing campaigns emphasised the health benefits of the avocado and, in a very clever move, positioned guacamole as the snack of choice while you watch the Super Bowl. Today, more than 45 million kilos of avocados are consumed on Super Bowl Sunday. The avocado spread across the pond, and we were soon eating guacamole in the UK, where annual imports increased in 2018 to almost six times what they were in

2000, at nearly 100,000 million kilos. In real terms, each UK citizen went from consuming just one avocado a year in 2000 to seven in 2018.

When we look back at the first 20 years of the twenty-first century, the dish that will sum up the zeitgeist is surely avocado on toast? Although avocado on toast pops up in recipe books much earlier than that and was suggested as an hors d'oeuvre as early as 1915, it was not until the 2010s that it became ubiquitous. The chef credited with 'inventing' avocado on toast is Bill Granger, who served the dish in Brisbane in the 1990s. Since then, everyone from Nigella Lawson to Gwyneth Paltrow has published a version of the recipe. It seemed like the perfect health food: indulgent yet healthy – and always pretty on Instagram.

Avocados are full of fats, but they are healthy fats.[139] The fruit is rich in potassium, fibre and vitamins B, E and C. The pop star Miley Cyrus had one tattooed on her bicep, and there are whole festivals dedicated to avocados. In text speak, it is shorthand for everything nutritious and pure and good.

As with all things that are branded perfect, there has been a backlash against avocados. When I give talks on my first book, *The Ethical Carnivore*, about eating meat, I often have audience members who want to talk not about meat but about avocados. They want to point out that vegetarians who do not eat meat for environmental reasons nevertheless eat 'exotic' foods like avocados that must have a high carbon footprint because they have been transported a long way. Ergo, vegetarians are hypocrites. I get it: people feel under attack for eating meat, and they want to lash out at what they see as self-righteous vegans. But are they correct about the carbon footprint?

---

[139] The type of fat in an avocado is mainly unsaturated (specifically, monounsaturated), which, when eaten in place of high-saturated-fat foods, can help maintain healthy cholesterol levels.

Assessing the carbon footprint of food is a notoriously complicated business, and it leads to a lot of head-scratching. Most calculations talk about the carbon dioxide equivalent (CO_2e) produced for every kilo of food produced. This is an expression not only of the global warming potential of the CO_2 emitted during the life cycle of the food but also the equivalent greenhouse gases, methane and nitrous oxide. Because methane and nitrous oxide have a greater global-warming impact, they will lead to a higher CO_2e. Then there are all the questions about what to include in the carbon footprint. Do you include the indirect emissions, or so-called 'toe-prints', in your calculation? So not only the fuel used in the combine harvester, but the fuel used in the machines used to maintain the combine harvester as well?

One of the best efforts to make sense of all this is the book *How Bad are Bananas?* by Mike Berners-Lee, a professor at the Institute for Social Futures at Lancaster University (and brother of Sir Tim Berners-Lee, the inventor of the world wide web), which breaks down the carbon footprint of our most popular foods and is used for most of the calculations in this book. Berners-Lee freely admits carbon footprinting is 'impossibly complex' but argues that, at the very least, being able to compare the impact of different foods enables us to make better choices. He compares our attempts to try to make sense of climate change to those of the great explorers trying to make sense of global travel: 'The situation we are in is like sailing round the world with a map from the 1700s,' he writes. 'How should we respond? Throw the map away and have nothing? Definitely not! Use a high-quality map of just a small part of the ocean and ignore the rest? No way. Use the maps we have but treat them with caution? Absolutely. Try to make better maps? Of course.'

Berners-Lee calculated that the carbon footprint of an avocado shipped to the UK from Peru, Chile or South Africa is 1.6kg of CO_2e per kg produced. Interestingly, avocados driven from Spain produce 1.8kg because of the use of trucks.

That compares to 83.8kg for beef imported from deforested land. Already, I can hear my audience member coming back to me: 'Aha! You see, that is beef imported from deforested land. What about the British pasture-fed organic beef I buy from my local farmers' market?' Sorry, but according to Berners-Lee, the figure for UK beef is still 25.5kg CO_2e per kg produced. The Sustainable Food Trust reckons the figure for organic, pasture-fed UK beef is closer to 18kg CO_2e per kg produced, which is much better than 83.3kg but it's still significantly more than an avocado imported from either Spain, South Africa or countries in South America.

The reason the carbon footprint of beef is so high is that the animals belch out methane, a greenhouse gas with a high global-warming impact. It also takes a lot more energy to feed, grow and transport a cow than to produce an avocado. Even chicken, pork and lamb have higher carbon footprints than avocados (although, again, how much higher depends on where the animal was raised, what it was fed, and how it was transported and processed).

In comparison, vegetables grown in the UK, such as broccoli and lettuce, have a carbon footprint of less than 1kg. Imported fruits and veg emit more carbon due to transport, so broccoli and grapes from Spain are 1.2kg CO_2e per kg. Then you are in the realm of avocados and other fruits imported from further afield but with a relatively low carbon footprint because they are transported by cargo ship in bulk. Bananas are 0.7kg because they are transported in such quantities, while avocados are 1.6kg. The next jump up is tomatoes grown in a hothouse in the UK at 4.6kg[140] and then fruit and veg transported by airfreight, which is up there with beef. Asparagus airfreighted from Peru is 18.5kg, according to the figures. So, yes, there's a stick for an angry omnivore to beat vegans with: an asparagus

---

[140] UK tomato producers claim the carbon footprint of hothouse tomatoes is falling because of the use of renewable energy and efficiencies in the energy system.

spear from Peru (though in my experience, most of them have thought it through and don't eat that either). In summary, avocados are not that bad compared to meat and airfreighted veg, but in terms of a carbon footprint, they are a lot worse than UK-grown potatoes.

There is also the question of seasonality. The average CO_2e for an avocado may be 1.6kg from Peru, but what about when they are out of season in that country and the British importers have to rely on avocados from Mexico with a much higher carbon footprint because they have been driven further overland to reach the port? Some companies, such as Riverford Organic, which sells veg boxes to customers around the country, have done the complicated calculations for you by adhering to company principles that dictate a food cannot go above a specific carbon footprint for them to sell it. That means that organic avocados are never in veg boxes between September and November when they would have to come from Mexico. This approach has been welcomed by customers keen to know their veg is low carbon without having to do the calculations in their heads themselves. But few companies are willing to be this transparent.

How is the average consumer expected to make sense of all this? The best we can expect is a carbon footprint label. In 2008, when I was environment correspondent for the *Daily Telegraph*, I reported on moves by PepsiCo to put carbon footprint labelling on packets of Walkers crisps. But the idea never took off. The public was not interested, and other companies did not follow suit. However, as climate change moves up the agenda, carbon labelling is back on the table. At the time of writing, Quorn are adding it to their products and Nestlé are considering doing the same.

Mike Berners-Lee wrote *How Bad Are Bananas?* in 2009 and he has continued to update the figures since. He was always realistic about the public taking their time to get their heads around carbon labelling; in the long run, he hopes it becomes a regular part of our shopping routine: a little bit like when we calculate the monetary cost of something in our head, we will also calculate the carbon cost. Ideally, we will walk around the shops understanding the carbon footprint of an avocado, among other fruit and veg, and what it means.

If, at this point, you are still scratching your head or perhaps throwing the book across the room, I wouldn't blame you. On top of considering the cost and the plastic packaging and the potential food waste and the animal welfare, now you are supposed to consider the carbon footprint too? How are you even supposed to trust this label when measuring the carbon footprint of foods is still an imperfect art? I would suggest imagining yourself on the boat with those eighteenth-century explorers and considering this map is the best we have.

The carbon footprint is all very well, but what about the other impacts of growing this food on the environment? Most avocado plantations are a monoculture of Hass avocados crowding out wildlife and diversity of other crops, including the hundreds of varieties of avocado available. The thirsty crop also uses up a lot of water, in many cases in areas of the world where climate change is making drought more likely. In 2008, around the same time as carbon footprinting took off, the WWF made the first attempt to measure the water footprint of the UK. As well as considering the water we use for drinking and sanitation, the water footprint considered the 'virtual water' we use, *i.e.* the water that has been used to grow the crops that make the food we eat, the beverages we drink and the clothes we wear. The report found that only 38 per cent of the UK's total water footprint comes from our own groundwater, reservoirs and rivers, while the rest is taken from the water systems of other countries. In particular, a large proportion of our water footprint in the UK is the water used to grow the imported fruits and vegetables we eat. This matters because many of the countries we import these vegetables and fruits from are under water stress themselves. For example, it takes 8.2 litres of water to grow a tomato in Spain – much more than growing a tomato in a greenhouse in the UK. The WWF is very concerned about this because over-exploitation of water is already threatening rare wildlife in Spain, such as the Iberian lynx.

The highlighting of our water footprint failed to sink in – perhaps because in the UK, we complain about how much it rains all the time – but ignoring the embedded water in what we eat could lead to shortages in the future as more countries suffer droughts because of climate change. The UK currently imports around 67 per cent of its fresh fruit and vegetables from overseas, with most coming from water-scarce countries like Spain, South Africa, Chile, Peru and Israel. If we use up that water, we will all go hungry.

The government and retailers are so concerned about this impending crisis that they recently asked Cranfield University to look more deeply into our reliance on other countries for water. It found that imported fruit and vegetables use 560 million cubic metres of freshwater per year. This figure has increased by 36 per cent from 1996 to 2015 as we switched from British seasonal vegetables and fruit, like potatoes and apples, to imported fruit, like mangoes and avocados. The UK's avocado intake alone from water-scarce countries is more than 25 million cubic metres annually – equivalent to 10,000 Olympic-sized swimming pools.

To make sense of this, I asked Cranfield University what the individual water footprint would be of an avocado from each of the five countries – Peru, Chile, South Africa, Mexico and Spain – that import the fruit into the UK. Based on other sources, they estimated that it takes around 85 litres to produce an avocado from Peru, where we source most of our avocados in the UK, 200 litres for an avocado from Chile, 190 for an avocado from South Africa, 50 litres from Spain and 66 litres from Mexico.

The Water Footprint Network (WFN), an organisation in the Netherlands committed to educating the world about the water footprint of food, estimates it takes on average 70 litres of water to grow one avocado. In comparison, the WFN reckons it takes on average 22 litres of water to grow an orange and five litres to grow a tomato. The WFN estimates that producing 1kg of beef requires approximately 15,000 litres of water, though there is considerable variation around this global average.

Yep, sorry, angry omnivore in the back row, avocados use a lot of water but nowhere near as much as beef. 'But wait,' says the audience member, 'where does the water come from?' Well, that is a good point. The water footprint of a cow raised in the Welsh Borders may be very high, but this is not a water-stressed area of the world, and rain will soon replenish supplies. In comparison, the water from an avocado farmed in Chile could be an area where people are suffering drought. The Cranfield University report made clear that the water footprint of a food was not just solely about calculating the *amount* of water in the water footprint but also needs to consider where that water is from. Countries like Chile, where the water came from aquifers that were not being replenished, were considered to have a much higher 'water scarcity' footprint.

In 2018, reports published in the *Guardian* and elsewhere claimed that demand for avocados, including in the UK, was driving drought in the Petorca region of Chile. Villagers claimed they were left without water to wash in or drink because water was being diverted to avocado plantations, and water shortages were leading to a human exodus from the area. According to the UN's World Water Development Report, which estimated that 5 billion people could suffer water shortages by 2050 due to climate change, problems like this could get a lot worse.

So, alongside carbon footprint, are we expected to know the water footprint of our food too? The WFN wants companies to make the water footprint more visible and, more importantly, to reduce the water footprint of their products. Professor Tim Hess, the professor at Cranfield University who led the study into water-related risk of the fruit and vegetable supply system in the UK, said consumers should be thinking about the water footprint of their food and the impact buying food like avocados is having on other parts of the world. He wants to see a shift to more sustainable sources and for the retailers to invest in infrastructure that protects the water sources in these areas. If we want to be healthier and eat more of our five-a-day, we need to ask questions about the water footprint of that fruit and veg – not only because of how it affects other people and threatens wildlife but because, if we don't, we are going to run out of food like avocados.

If the headlines are anything to go by, avocados are as bad as 'blood diamonds' in terms of the damage wrought to communities where the fruit is grown. In Mexico, the world's largest producer of avocados, it is alleged that drug cartels extort cash and make the lives of farmers in the industry a misery. These stories first emerged in the late 2010s. The avocado industry had proliferated in Mexico following a trade agreement with the US in the 1990s. Within a couple of decades, Mexican avocados were the new 'green gold', and the country was providing the US with half its avocados. Like a lot of industries in Mexico, the drug cartels followed the money. Reports started to emerge of horrific violence against avocado farmers, especially in Michoacán state, which produces over 80 per cent of Mexico's avocados. The drug cartels were reportedly forcing producers to pay for every kilo they exported or face the consequences. If they refused to pay the protection money, they were threatened with violence, and there were reports of kidnappings and murder. The local community was forced to set up a volunteer 'avocado police' to protect the orchards and packing houses.

In 2018, Netflix aired a documentary called *Rotten* about the avocado industry, reminiscent of *Narcos*, its fictional output about drug trafficking. In UK newspapers, there was a series of articles about blood avocados culminating, bizarrely, in a story linking the Duchess of Sussex to the problem. The *Daily Mail* claimed Meghan's 'favourite snack, beloved of millennials', was fuelling human rights abuses, drought and murder. Meanwhile, avocados from other countries also hit the headlines. In 2020, the *Sunday Times* ran a series of articles highlighting allegations of human rights abuses at a Kenyan avocado farm that supplied UK supermarkets. The reports claimed security guards at British-owned Kakuzi, a huge avocado farm north of Nairobi, had used extreme violence against the local community. The 79 claims included allegations of rape, beatings and, in one case, the battering of a young man to death. It led to four UK supermarkets severing their supplies from the company.

The reports also led to many UK restaurants taking avocado off the menu. Wildflower Restaurant in Peckham, which has since become a pop-up restaurant, suggested we are now entering a 'post-avocado era'. The famous Irish chef JP McMahon also stopped serving avocados in his Michelin-starred restaurants, branding the fruit the 'blood diamonds of Mexico' (though he occasionally serves seasonal organic Spanish avocados). Tincan Coffee in Bristol has replaced 'avo' with pea guacamole. The restaurant chain Wahaca has recently launched a new avocado-free 'wahacamole' made with Hodmedod's fava beans (see chapter one) in response to demand for a more climate-friendly guacamole.

Although Mexico is by far the world's largest producer of avocado, the UK relies on imports from elsewhere, with Peru, South Africa, Chile, Israel and Spain (in that order) accounting for 84 per cent of the avocados bought into the UK over the last five years, according to Cranfield University. The biggest concern for all these countries is water, though, in the past, all have had human rights issues.

If you want to be sure of the source of your avocado, Fairtrade avocados are becoming increasingly common. At the moment, there are 13 Fairtrade co-operatives across seven different countries selling avocados on Fairtrade terms. There are plans for more, but few are available in the UK. For now, 'blood avocados' remain a genuine issue of concern.

Have I made you feel anxious about eating avocados? The fact is that eating most things nowadays makes us anxious. Millennials have perhaps had it hardest. In 2017, avocado on toast became the focal point for criticism of this generation when Tim Gurner, an Australian millionaire property developer, suggested that millennials save their money to buy their first home instead of squandering it on overpriced breakfasts. The #avocadotoast meme quickly went from being a symbol of millennial excess to the focus of ridicule as posts on Twitter pointed out how many avocados on toast it would take for millennials to afford a home in an inflated property market created by baby boomers. Then came that criticism of Meghan and the millennials 'fuelling climate change' by what they eat for breakfast. Finally, they were branded 'snowflakes' for worrying about blood avocados.

Is it any wonder millennials are anxious, and that anxiety is leaking into how they eat? The link between the media, anxiety and disordered eating is being discussed more and more by health professionals. Never before have we had so much food to eat, watched so many cookery programmes or read so many cookery books. Or looked at so many pictures of food on social media. Yet, for many people, food is not a source of joy but a source of worry. Eating disorders are on the rise.[141] This is not meant to be something a 'food writer' writes about. Generally, books about food celebrate ingredients, share recipes and talk about how healthy food can be. Recently, more investigative books have been written about our diet's impact on the environment. Yet we seldom write about how this onslaught of information about food is making us feel. Are all these investigations and revelations making us eat a better diet, or are they just making us all terribly, terribly anxious?

The avocado has become a symbol of 'clean eating'. It is on the branding and in many of the recipes shared by the stars of the movement. It is also the symbol of all that is wrong with the wellness industry. An article on the history of clean eating by food historian Bee Wilson describing the impact on some of the victims of the wellness industry – including people who lost thousands of pounds trying to cure cancer through diet and those with eating disorders who took some of the messages too far – used a rotten avocado for illustration. Like bananas and green beans and potatoes, the avocado has a backstory as messy and complex as any global commodity. And, like most food, it depends on the context in which you eat it. None of this means that avocados are suddenly not good for you – it means that they are not perfect.

Renee McGregor knows better than anyone how emotionally charged the debate about clean eating can be. The dietician, who has worked with the British Olympic and Paralympic teams, has long been interested in helping people to eat a balanced diet, but when she suggested at the

---

[141] More young people than ever before are receiving treatment for eating disorders, according to the NHS.

Cheltenham Book Festival that this could include meat and dairy, she was booed on stage. It led her to think deeply about what is making people feel so dogmatic about food. She was increasingly seeing people coming into her clinic who had become vegan or started cutting out processed foods for understandable health and environmental reasons but had then restricted their diet beyond what is safe for the human body. Renee believes more people than ever before are suffering from orthorexia, where sufferers can only eat what they deem 'pure' or 'perfect' and so begin to dangerously restrict their diets. She blames much of the problem on social media peddling a 'perfect' way of eating, including being environmentally 'perfect'. It is not difficult for me to find an example of this in a chatroom for people recovering from eating disorders. Someone admitted that having spent so long learning to relax about calories from food, they now felt anxious about the environmental impact of what they were eating. A fellow survivor replied more eloquently than I ever could: 'You can't help the planet if you are dying.'

Of course, we need information. I hope you can see from this chapter that eating avocados has implications for carbon and water and, in some cases, the lives of others. You can think about where avocados are from, you can educate yourself and make decisions, you can replace them with alternatives or not eat them at all. But don't make yourself ill worrying about it.

Pixie Turner, a registered nutritionist, has experienced what it feels like to be under fire just for eating. Following a health scare in her early 20s, she became interested in healthy eating and soon gravitated toward the new wellness scene. She was @plantbased_pixie on Instagram for a few years before realising that the pressure to post a constant stream of 'perfectly healthy' smoothies and salads was taking her away from her friends, affecting her health and making her unhappy. Switching to @pixienutrition, she came under criticism for moving away from a vegan and 'clean' diet free

AVOCADO ANXIETY

of processed foods. Speaking about how it made her feel, she blames the constant pressure to be perfect for distorting her relationship with food.

'The worst part is you are never good enough. You can never reach peak wellness,' Pixie says. 'For someone who already has low self-esteem, it can push you down further and make you feel worthless.'

Having qualified as a psychotherapist, Pixie now helps others to develop a healthy relationship with eating by moving away from 'good or bad' foods and learning to eat more intuitively based on the acceptance that we can never be perfect.

I know what it is like to feel anxious about food because a lot of the time, that is how I feel. After becoming a food writer, I wrote a piece about bulimia. I felt uncomfortable with the notion that anyone – even someone who writes about food – has an unblemished relationship with what they eat. To me, it is crucial people always get the full, true story. As a teenager, I made myself sick because I was afraid, and I felt I had no way to vent that emotion. I stopped after many years because I learned to deal with my emotions. I wrote about it in the *Observer* and got a massive response, including from other food writers, bloggers, chefs and even doctors who had been through something similar. I still can't read that article back, but I'm glad I did it. I don't have an entirely straightforward relationship with food now. Like many people, I eat when I am stressed or anxious. For me, it is a way to deal with difficult emotions, perhaps not the best way, but something I try to forgive myself for.

I don't want to attack people for what they eat; doing that makes people ill. They do not listen, and they turn away. Food shaming doesn't empower people; it can shut them down and makes them binge, guiltily. Anxiety is harmful in the context of food and eating because you need to use your intuition to eat well, and you can't use your intuition if you feel frozen with worry. I am done with attacking myself or anyone else for eating 'good' or 'bad' food. It is just food; messy, complicated, tasty, energy-giving, nourishing food.

The important thing for me is that people understand the complex stories of where their food is from, that they even enjoy reading those stories, and most of all, that they feel empowered to make decisions rather than anxious. However good it looks on Instagram, the avocado can never be the perfect food, any more than I can be the perfect person. But maybe the real avocado, with its complicated backstory, social media presence and emotional resonance, is the perfect food to represent our age of anxiety?

Further reading

'UK Water footprint: The impact of the UK's food and fibre consumption on global water resources', WWF, 2008

How Bad Are Bananas?: The Carbon Footprint of Everything by Mike Berners-Lee (Profile Books, 2010)

Orthorexia: When Healthy Eating Goes Bad by Renee McGregor (Nourish Books, 2017)

'My Double Life as a Food Writer and Bulimic', Louise Gray, *Observer*, 11 March 2018

'The Exposure of a fresh fruit and vegetable supply chain to global water-related risks', Tim Hess and Chloe Sutcliffe, Cranfield University, Water International, 2018

The Insta-Food Diet: How Social Media Has Shaped the Way We Eat by Pixie Turner (Anima, 2020)

The Way We Eat Now: Strategies for Eating in a World of Change by Bee Wilson (Fourth Estate, 2020)

For more information and confidential support on eating disorders: beateatingdisorders.org.uk/

Ecovado[142] (smashed broad beans) on toast

Okay, confession, I developed this recipe specifically to share on Instagram. I came up with it while writing about avocados for *Wicked Leeks* magazine. I wanted to make something that was as bright and pretty as avocado on toast but without the same water footprint. I am not going to tell anyone never to eat an avocado again. But, given the pressure on water in other parts of the world, it would help if we ate fewer avocados. As the Cranfield University report points out, the UK can't just rely on other countries' water supplies to grow food for us; we have to produce our own food as well. As we saw in chapter one, UK-grown broad beans are good for the environment because the plant needs less nitrogen fertiliser. This recipe is also an excellent opportunity to add some plant-based protein to your diet. And show off on Instagram if you want to.

- 3 tbsp of frozen broad beans
- 1 tbsp of frozen peas
- 1 tbsp of cold pressed rapeseed oil
- a handful of parsley stalks

1. Boil the peas and broad beans for about four minutes.
2. Drain the vegetables, then add them to a blender with the oil and parsley and whizz everything up.
3. While it is still in the blender, you could add a pinch of ground coriander, a squeeze of lemon or lime or whatever you add to your usual avocado on toast.
4. Spread the blended mixture on some toasted sourdough, grab a frothy coffee, take a photo to post on Insta, #avocadoanxiety, and then actually enjoy eating it.

---

[142] Ecovado is what Arina Shokouhi, a graduate student at Central St Martins, called an avocado alternative also made with broad beans.

Seeds

'I am little concerned with beauty or perfection.'
Émile Zola

If you want to experience the cut and thrust of the fruit and vegetable trade, there is one place where it still exists, Rungis in Paris. While other cities have let their wholesale food markets fade out, the French have held on to their gastronomic heritage and market share by building an international trading complex on the fringes of their capital city. Rungis is slightly larger than the Principality of Monaco; it has its own train station and motorway exit and boasts the largest turnover of any wholesale market in the world.

It is the closest I will ever get to the kind of wholesale markets my great-grandfather Willie Rankin would have frequented as an Edinburgh greengrocer. So, on a cold winter's morning, I make the journey to see what the fruit and vegetable trade looks like today. Driving off the motorway in the middle of the night, I feel like I am entering a parallel universe. While the rest of Paris sleeps, another city has woken up. Lorries roar back and forth,

forklift trucks beep as they reverse, neon lights advertise
market stalls, and workers pour in and out of the many
restaurants on site. I put on a white coat and hairnet, the
uniform of everyone else in this strange city, and set out
across 'town'. A bus takes me past the slop and smell of the
fish market and through the alleyways of the meat market,
where butchers display the bulging eyeballs of *tête de veau*,
or calves' heads, for the Instagram tourists. Strangely, the
fruit market is the quietest place, as though the traders know
they don't need to joke or shout or make excuses for their
bloody produce. Here the smells are fragrant and fresh. In a
warehouse the size of a football pitch, every fruit and
vegetable you have ever heard of – and some that you
haven't – from more than 60 countries around the world
stretch out into the distance like the rainbows in my
daughter's story books.

In preparation for the trip, I have been reading Émile
Zola's famous book *The Belly of Paris*, all about the original
wholesale markets of Paris, Les Halles. He famously
described the fruits and vegetables as like a symphony: 'the
bunches of spinach, sorrel and artichokes, piles of peas and
beans, mounds of cos lettuces, tied up with straw, sounded
every note in the scale of greens, from the lacquered green
of the pods to the coarse green of the leaves; a continuous
rising and falling of notes that died away then rose again to
the top of the scale.' I can see what he means; I can even
hear the music. But it is more like a pop song. Perhaps it is
the artificial lights, but the colours seem brighter, blockier.
The lettuces are one neon bright green, the endives iceberg
white, the carrots almost an atomic orange. The asparagus
comes wrapped in clear blue cellophane, not twine, and the
peaches are laid in purple polystyrene rather than moss.
Magenta dragon fruit and scarlet rambutan add exotic tones
to the palette. Moving around the market like robots are
men in Day-Glo jackets constantly murmuring into mobile
phones. The colours pulse rather than build to a symphony.

In his ecstatic climax, influenced by art criticism of the time, Zola talks about the 'sweet balsamic scent of the dawn', the sunrise blazing on the 'luxuriant fullness of the bundles of artichokes' and the 'turnips incandescent' in the pink light. The turnips here are certainly better looking than a pile of muddy neeps in Scotland, but they are not incandescent. The colours are bright and fresh but somehow less like a painting. These blocks of Clarendon colour are more like a photo or even an Instagram feed. It is no longer a belly gurgling with bacteria and life. It is more sterile, more controlled, like a screen, something outside the body, a computer perhaps that we can control at the tap of a button.

Like the paintings of the day, *The Belly of Paris* was about more than the descriptions of fruit and vegetables; it was the truth behind these scenes. While Zola rejoiced in the colour and vitality and greed and sexiness of the marketplace, he was also concerned about who the free market was leaving behind. Alongside his descriptions of the cabbages 'shining with well being' were vegetable peelings and manure on the floor, a reminder of the cycle of life and death that will 'rise again as perfect produce'. Tramps beg for scraps, and much of the fruit is overripe and ready to explode or already rotten, just like the corrupt government of the time.

I wonder what Rungis could tell us about the state of the world today? The perfection of the fruits and vegetables certainly reflects the advances in technology. Any rotten fruit is tidied away each day and used to power an incinerator that heats not only Rungis but the nearby airport. The smells are all fresh and zingy. Ripeness is now something to be controlled by manipulating the plant hormone ethylene. Exotic foods, like prickly pears and starfruit, which would never have been available before refrigeration, sit alongside new breeds like the 'limequat' and 'tangelo'. Technology has created this spectacle, not nature. Well, technology and nature. Breeding has produced watermelons with yellow flesh, purple cauliflowers and bright pink carrots. Soon there could be purple genetically modified tomatoes.

Unlike the markets Willie Rankin would have frequented, this one is not limited by seasons. Here you can get anything you want, from anywhere. It is deepest winter, before most fruits and vegetables are at their best and after most have run out in storage, but in this new universe, it is Permanent Global Summertime. There is every fruit and vegetable you have ever wanted – asparagus from Peru, green beans from Kenya, strawberries from Egypt. I can't help wondering how much carbon it has taken to fly them all here. On an individual level, perhaps greenhouse gas emissions from food miles are not the most significant part of your carbon footprint. But globally, growing and producing food is having a huge impact. Farming and food production are responsible for more than a third of our greenhouse gas emissions.[143]

The pavilion is still chilly in the early morning air except for the 'banana room', a closed-off section kept at a higher temperature to ripen the green bananas that arrive from abroad. It smells of foam banana sweets. I ask if the bananas are Fairtrade or 'Commerce Équitable', but the market traders don't seem to understand what I am talking about or pretend not to. I notice the bananas are all Cavendish, and I wonder how long it will be before other varieties have to be introduced to ensure their survival.

There is such diversity on display, not only purple beetroots but yellow and red and orange and candy-striped. It makes me think of the diversity of food and how we are losing it. In the UK, we struggle to eat five portions of fruit and vegetables a day, never mind trying more than five different types of fruits and vegetables.

---

[143] Food systems were responsible for 34 per cent of all human-caused greenhouse gas emissions in 2015, according to a study, published in Nature Food.

Local produce fills the last pavilion, stacked with boxes of bouquet garnis, lavender from Provence and piles of purple garlic. Suddenly it smells like Zola's market, like France. But unlike Zola, I don't know the farmer who grew this produce. Was it a Frenchman? An Eastern European? A robot? What kind of soil was it grown in? Where did the water come from? I leave Rungis with more questions than answers.

The original English title of *The Belly of Paris* was *The Fat and the Thin*. Zola's book tells the story of Florent, a fugitive on the run from the watching eyes of the Napoleonic Empire. He is the 'thin', the tortured artist trying to make sense of the world, while the complacent 'fat' consumers around him, well, consume and get fat. His book was a warning about the greed of the free market, and in many ways, it was a foretelling of today. While my Instagram feed shows nothing but pretty pictures of fruit and vegetables, I am aware of the stories it is not telling of the chemicals used in growing these crops, of the unfair labour, of the fossil fuels. It is not just environmental concerns. As the cost of living crisis hits, for many people, the question of where fruit and veg come from is irrelevant; the more important question is can we afford it? According to the National Food Strategy, unhealthy food is cheaper per calorie than healthy food, with potatoes and broccoli costing more than six times more per calorie. In Tower Hamlets in London, fruit and veg vouchers are being prescribed by the NHS for the first time to help struggling families eat a healthy diet. The Peas Please campaign was recently set up by the Food Foundation to try and get everyone in the UK to eat more veg. Just as in Zola's day, the bourgeoisie still enjoys the best the free market has to offer; whether it is superfood or clean food, the poor still struggle to eat well. *Plus ça change …*

Rungis leaves me exhausted. It is not just the assault of colour and noise so early in the morning – it is the sheer information overload. In comparison, early morning Paris seems muted and more elegant than ever, the only fruit on display presented on top of a delicate patisserie I devour inelegantly in the street.

It is still early morning, and I let my contemplative mood take me along the Seine to the Pont des Arts. I mistakenly think the Louvre will be empty. Of course, it is packed, the excitement of school children echoing off the upside-down glass pyramid. I avoid the crowds and the queues to see *Mona Lisa* and head straight for the Richelieu Wing, with its racing-green walls and quiet corners. This is where most of the seventeenth-century Dutch paintings are, the golden age of still life. I find it peaceful to look at a simple object captured in time and space. It is one of the few times in life we are forced to sit and stare, and as I am staring, I start to notice something strange. Every piece of fruit, every vegetable is blemished in some way, whether it has a caterpillar crawling up a stem, or there is fungus on a leaf or a bruise on an apple.

The fruit in still life paintings is never perfect. The peaches are not blushing pink but shades of rose and brown, the lemons are misshapen, the grapes wet with dew, the pomegranates half-eaten. There are thorny gooseberries, lumpen quince and unripe plums. There is a grasshopper on a pear, a beetle on a melon and an earwig on a fig. The still lifes in the Louvre are somehow more life-like than some of the perfect fruit on display in Rungis. It makes me think about what we have done to rid ourselves of these insects and diseases, these bruises and blemishes.

It shows the reality of farming and perhaps the reality of life. It wasn't just that Van Dyck and Snyders and Mignon could find no perfect fruit to paint or because they wanted to show off their considerable talent for detail; they were trying to make a point. Like Zola, their paintings were about more than the eye could see. They were about youth and beauty, decadence and decline.

If there is one thing motherhood teaches you, it is that 'perfect' does not exist; at some point, you learn to ignore the voices saying 'not good enough' and instead try to be simply 'good enough'. When she wrote *The Gastronomical Me* in 1943 – an excellent book with an excruciatingly bad title – M.F.K. Fisher was also experiencing early motherhood. She needed the money, and she knew how to write a perfectly decent commercial cookbook. Indeed, she had written one already. But she did not choose to do that; she chose to take a risk and write about food in a completely different way. Read *The Gastronomical Me* and you realise Fisher is not writing about food but about life and death. After experiencing everything she had been through – war, betrayal, grief – I don't think she had the stomach to measure out ingredients or note down methods. Instead, she writes about the moments she had really lived, and for Fisher, that is nearly always expressed through food. There is the peach pie enjoyed with a beloved father, the first oyster shortly before a lesbian kiss and the champagne on a train hurtling towards war and fascism. She understood that food was a story, and perhaps, in those moments when one chapter of her life was ending, she wanted to tell the story of her life so far.

On becoming a mother, I thought my story would be about how to feed a young child in a way that does not damage the world. I hope there are a few answers here about how we might reduce our carbon footprint and even improve the environment through our food choices. Among other things, we can eat more plant protein, buy Fairtrade bananas, order an organic veg box and cut down on food waste. But the truth is that my daughter is already living in a world where climate change is happening, genetically modified foods are out there, chemicals are used on plants and food is wasted. She will have to face up to all of these issues, both of us will. Simply being anxious about it will not help; understanding the stories of how our food is produced and taking action where we can will.

Food is not a post on Instagram, an instant. It is a story, and stories are powerful. It is the story of farmers regenerating the soil and scientists fighting a banana pandemic. It is the community orchards protecting the diversity we all need to help us fight climate change. It is cutting down on chemicals by using insects to control pests and bringing back nature on farms. It is the allotments producing vegetables in cities and the foragers picking fruit from hedgerows. It is the stories I will tell my daughter and the recipes I put in that battered old orange and brown recipe book; it is the seeds I will plant in the ground.

Acknowledgements

We all eat, but few of us get the opportunity to understand how our food is produced or to say thank you to the farmers, scientists and chefs behind our meals. In its own small way, my book is an effort to do this. Firstly, the farmers, in particular Mike Stringer, James Thorp, Cedric Porter, Jim Shanks, Charles Shropshire, Kirstie Perfitt, Martin Hammod, Lochy Porter (and all the people who pick seasonal fruit all-year-round), Kettle Produce and Ali Capper. I guess I should also add my father, Duncan Gray, who taught me to appreciate farmers but also to answer back to them. Next, the scientists, in particular Mike Berners-Lee, Wendy Russell, Fernando García-Bastidas, Madalina Neacsu, Dan Bebber, John Crawford, David Griffiths, Don Pettit, Jill Edmondson and Tim Biddlecombe. The chefs, in particular Jenny Chandler, Sumayya Usmani and Dennis Mwakulua. The campaigners fighting for a better food system, in particular Gavin Wren, Mary Nyale (Farm Africa), Alistair Smith (Banana Link), Harriet Lamb, Jackie Turner (Bananageddon), Mike Small, Incredible Edible, LEAF, Soil Association, Feedback, WRAP, Ellen MacArthur Foundation, Cyrenians, Sustain: the alliance for better food and farming, Empty Kitchens Full Hearts, Common Ground, National Food Strategy, National Allotment Society, Marcher Apple Network, The Orchard Project and BEAT Eating Disorders Charity. All gardeners, particularly the plot holders at Inverleith Allotments, especially Stewart McKenzie and Cathy Bell and everyone at the Blue Door Garden, especially Diana Gray-Buchanan. The 'witches' Jennifer Lane, Soraya Bishop, Ally Hurcikova, Kirstie Campbell and my illustrator Tiffany Francis-Baker. This book would not have been possible without my family and friends and their ability to endure odd suppers or recipe-test weird meals, especially Issy Macdonald and Ailsa Sheldon. My dear friend Fiona Macgregor has kept me sane (just about) through the pandemic and much else. My agent Jenny Brown has been so supportive of my writing, and my writing pals Cal Flyn and Emily Beament have been helpful early readers. I am so lucky to have an editor at Bloomsbury, Julie Bailey, who sees the link between food and the environment and wants to commission and ensure good writing about it. I am grateful to my paternal family, who I am proud to say are farmers, and my maternal family, who I am proud to say were once greengrocers, including the long-lost Rankin cousins Dorothy McQueen and David Gillon, who helped me discover our heritage as Edinburgh greengrocers. When my late mother was born, my grandfather phoned the fruit market in Edinburgh because it was the early hours of the morning, and he knew his father-in-law, Willie Rankin, would be awake to hear the good news. Marianne Rankin Gray (née Flockhart) received a Rankins' fruit and veg box her whole life. She loved fruit, and she passed that love on to me. Thank you, Mummy. Finally, Luke, who really gave me roots and Ada, I ask you to eat your greens because I love you.

Permissions

Index